TRUEBLOOD™

SHAKE FOR ME

TRUE BLOOD created by
Alan Ball

story by
Annie Nocenti and **Michael McMillian**

script by
Michael McMillian and **Annie Nocenti**
(issue #6)

art by
Michael Gaydos, Greg Scott,
and **Beni Lobel**

colors by
Marcelo Maiolo and **Esther Sanz**

letters by
Neil Uyetake

series edits by
Denton J. Tipton

story editor for HBO
Gianna Sobol

collection cover by
Tim Bradstreet

collection edits by
Justin Eisinger and **Alonzo Simon**

collection design by
Neil Uyetake

Special thanks to Janis Fein, James Costos, Benjamin Hayes, Stacey Abiraj, and everyone else at HBO for their invaluable assistance.

IDW founded by Ted Adams, Alex Garner, Kris Oprisko, and Robbie Robbins

ISBN: 978-1-61377-630-8

16 15 14 13 1 2 3 4

IDW

Ted Adams, CEO & Publisher
Greg Goldstein, President & COO
Robbie Robbins, EVP/Sr. Graphic Artist
Chris Ryall, Chief Creative Officer/Editor-in-Chief
Matthew Ruzicka, CPA, Chief Financial Officer
Alan Payne, VP of Sales
Dirk Wood, VP of Marketing
Lorelei Bunjes, VP of Digital Services

Become our fan on Facebook **facebook.com/idwpublishing**
Follow us on Twitter **@idwpublishing**
Check us out on YouTube **youtube.com/idwpublishing**
www.IDWPUBLISHING.com

HBO

Originally published as TRUE BLOOD Issues #6–10.

TRUEBLOOD ™
SHAKE FOR ME

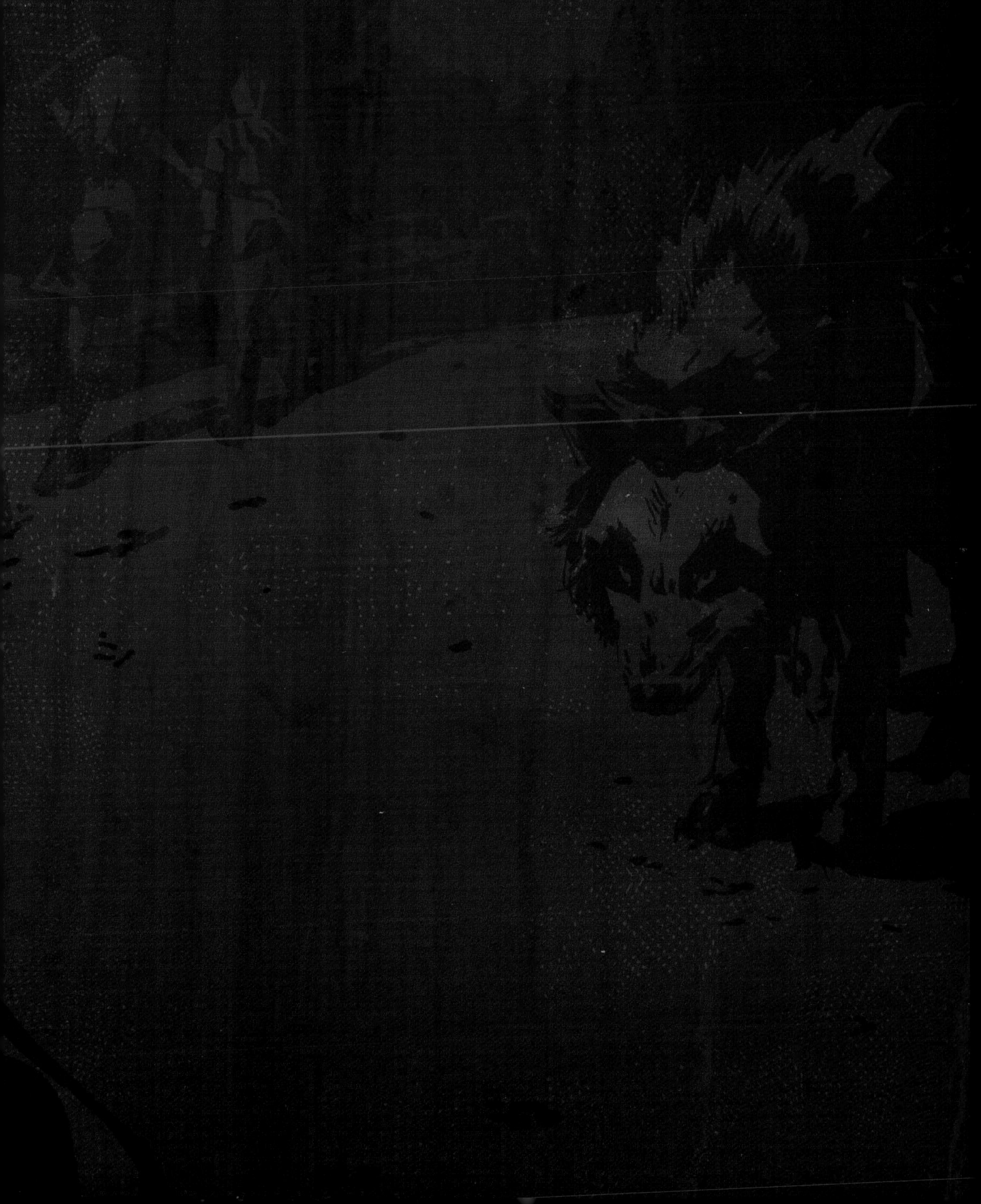

CHAPTER 1

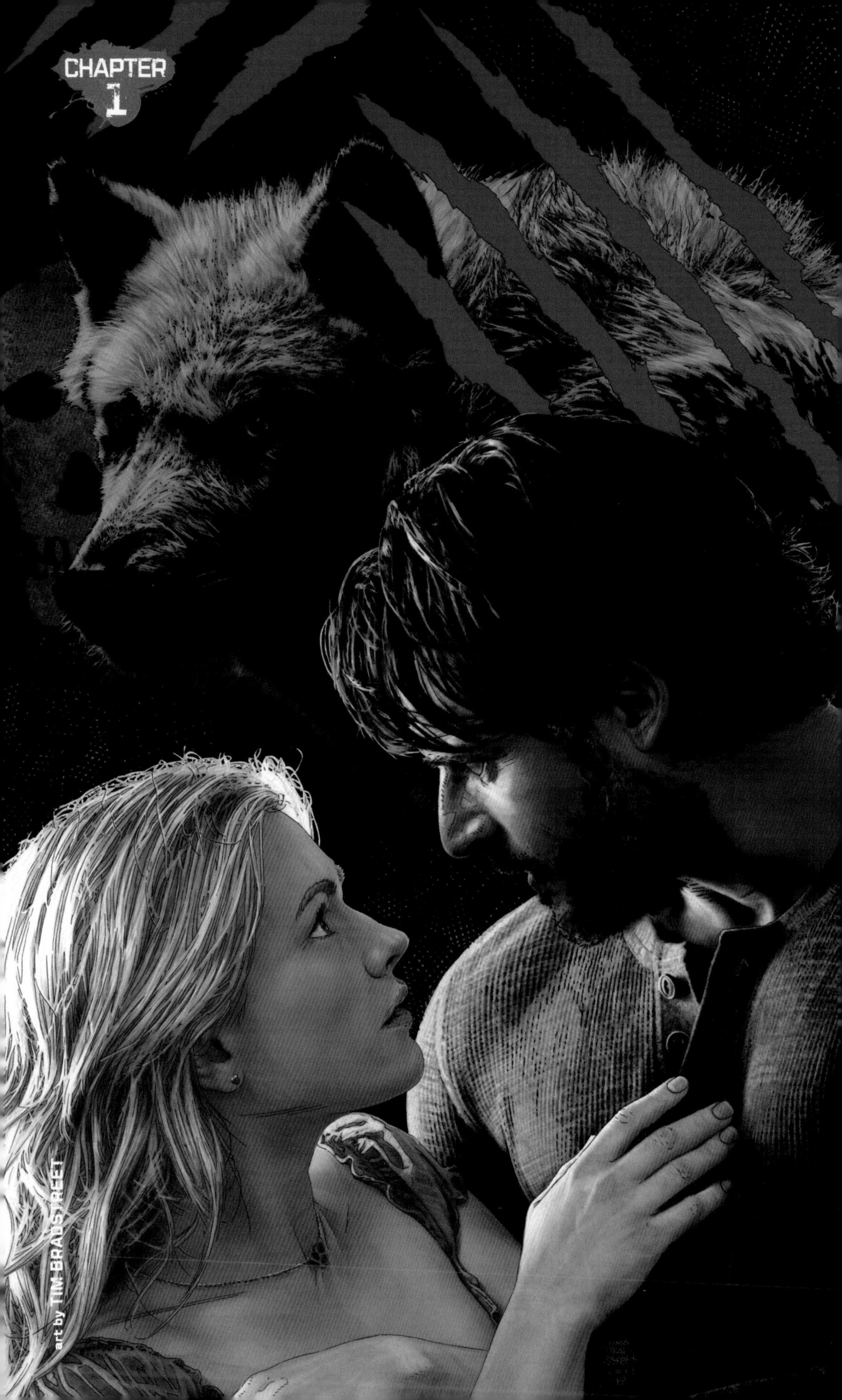

art by TIM BRADSTREET

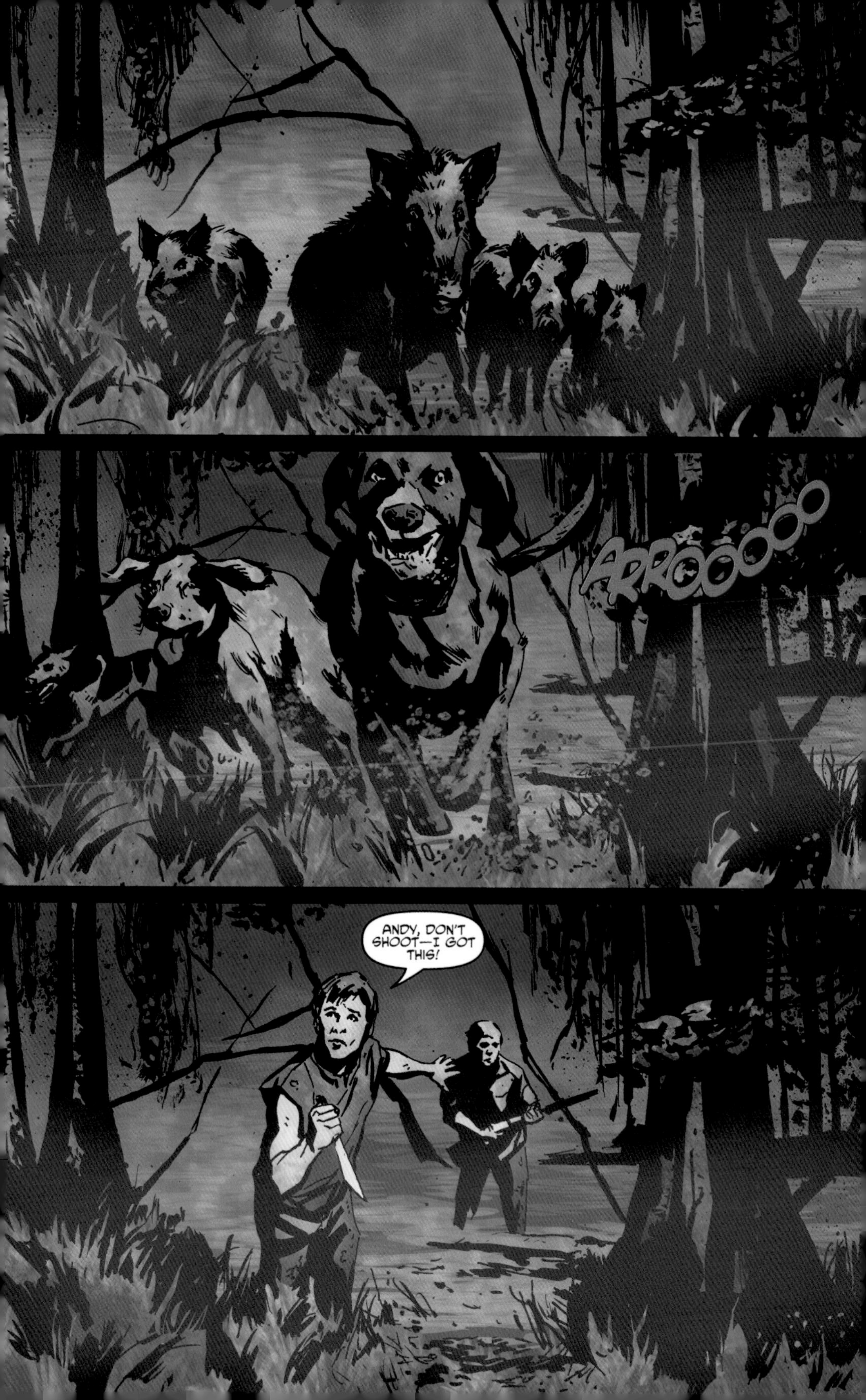
ARROOOOOO
ANDY, DON'T SHOOT—I GOT THIS!

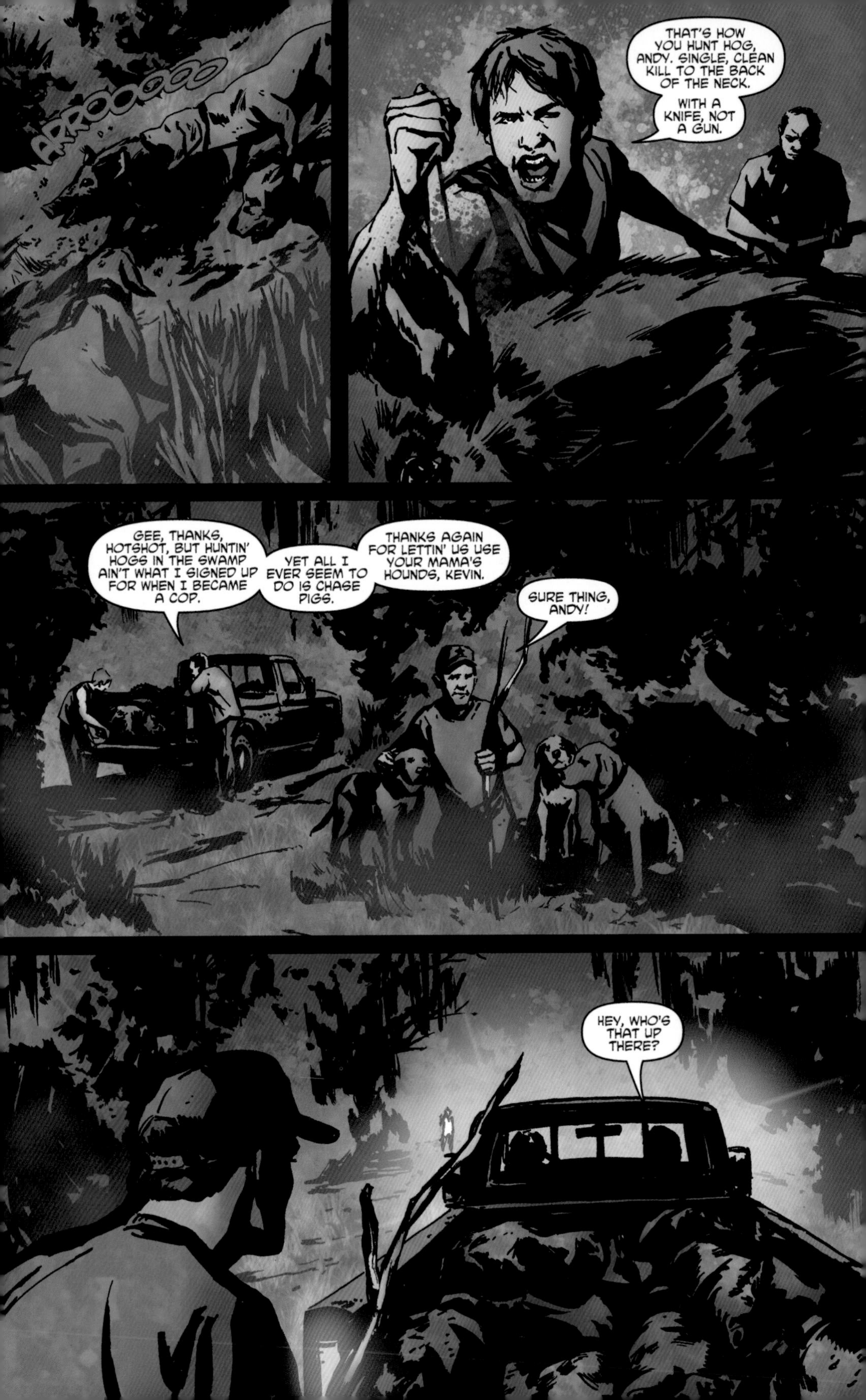
ARROOOOOO
THAT'S HOW YOU HUNT HOG, ANDY. SINGLE, CLEAN KILL TO THE BACK OF THE NECK.
WITH A KNIFE, NOT A GUN.
GEE, THANKS, HOTSHOT, BUT HUNTIN' HOGS IN THE SWAMP AIN'T WHAT I SIGNED UP FOR WHEN I BECAME A COP.
YET ALL I EVER SEEM TO DO IS CHASE PIGS.
THANKS AGAIN FOR LETTIN' US USE YOUR MAMA'S HOUNDS, KEVIN.
SURE THING, ANDY!
HEY, WHO'S THAT UP THERE?

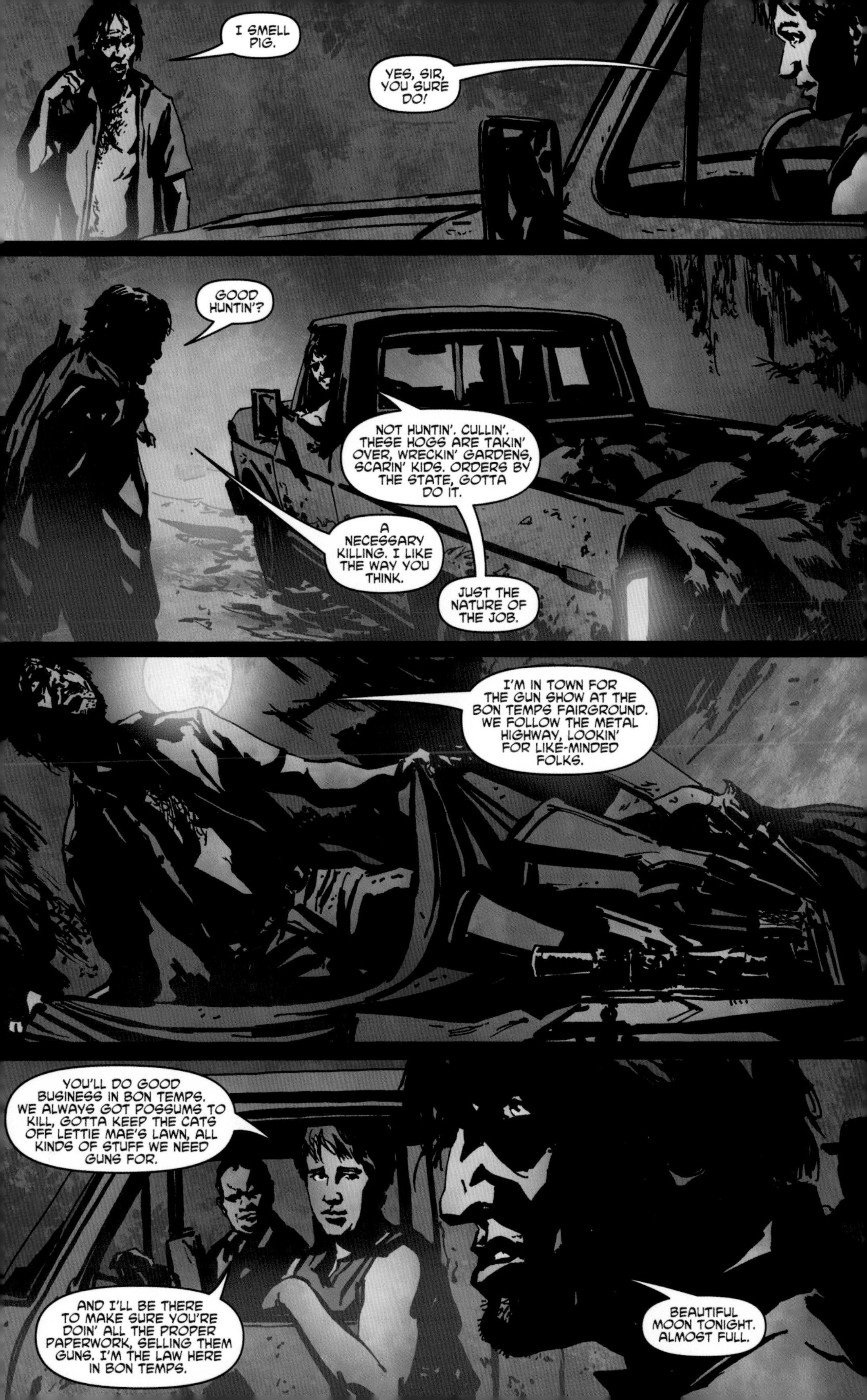
I SMELL PIG.
YES, SIR, YOU SURE DO!
GOOD HUNTIN'?
NOT HUNTIN'. CULLIN'. THESE HOGS ARE TAKIN' OVER, WRECKIN' GARDENS, SCARIN' KIDS. ORDERS BY THE STATE, GOTTA DO IT.
A NECESSARY KILLING. I LIKE THE WAY YOU THINK.
JUST THE NATURE OF THE JOB.
I'M IN TOWN FOR THE GUN SHOW AT THE BON TEMPS FAIRGROUND. WE FOLLOW THE METAL HIGHWAY, LOOKIN' FOR LIKE-MINDED FOLKS.
YOU'LL DO GOOD BUSINESS IN BON TEMPS. WE ALWAYS GOT POSSUMS TO KILL, GOTTA KEEP THE CATS OFF LETTIE MAE'S LAWN, ALL KINDS OF STUFF WE NEED GUNS FOR.
AND I'LL BE THERE TO MAKE SURE YOU'RE DOIN' ALL THE PROPER PAPERWORK, SELLING THEM GUNS. I'M THE LAW HERE IN BON TEMPS.
BEAUTIFUL MOON TONIGHT. ALMOST FULL.

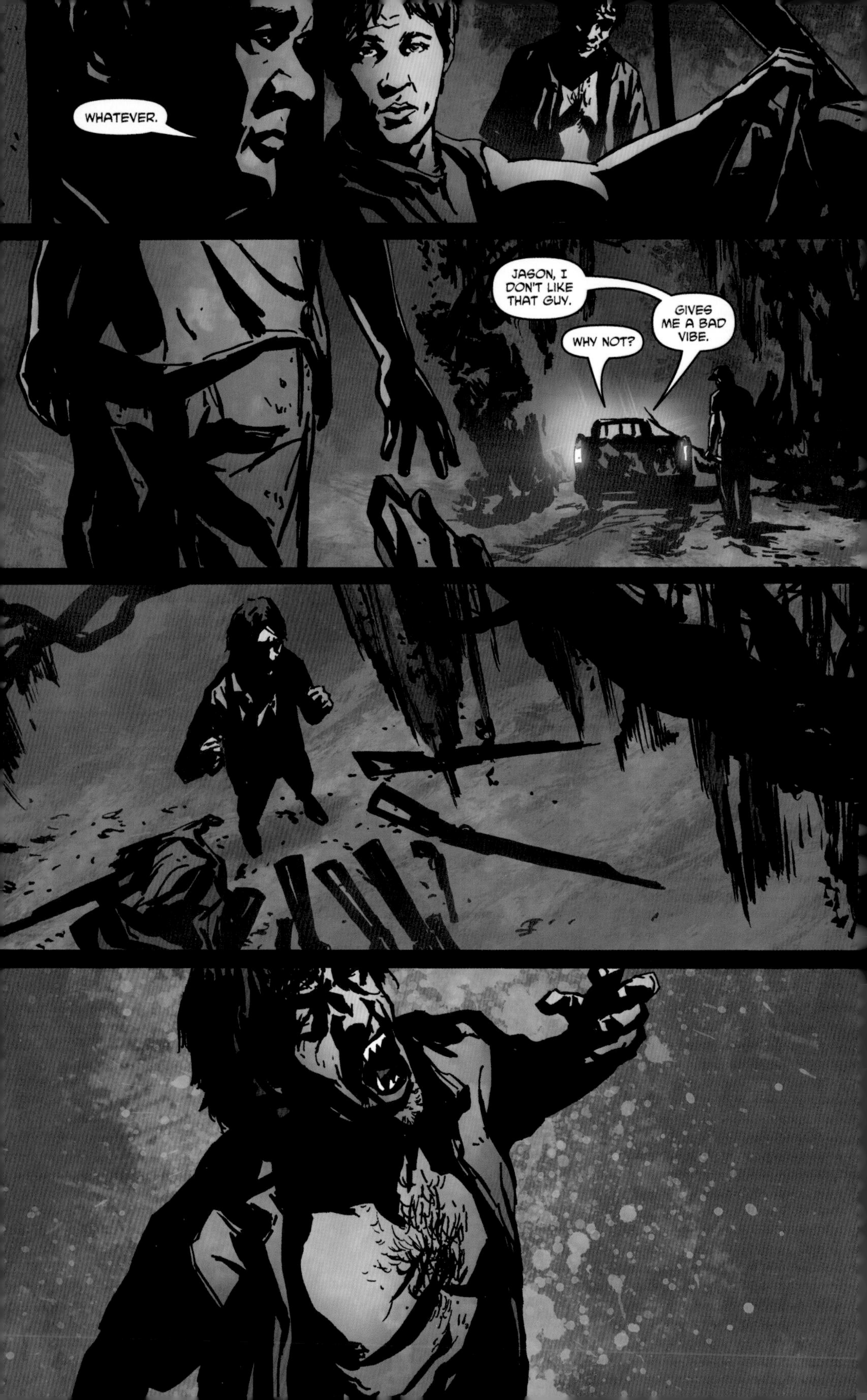
WHATEVER.
JASON, I DON'T LIKE THAT GUY.
WHY NOT?
GIVES ME A BAD VIBE.

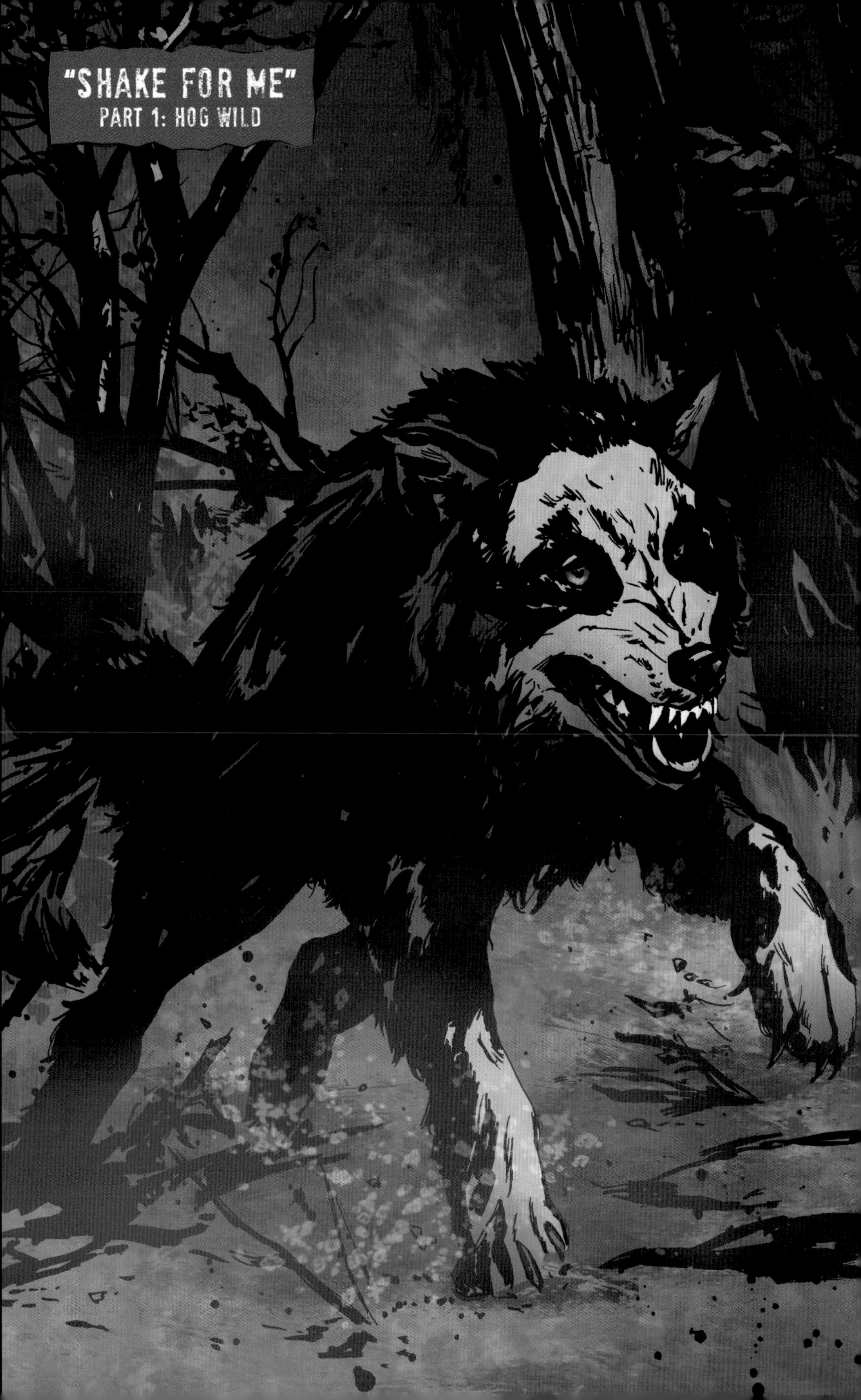
"SHAKE FOR ME"
PART 1: HOG WILD

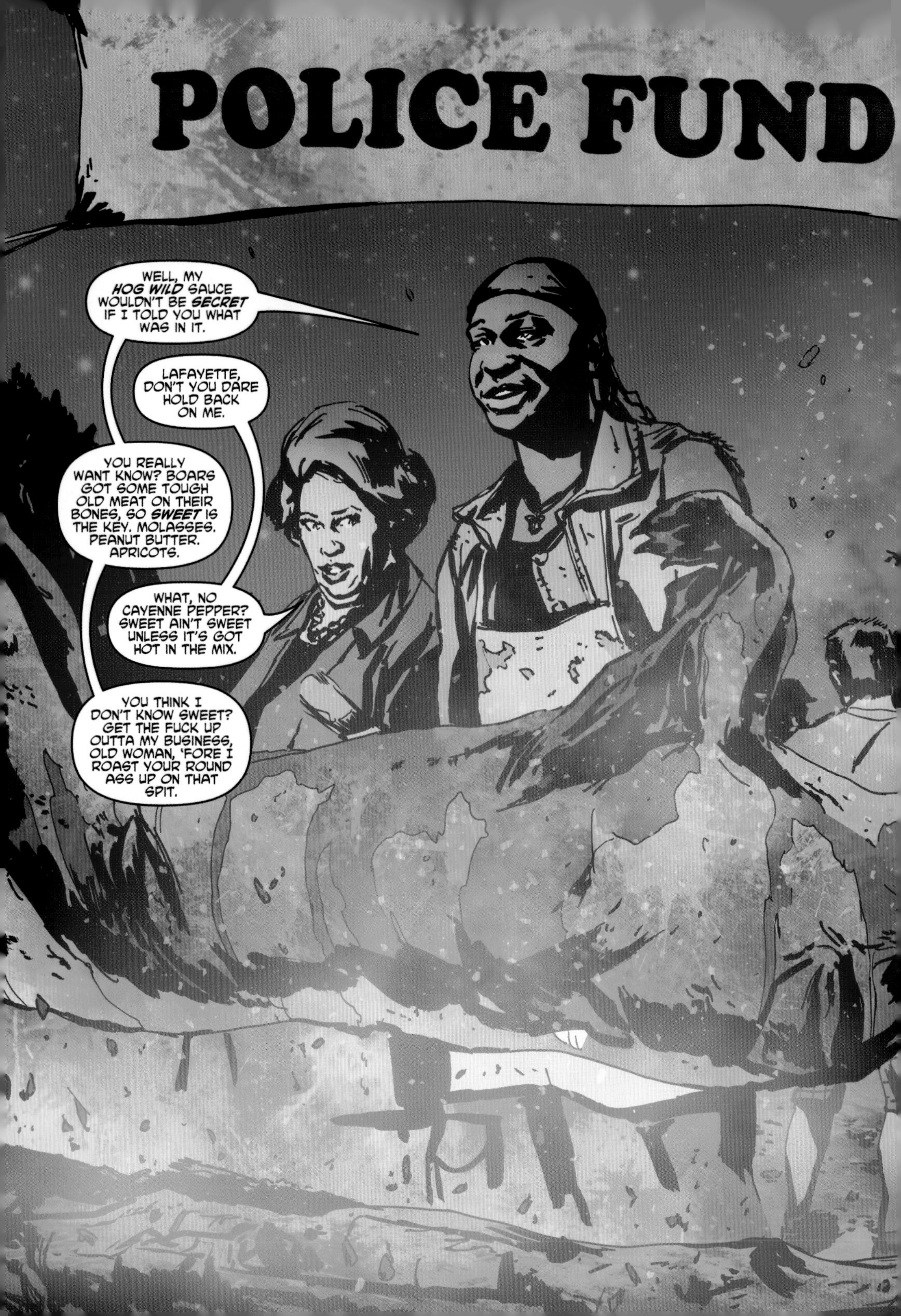
POLICE FUND
WELL, MY HOG WILD SAUCE WOULDN'T BE SECRET IF I TOLD YOU WHAT WAS IN IT.
LAFAYETTE, DON'T YOU DARE HOLD BACK ON ME.
YOU REALLY WANT KNOW? BOARS GOT SOME TOUGH OLD MEAT ON THEIR BONES, SO SWEET IS THE KEY. MOLASSES. PEANUT BUTTER. APRICOTS.
WHAT, NO CAYENNE PEPPER? SWEET AIN'T SWEET UNLESS IT'S GOT HOT IN THE MIX.
YOU THINK I DON'T KNOW SWEET? GET THE FUCK UP OUTTA MY BUSINESS, OLD WOMAN, 'FORE I ROAST YOUR ROUND ASS UP ON THAT SPIT.

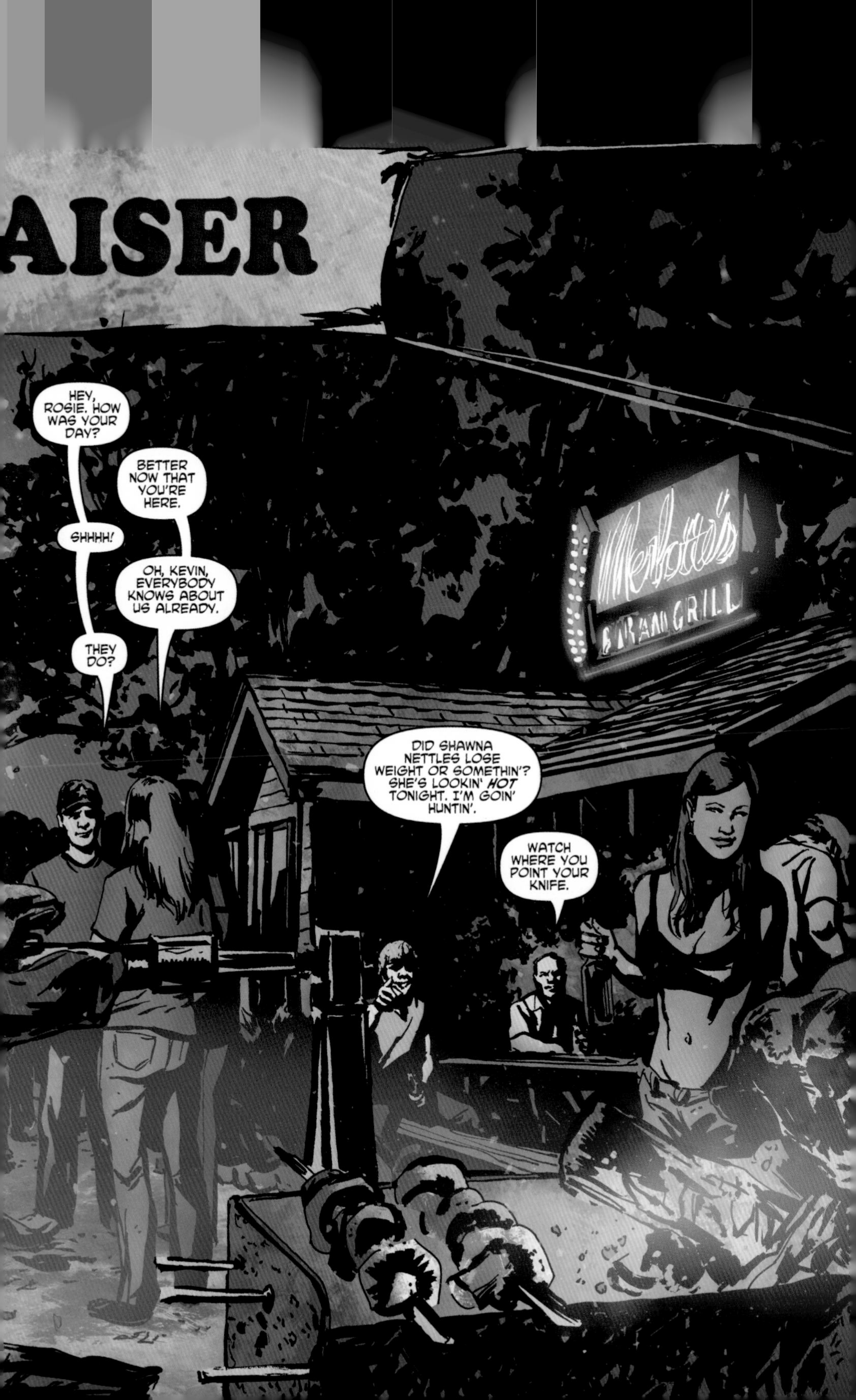
AISER
HEY, ROSIE. HOW WAS YOUR DAY?
BETTER NOW THAT YOU'RE HERE.
SHHHH!
OH, KEVIN, EVERYBODY KNOWS ABOUT US ALREADY.
THEY DO?
GRILL
DID SHAWNA NETTLES LOSE WEIGHT OR SOMETHIN'? SHE'S LOOKIN' HOT TONIGHT. I'M GOIN' HUNTIN'.
WATCH WHERE YOU POINT YOUR KNIFE.

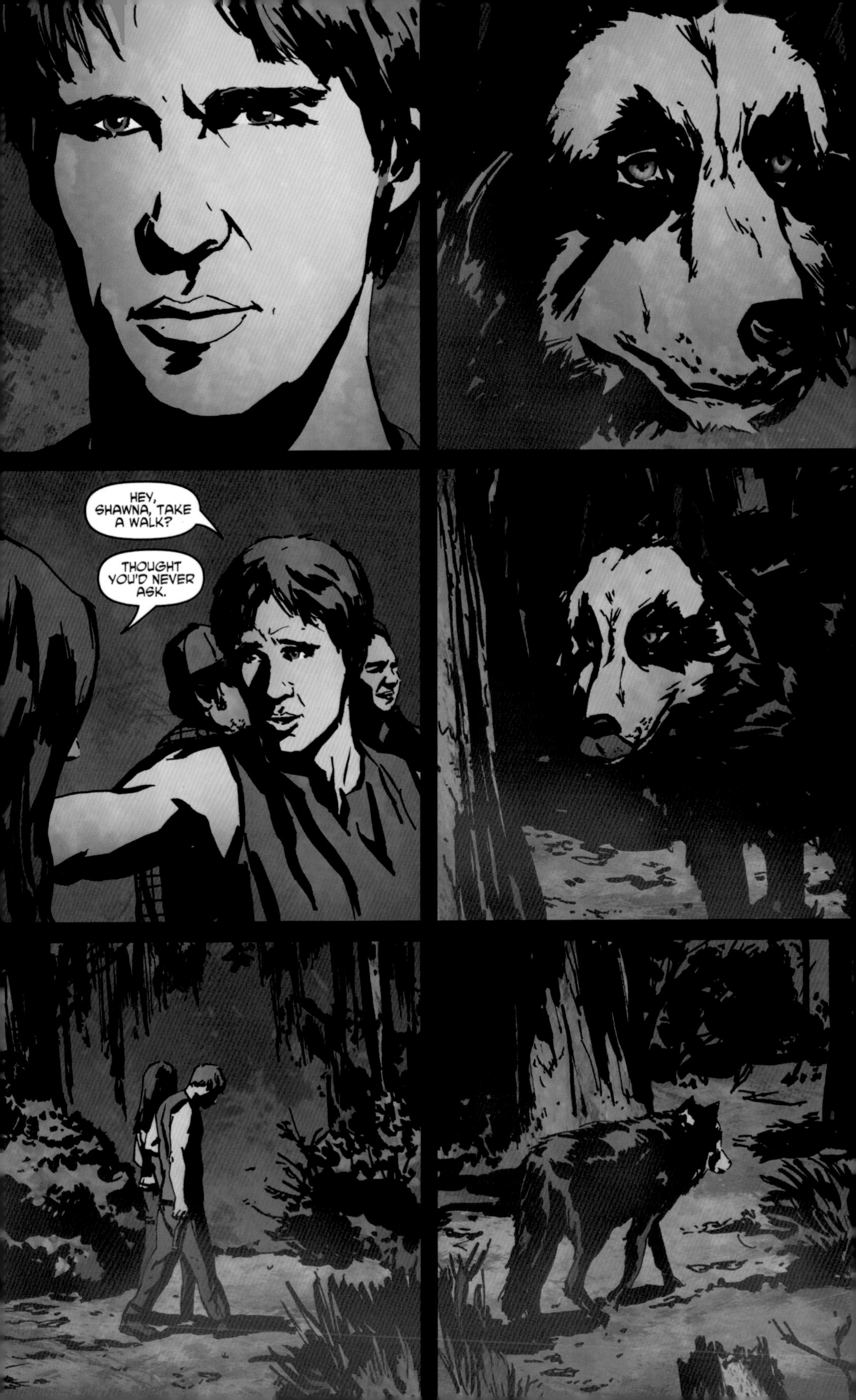
HEY, SHAWNA, TAKE A WALK?
THOUGHT YOU'D NEVER ASK.

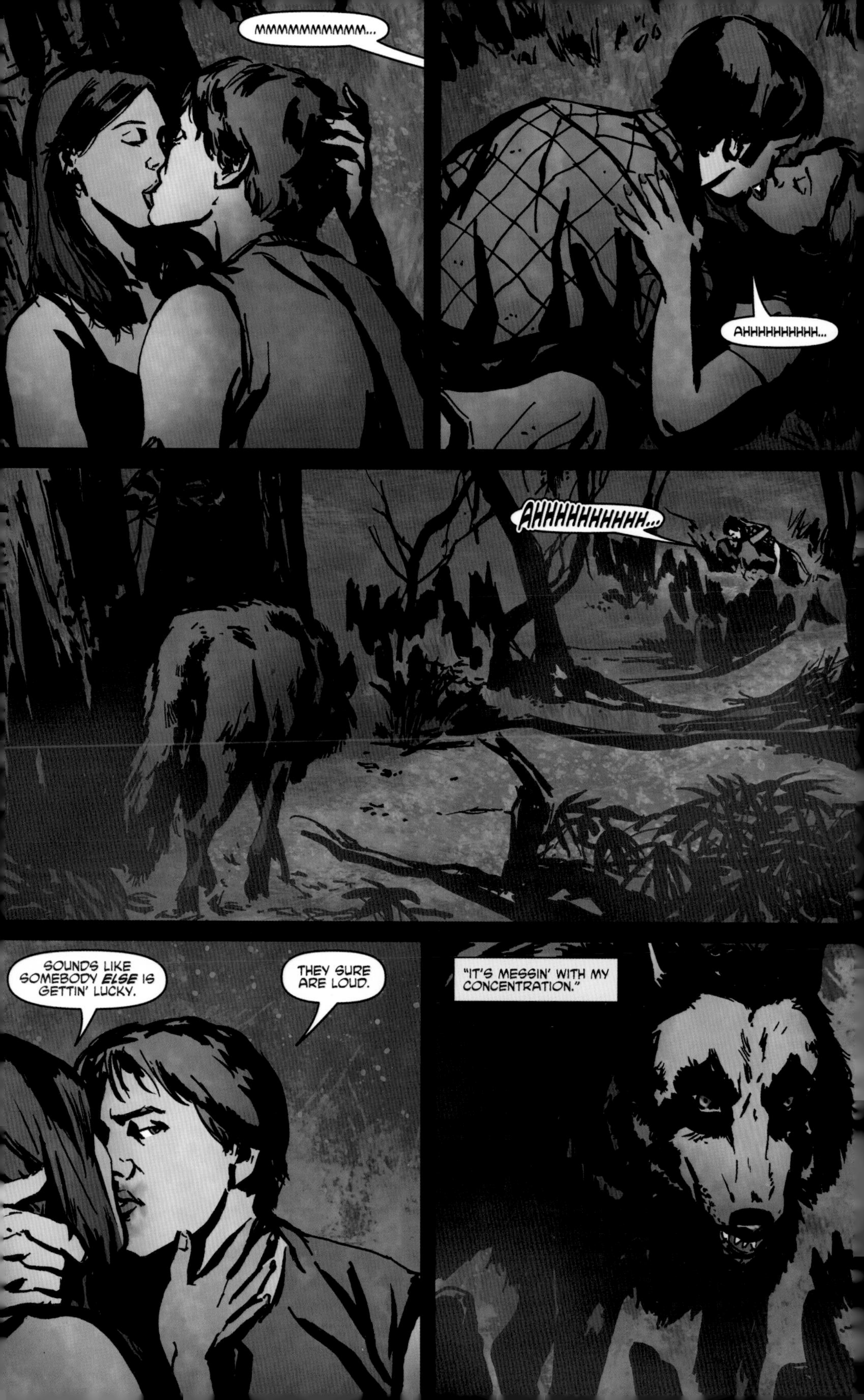
MMMMMMMMMMM...
AHHHHHHHHHH...
AHHHHHHHHHH...
SOUNDS LIKE SOMEBODY ELSE IS GETTIN' LUCKY.
THEY SURE ARE LOUD.
"IT'S MESSIN' WITH MY CONCENTRATION."

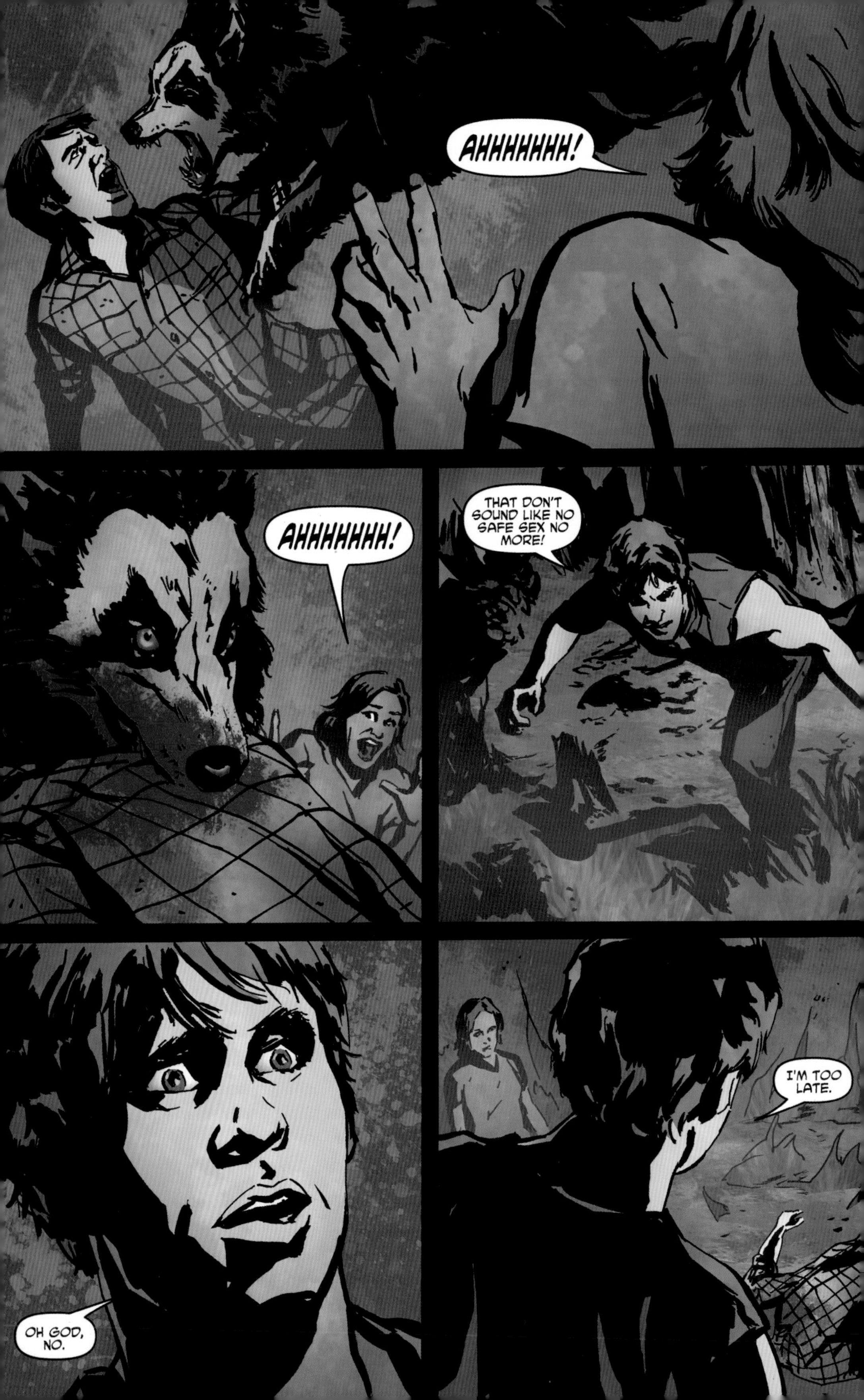
AHHHHHHH!
AHHHHHHH!
THAT DON'T SOUND LIKE NO SAFE SEX NO MORE!
OH GOD, NO.
I'M TOO LATE.

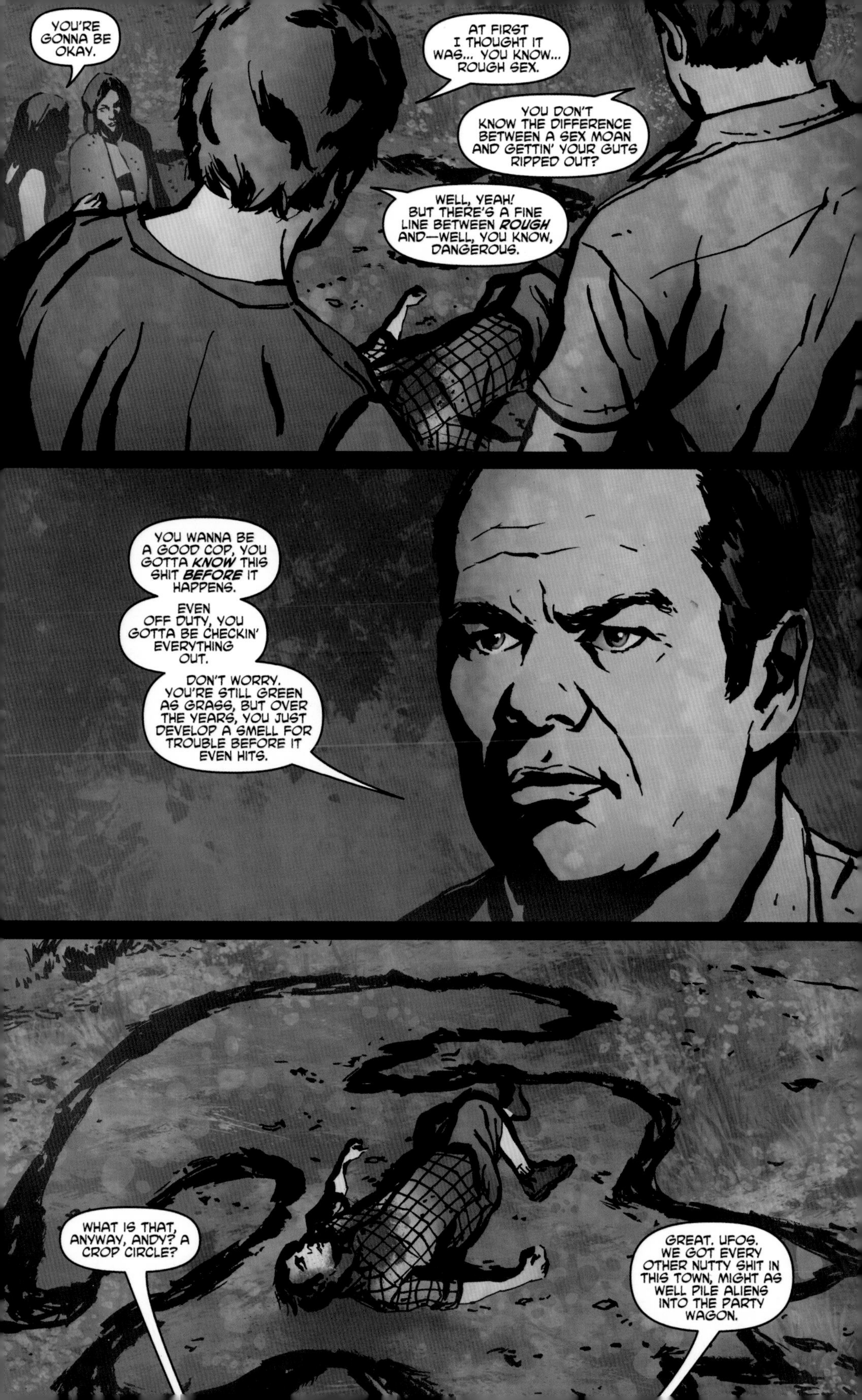
YOU'RE GONNA BE OKAY.
AT FIRST I THOUGHT IT WAS... YOU KNOW... ROUGH SEX.
YOU DON'T KNOW THE DIFFERENCE BETWEEN A SEX MOAN AND GETTIN' YOUR GUTS RIPPED OUT?
WELL, YEAH! BUT THERE'S A FINE LINE BETWEEN *ROUGH* AND—WELL, YOU KNOW, DANGEROUS.
YOU WANNA BE A GOOD COP, YOU GOTTA *KNOW* THIS SHIT *BEFORE* IT HAPPENS.
EVEN OFF DUTY, YOU GOTTA BE CHECKIN' EVERYTHING OUT.
DON'T WORRY. YOU'RE STILL GREEN AS GRASS, BUT OVER THE YEARS, YOU JUST DEVELOP A SMELL FOR TROUBLE BEFORE IT EVEN HITS.
WHAT IS THAT, ANYWAY, ANDY? A CROP CIRCLE?
GREAT. UFOS. WE GOT EVERY OTHER NUTTY SHIT IN THIS TOWN, MIGHT AS WELL PILE ALIENS INTO THE PARTY WAGON.

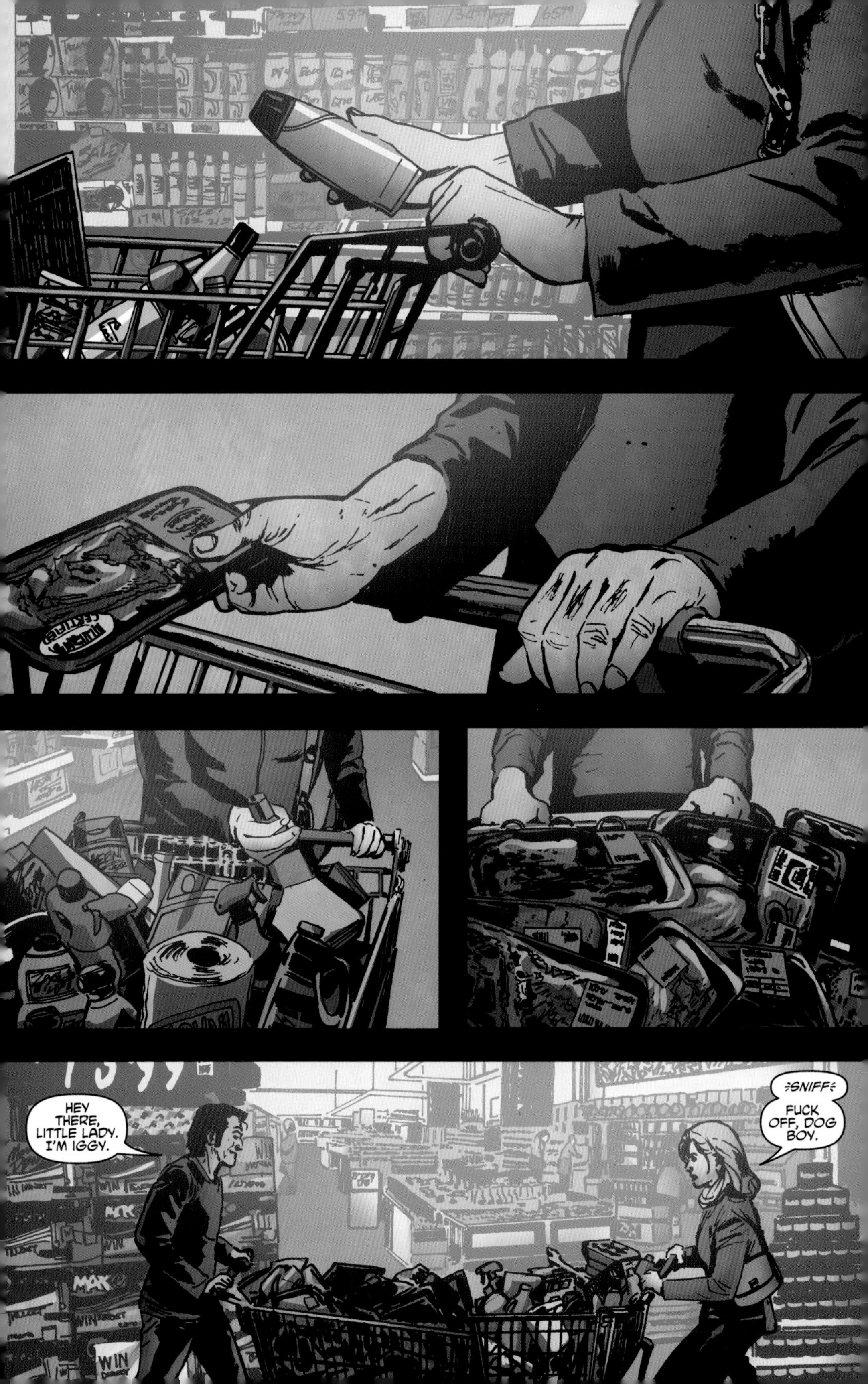
HEY THERE, LITTLE LADY. I'M IGGY.
SNIFF
FUCK OFF, DOG BOY.

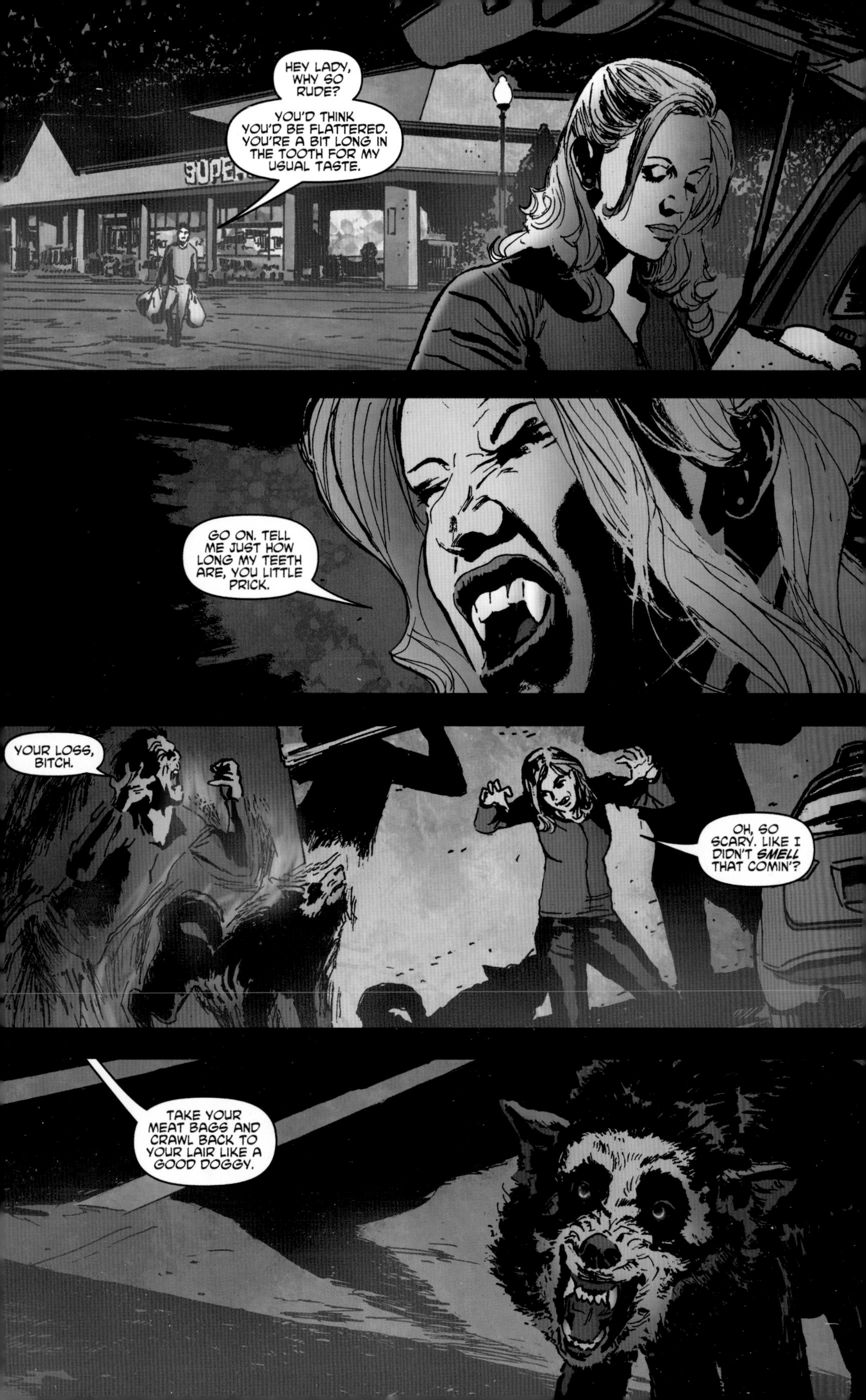
HEY LADY, WHY SO RUDE?
YOU'D THINK YOU'D BE FLATTERED. YOU'RE A BIT LONG IN THE TOOTH FOR MY USUAL TASTE.
GO ON. TELL ME JUST HOW LONG MY TEETH ARE, YOU LITTLE PRICK.
YOUR LOSS, BITCH.
OH, SO SCARY. LIKE I DIDN'T SMELL THAT COMIN'?
TAKE YOUR MEAT BAGS AND CRAWL BACK TO YOUR LAIR LIKE A GOOD DOGGY.

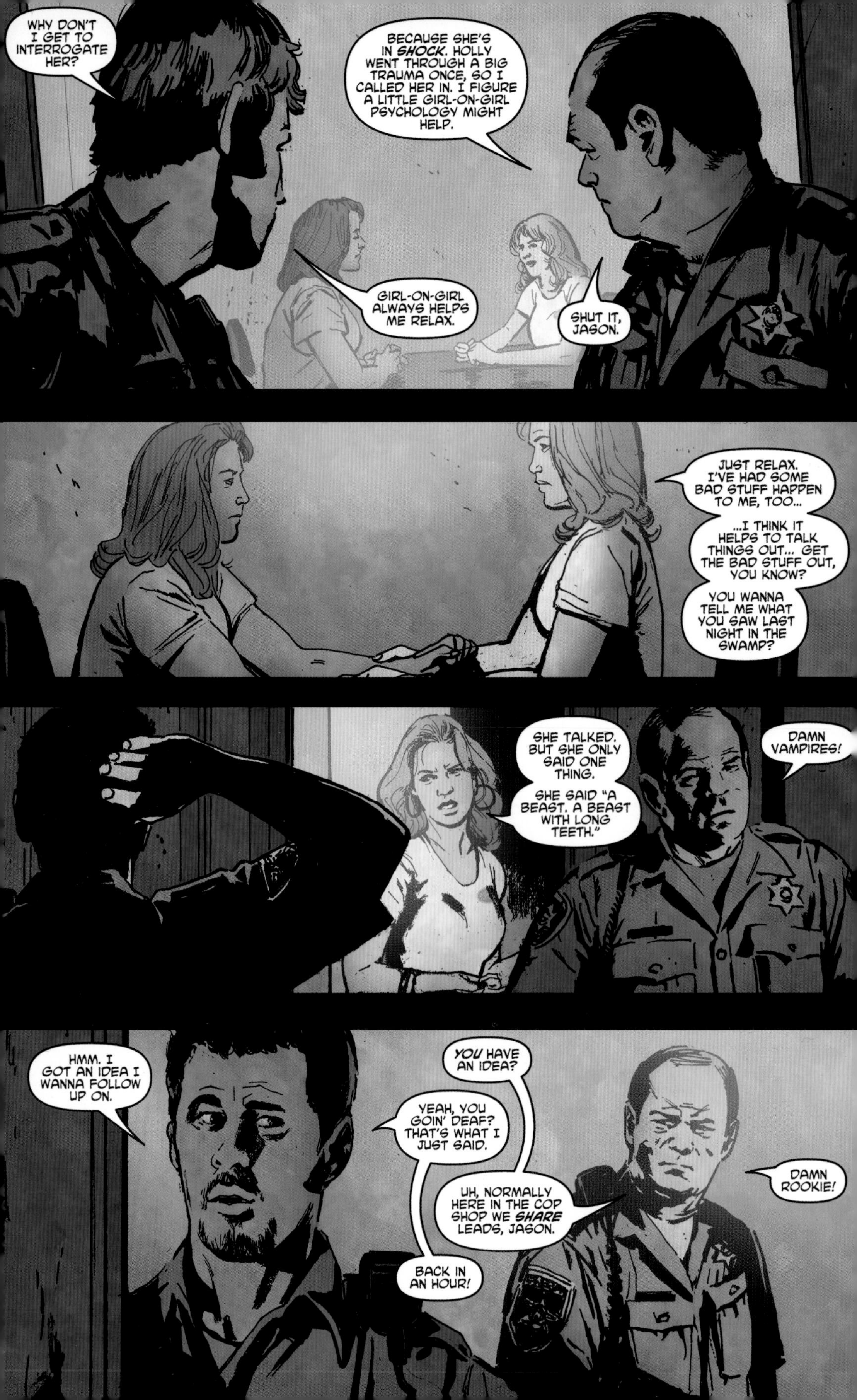
WHY DON'T I GET TO INTERROGATE HER?
BECAUSE SHE'S IN SHOCK. HOLLY WENT THROUGH A BIG TRAUMA ONCE, SO I CALLED HER IN. I FIGURE A LITTLE GIRL-ON-GIRL PSYCHOLOGY MIGHT HELP.
GIRL-ON-GIRL ALWAYS HELPS ME RELAX.
SHUT IT, JASON.
JUST RELAX. I'VE HAD SOME BAD STUFF HAPPEN TO ME, TOO...
...I THINK IT HELPS TO TALK THINGS OUT... GET THE BAD STUFF OUT, YOU KNOW?
YOU WANNA TELL ME WHAT YOU SAW LAST NIGHT IN THE SWAMP?
SHE TALKED. BUT SHE ONLY SAID ONE THING.
SHE SAID "A BEAST. A BEAST WITH LONG TEETH."
DAMN VAMPIRES!
HMM. I GOT AN IDEA I WANNA FOLLOW UP ON.
YOU HAVE AN IDEA?
YEAH, YOU GOIN' DEAF? THAT'S WHAT I JUST SAID.
UH, NORMALLY HERE IN THE COP SHOP WE SHARE LEADS, JASON.
BACK IN AN HOUR!
DAMN ROOKIE!

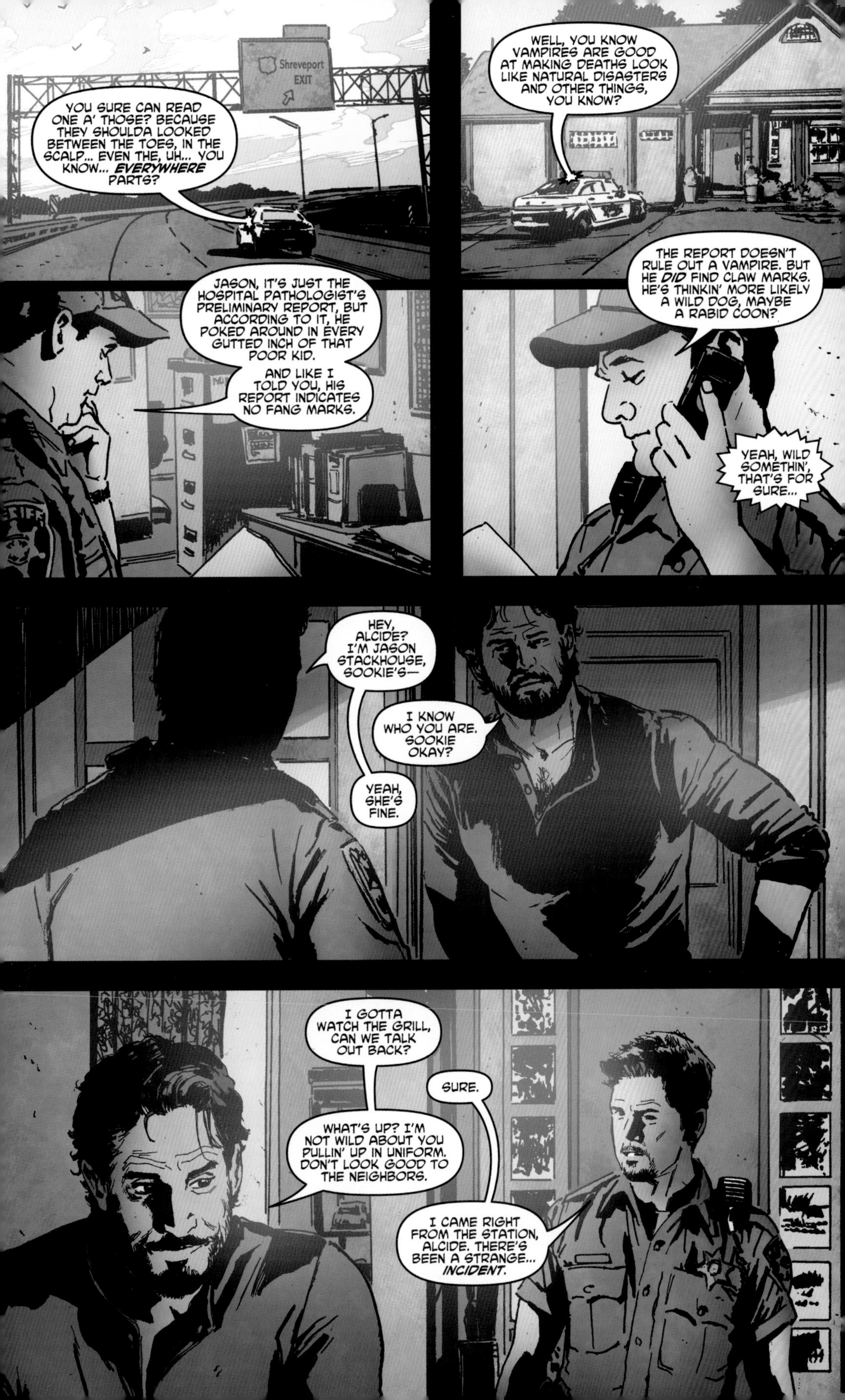
Shreveport
EXIT
YOU SURE CAN READ ONE A' THOSE? BECAUSE THEY SHOULDA LOOKED BETWEEN THE TOES, IN THE SCALP... EVEN THE, UH... YOU KNOW... EVERYWHERE PARTS?
WELL, YOU KNOW VAMPIRES ARE GOOD AT MAKING DEATHS LOOK LIKE NATURAL DISASTERS AND OTHER THINGS, YOU KNOW?
JASON, IT'S JUST THE HOSPITAL PATHOLOGIST'S PRELIMINARY REPORT, BUT ACCORDING TO IT, HE POKED AROUND IN EVERY GUTTED INCH OF THAT POOR KID.
AND LIKE I TOLD YOU, HIS REPORT INDICATES NO FANG MARKS.
THE REPORT DOESN'T RULE OUT A VAMPIRE. BUT HE DID FIND CLAW MARKS. HE'S THINKIN' MORE LIKELY A WILD DOG, MAYBE A RABID COON?
YEAH, WILD SOMETHIN', THAT'S FOR SURE...
HEY, ALCIDE? I'M JASON STACKHOUSE, SOOKIE'S—
I KNOW WHO YOU ARE. SOOKIE OKAY?
YEAH, SHE'S FINE.
I GOTTA WATCH THE GRILL, CAN WE TALK OUT BACK?
SURE.
WHAT'S UP? I'M NOT WILD ABOUT YOU PULLIN' UP IN UNIFORM. DON'T LOOK GOOD TO THE NEIGHBORS.
I CAME RIGHT FROM THE STATION, ALCIDE. THERE'S BEEN A STRANGE... INCIDENT.

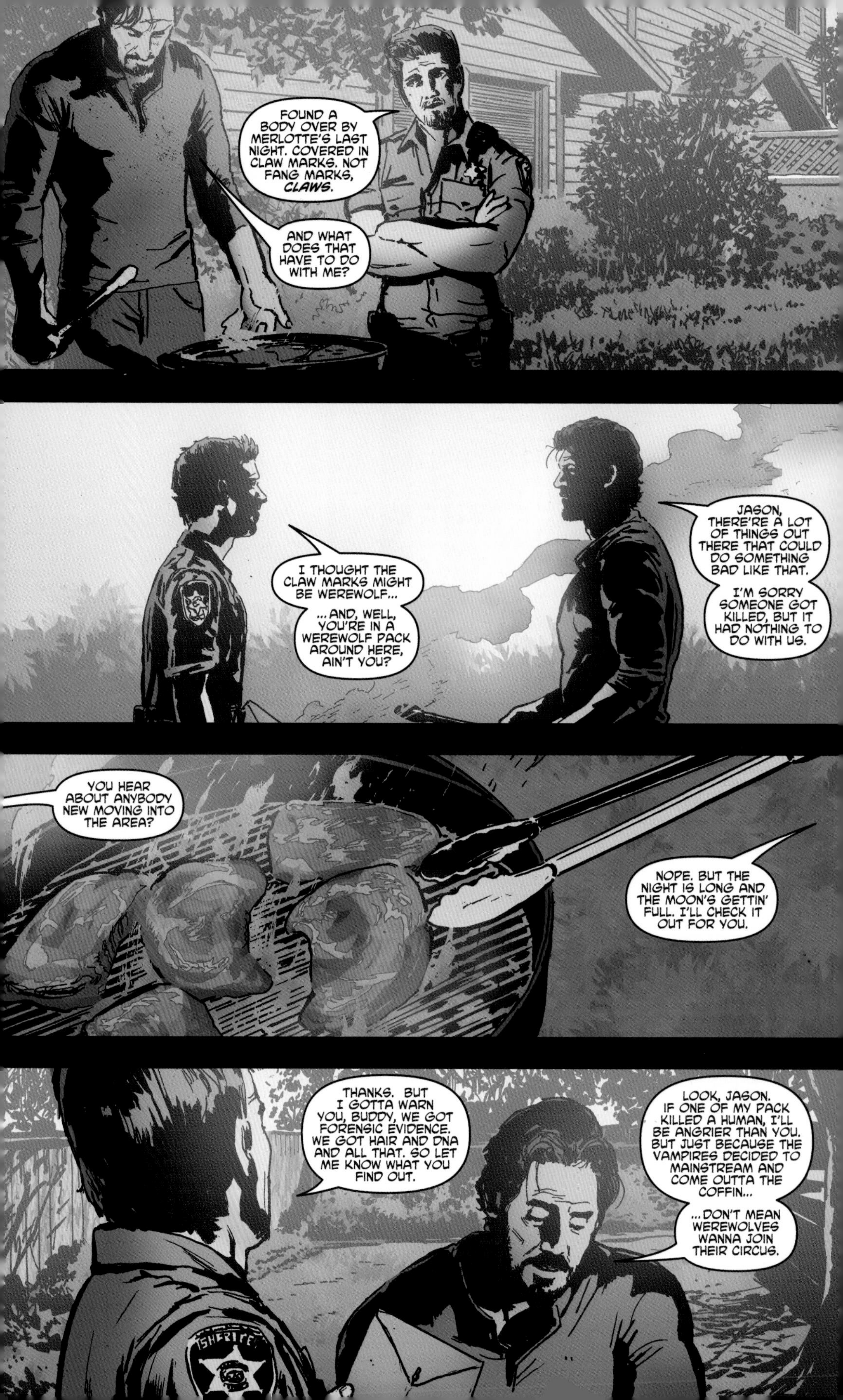
FOUND A BODY OVER BY MERLOTTE'S LAST NIGHT. COVERED IN CLAW MARKS. NOT FANG MARKS, *CLAWS*.
AND WHAT DOES THAT HAVE TO DO WITH ME?
I THOUGHT THE CLAW MARKS MIGHT BE WEREWOLF...
...AND, WELL, YOU'RE IN A WEREWOLF PACK AROUND HERE, AIN'T YOU?
JASON, THERE'RE A LOT OF THINGS OUT THERE THAT COULD DO SOMETHING BAD LIKE THAT.
I'M SORRY SOMEONE GOT KILLED, BUT IT HAD NOTHING TO DO WITH US.
YOU HEAR ABOUT ANYBODY NEW MOVING INTO THE AREA?
NOPE. BUT THE NIGHT IS LONG AND THE MOON'S GETTIN' FULL. I'LL CHECK IT OUT FOR YOU.
THANKS. BUT I GOTTA WARN YOU, BUDDY, WE GOT FORENSIC EVIDENCE. WE GOT HAIR AND DNA AND ALL THAT. SO LET ME KNOW WHAT YOU FIND OUT.
LOOK, JASON. IF ONE OF MY PACK KILLED A HUMAN, I'LL BE ANGRIER THAN YOU. BUT JUST BECAUSE THE VAMPIRES DECIDED TO MAINSTREAM AND COME OUTTA THE COFFIN...
...DON'T MEAN WEREWOLVES WANNA JOIN THEIR CIRCUS.
SHERIFF

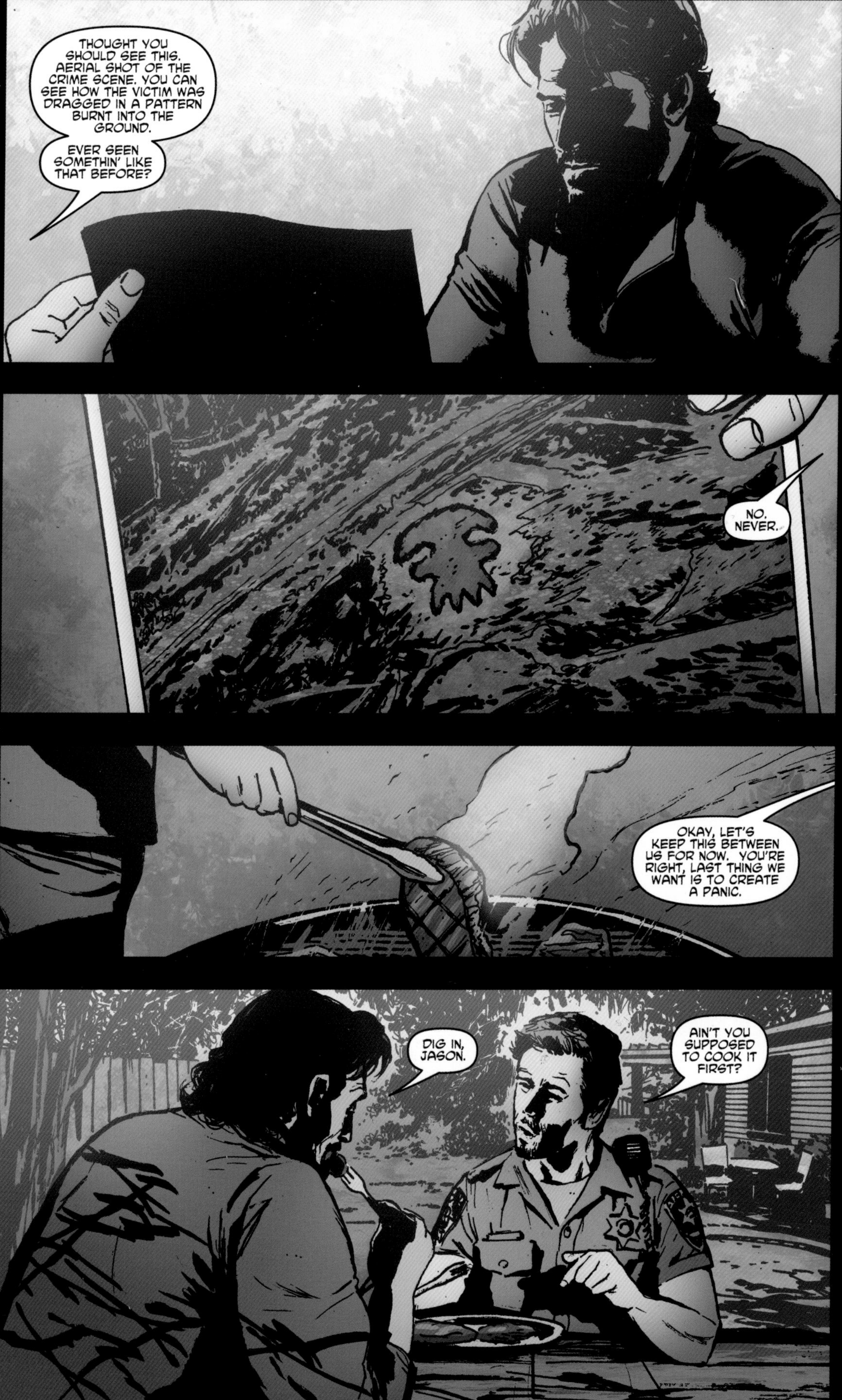
THOUGHT YOU SHOULD SEE THIS. AERIAL SHOT OF THE CRIME SCENE. YOU CAN SEE HOW THE VICTIM WAS DRAGGED IN A PATTERN BURNT INTO THE GROUND.
EVER SEEN SOMETHIN' LIKE THAT BEFORE?
NO. NEVER.
OKAY, LET'S KEEP THIS BETWEEN US FOR NOW. YOU'RE RIGHT, LAST THING WE WANT IS TO CREATE A PANIC.
DIG IN, JASON.
AIN'T YOU SUPPOSED TO COOK IT FIRST?

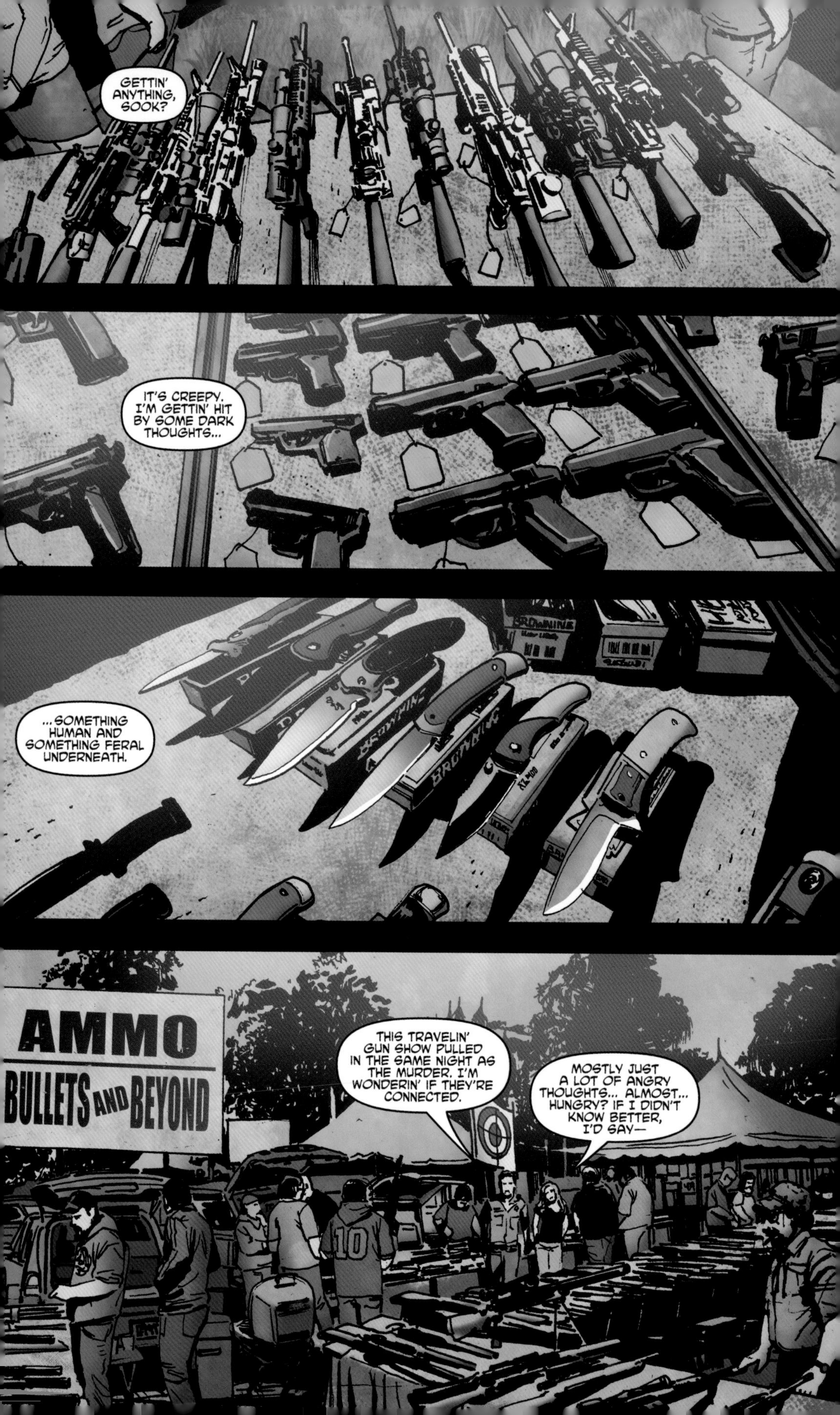
GETTIN' ANYTHING, SOOK?
IT'S CREEPY. I'M GETTIN' HIT BY SOME DARK THOUGHTS...
...SOMETHING HUMAN AND SOMETHING FERAL UNDERNEATH.
AMMO
BULLETS AND BEYOND
THIS TRAVELIN' GUN SHOW PULLED IN THE SAME NIGHT AS THE MURDER. I'M WONDERIN' IF THEY'RE CONNECTED.
MOSTLY JUST A LOT OF ANGRY THOUGHTS... ALMOST... HUNGRY? IF I DIDN'T KNOW BETTER, I'D SAY—

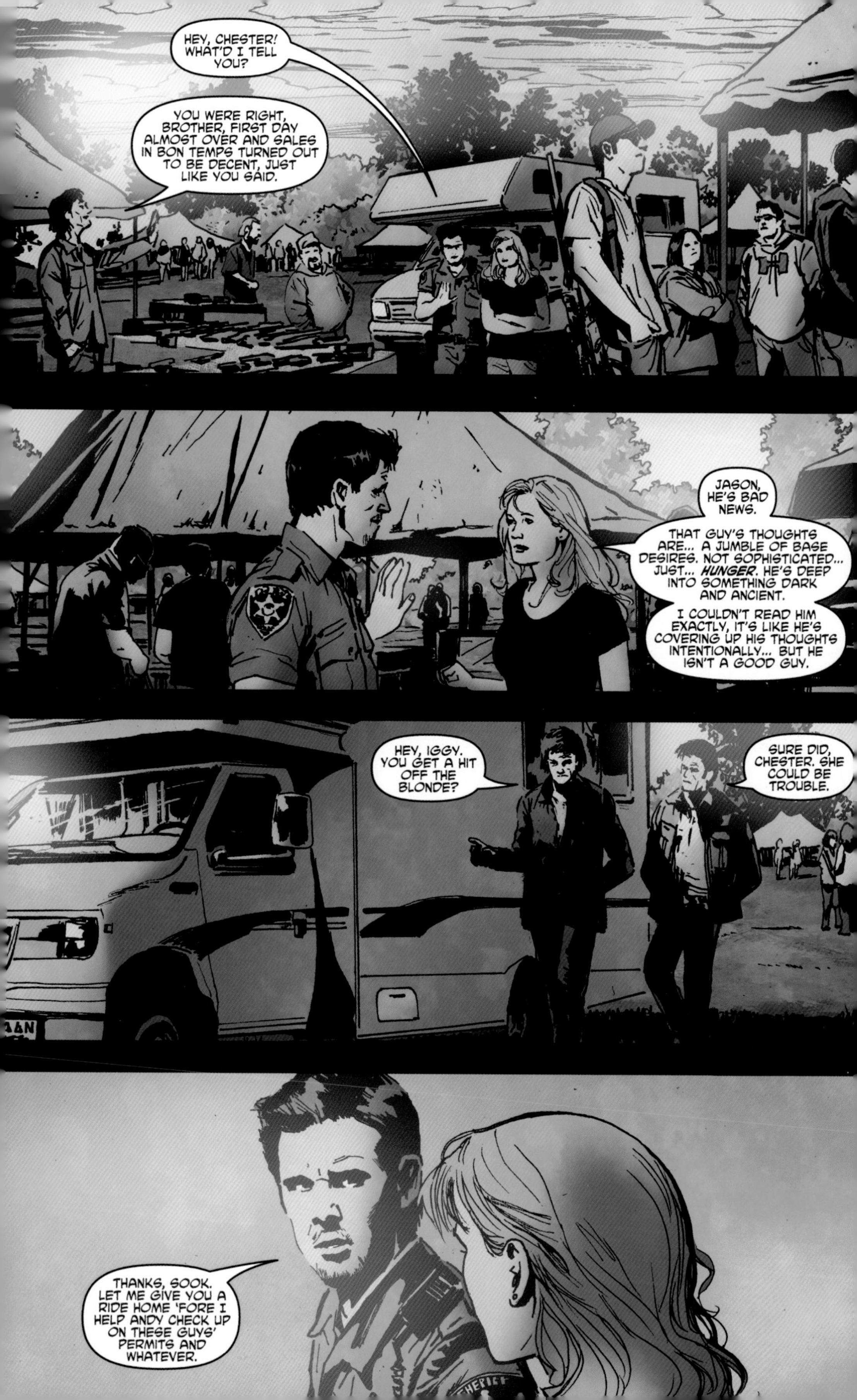
HEY, CHESTER! WHAT'D I TELL YOU?
YOU WERE RIGHT, BROTHER, FIRST DAY ALMOST OVER AND SALES IN BON TEMPS TURNED OUT TO BE DECENT, JUST LIKE YOU SAID.
JASON, HE'S BAD NEWS.
THAT GUY'S THOUGHTS ARE... A JUMBLE OF BASE DESIRES. NOT SOPHISTICATED... JUST... HUNGER. HE'S DEEP INTO SOMETHING DARK AND ANCIENT.
I COULDN'T READ HIM EXACTLY, IT'S LIKE HE'S COVERING UP HIS THOUGHTS INTENTIONALLY... BUT HE ISN'T A GOOD GUY.
HEY, IGGY. YOU GET A HIT OFF THE BLONDE?
SURE DID, CHESTER. SHE COULD BE TROUBLE.
THANKS, SOOK. LET ME GIVE YOU A RIDE HOME 'FORE I HELP ANDY CHECK UP ON THESE GUYS' PERMITS AND WHATEVER.

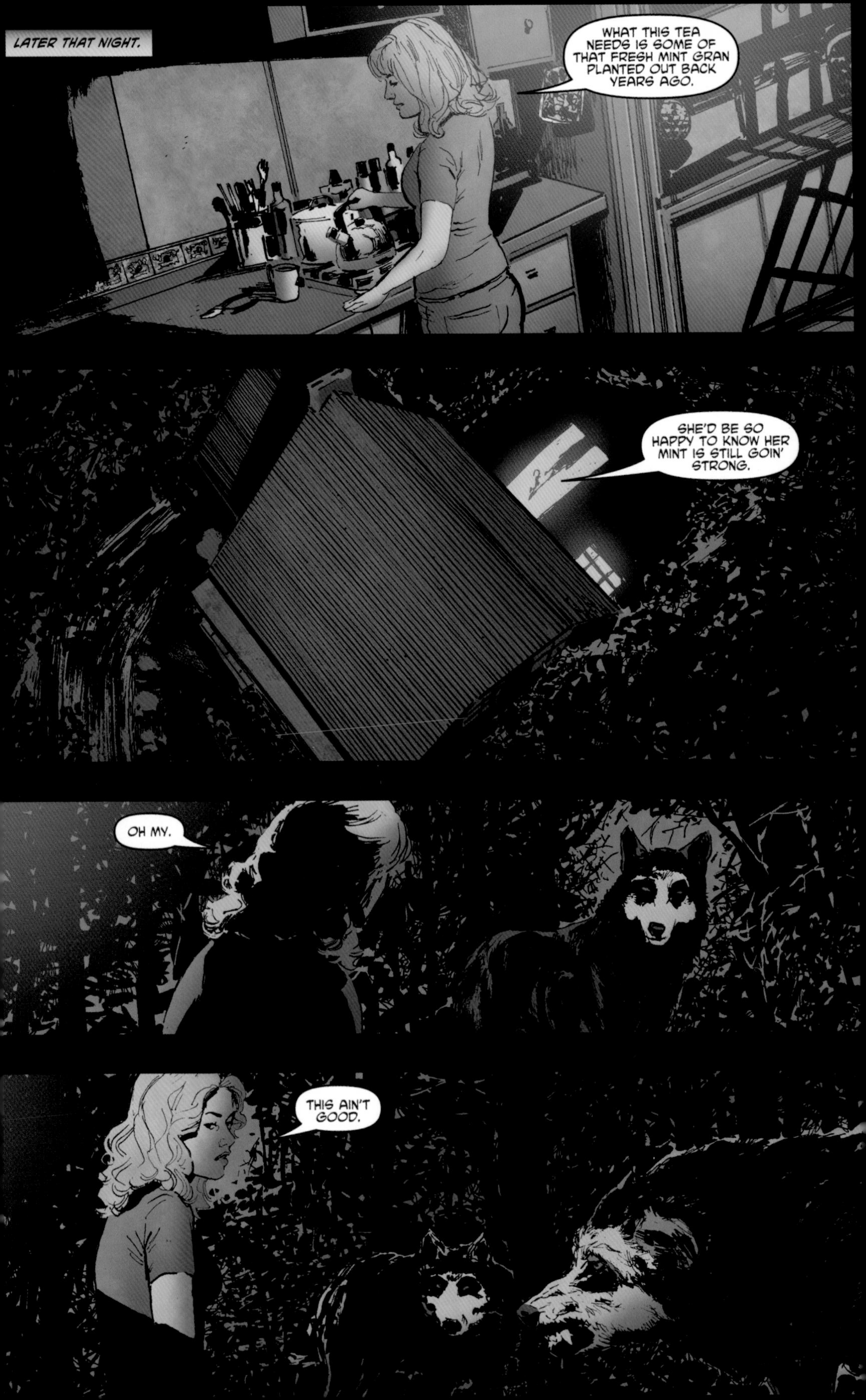
LATER THAT NIGHT.
WHAT THIS TEA NEEDS IS SOME OF THAT FRESH MINT GRAN PLANTED OUT BACK YEARS AGO.
SHE'D BE SO HAPPY TO KNOW HER MINT IS STILL GOIN' STRONG.
OH MY.
THIS AIN'T GOOD.

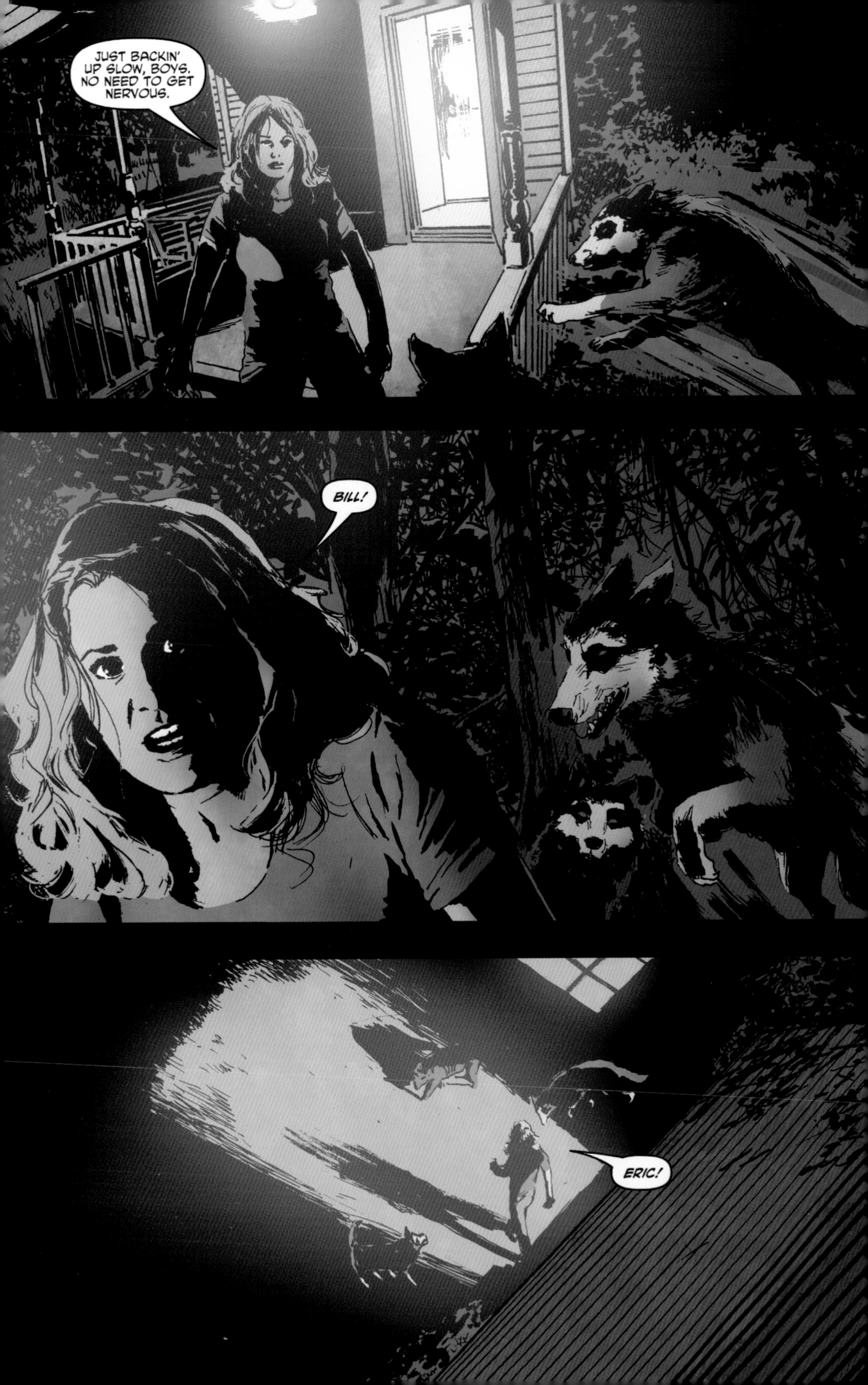
JUST BACKIN' UP SLOW, BOYS. NO NEED TO GET NERVOUS.
BILL!
ERIC!

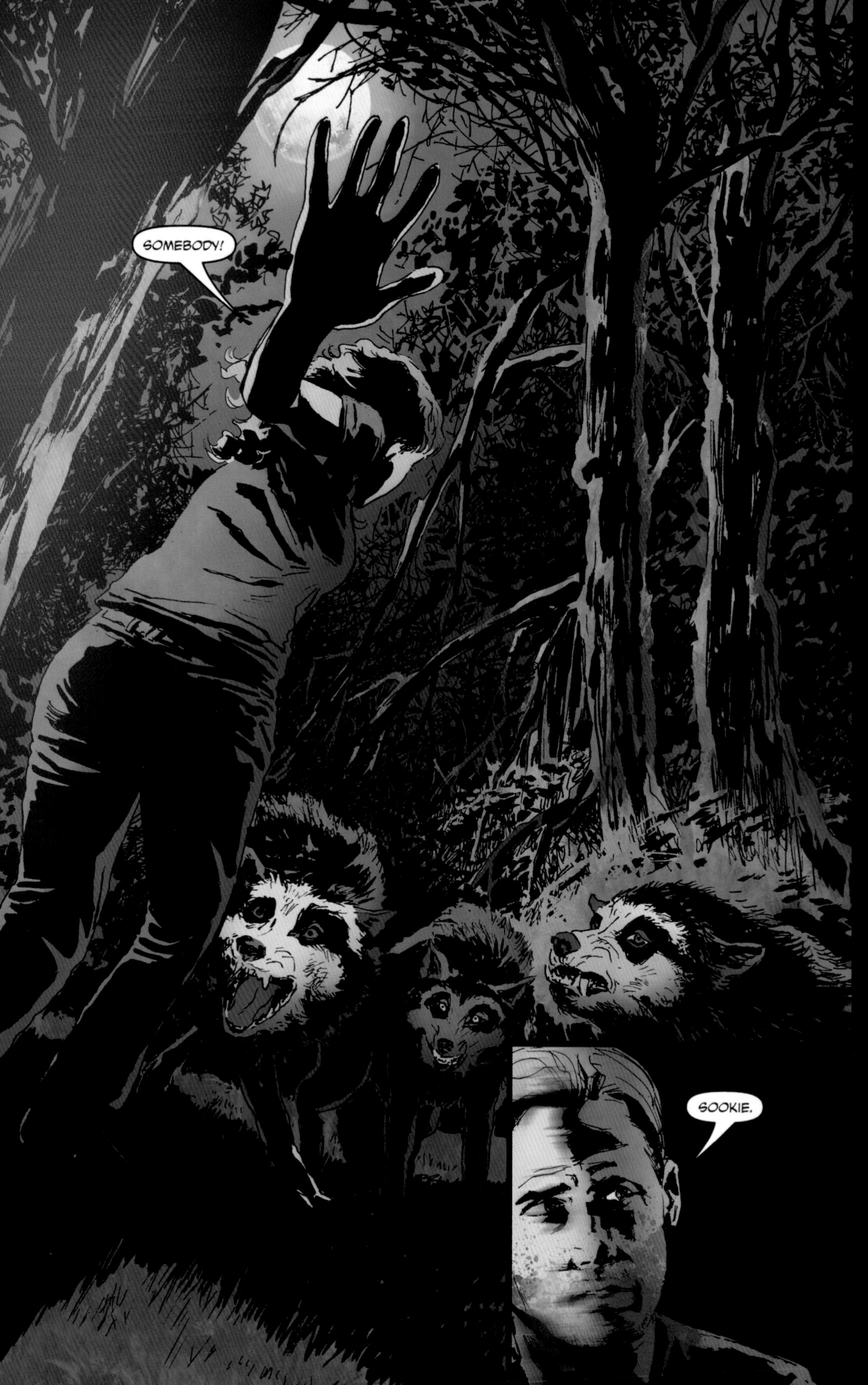
SOMEBODY!
SOOKIE.

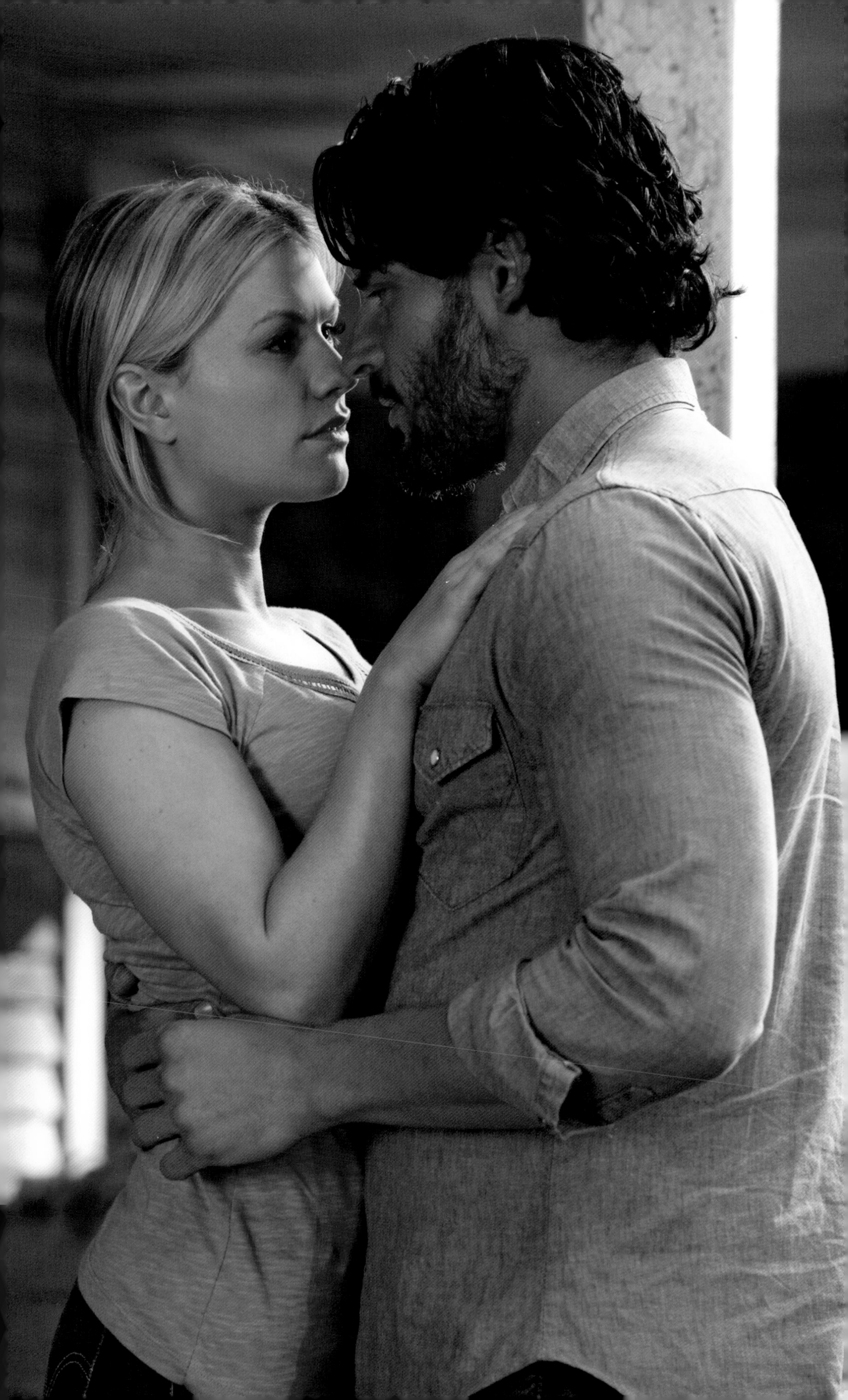

CHAPTER 2

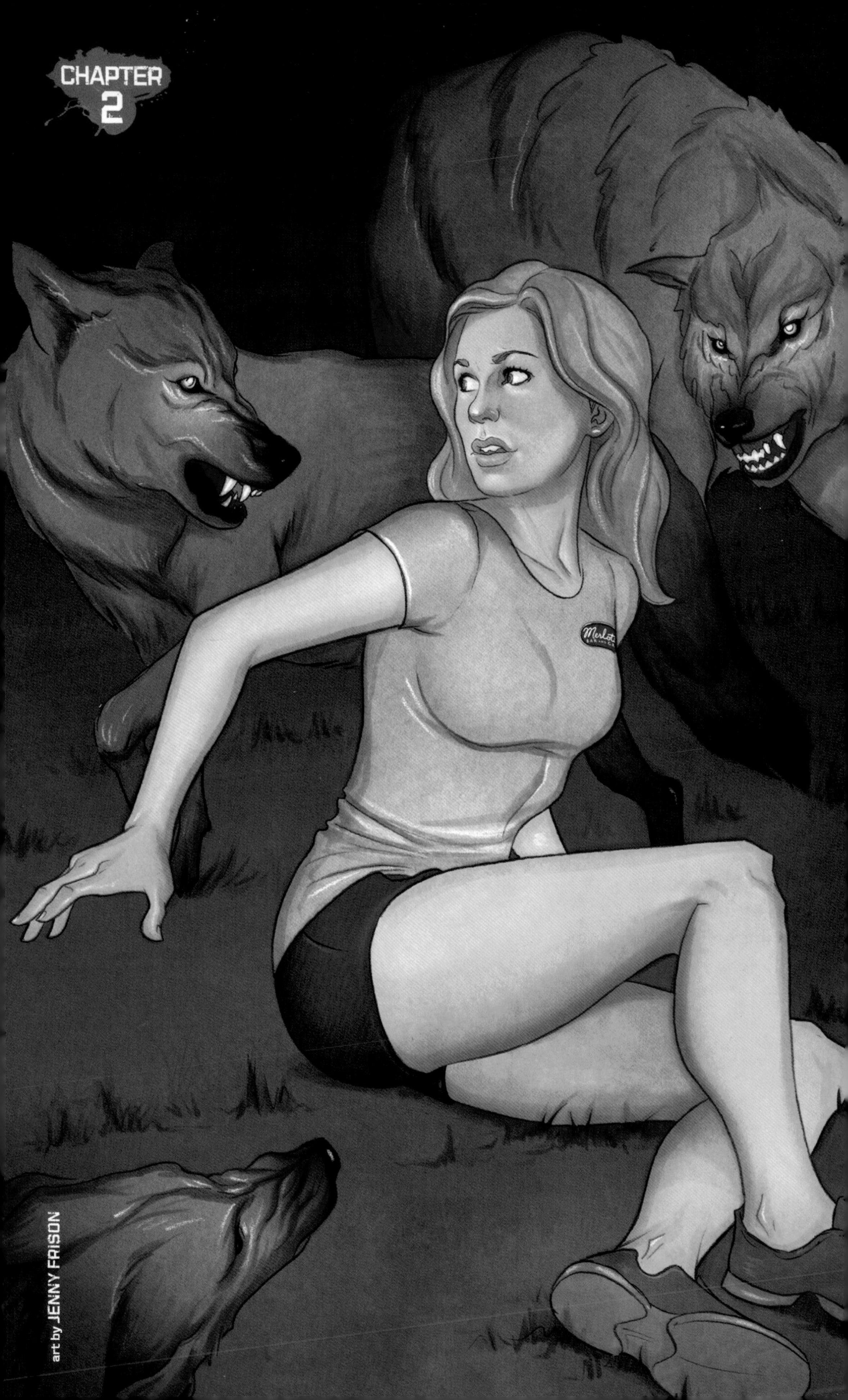

art by JENNY FRISON

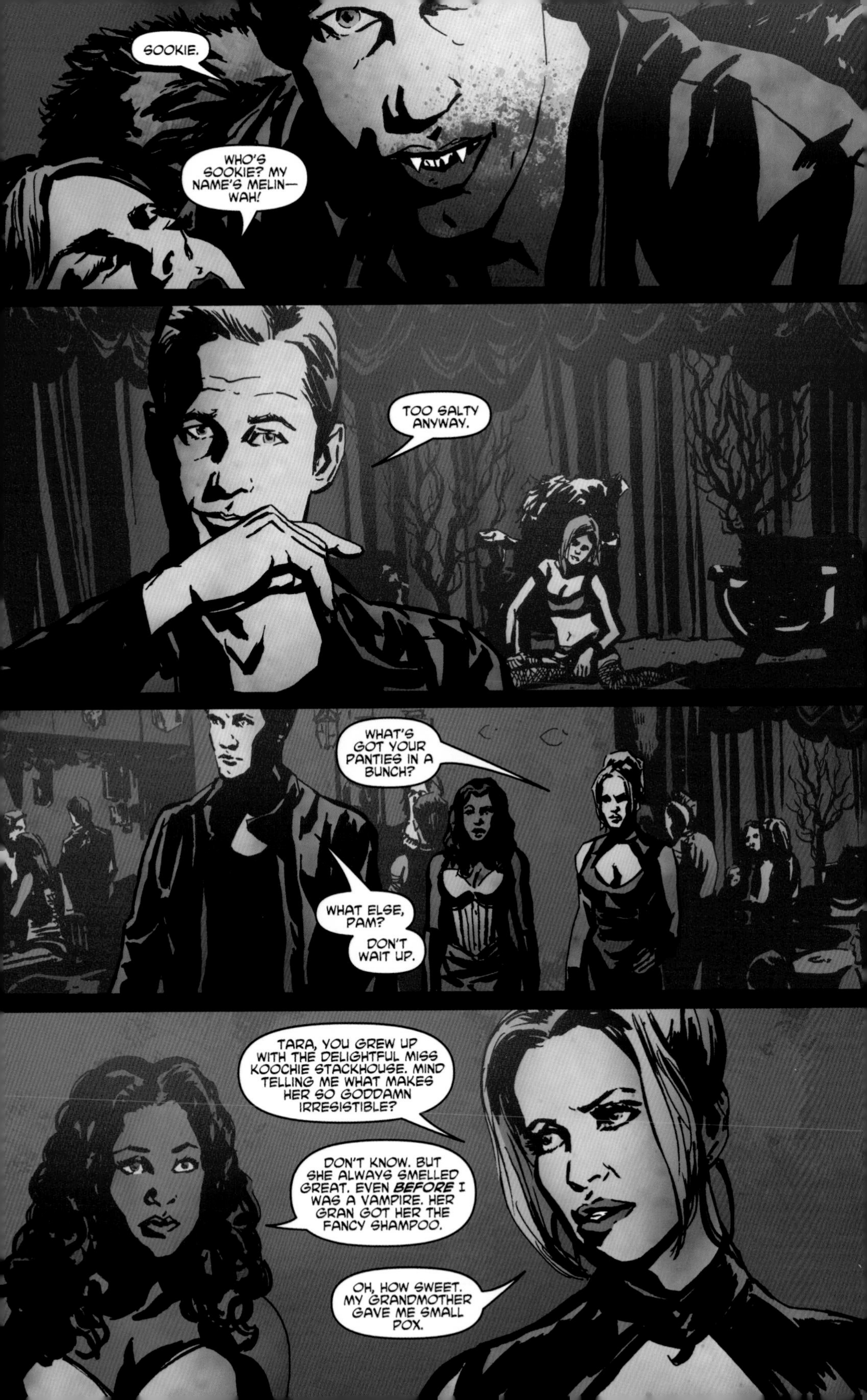

SOOKIE.
WHO'S SOOKIE? MY NAME'S MELIN—WAH!
TOO SALTY ANYWAY.
WHAT'S GOT YOUR PANTIES IN A BUNCH?
WHAT ELSE, PAM?
DON'T WAIT UP.
TARA, YOU GREW UP WITH THE DELIGHTFUL MISS KOOCHIE STACKHOUSE. MIND TELLING ME WHAT MAKES HER SO GODDAMN IRRESISTIBLE?
DON'T KNOW. BUT SHE ALWAYS SMELLED GREAT. EVEN *BEFORE* I WAS A VAMPIRE. HER GRAN GOT HER THE FANCY SHAMPOO.
OH, HOW SWEET. MY GRANDMOTHER GAVE ME SMALL POX.

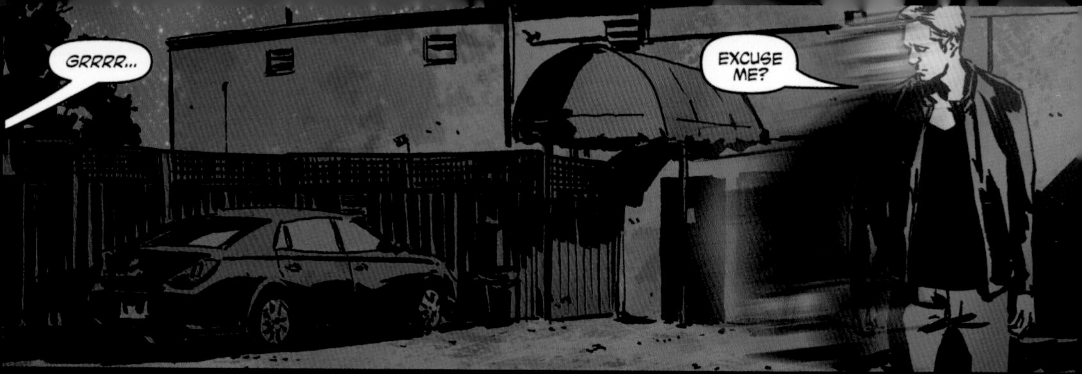
GRRRR...
EXCUSE ME?

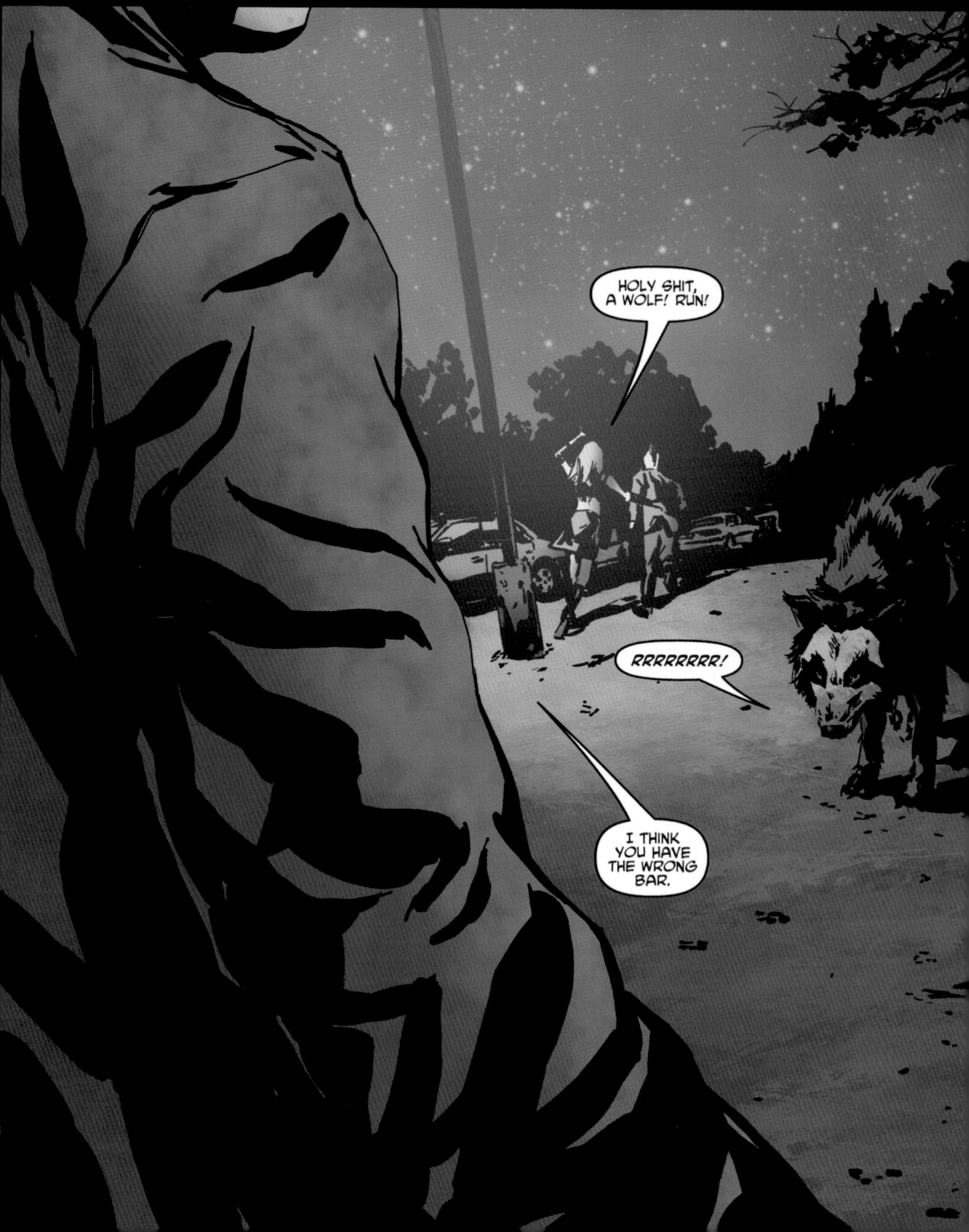
HOLY SHIT, A WOLF! RUN!
RRRRRRRR!
I THINK YOU HAVE THE WRONG BAR.

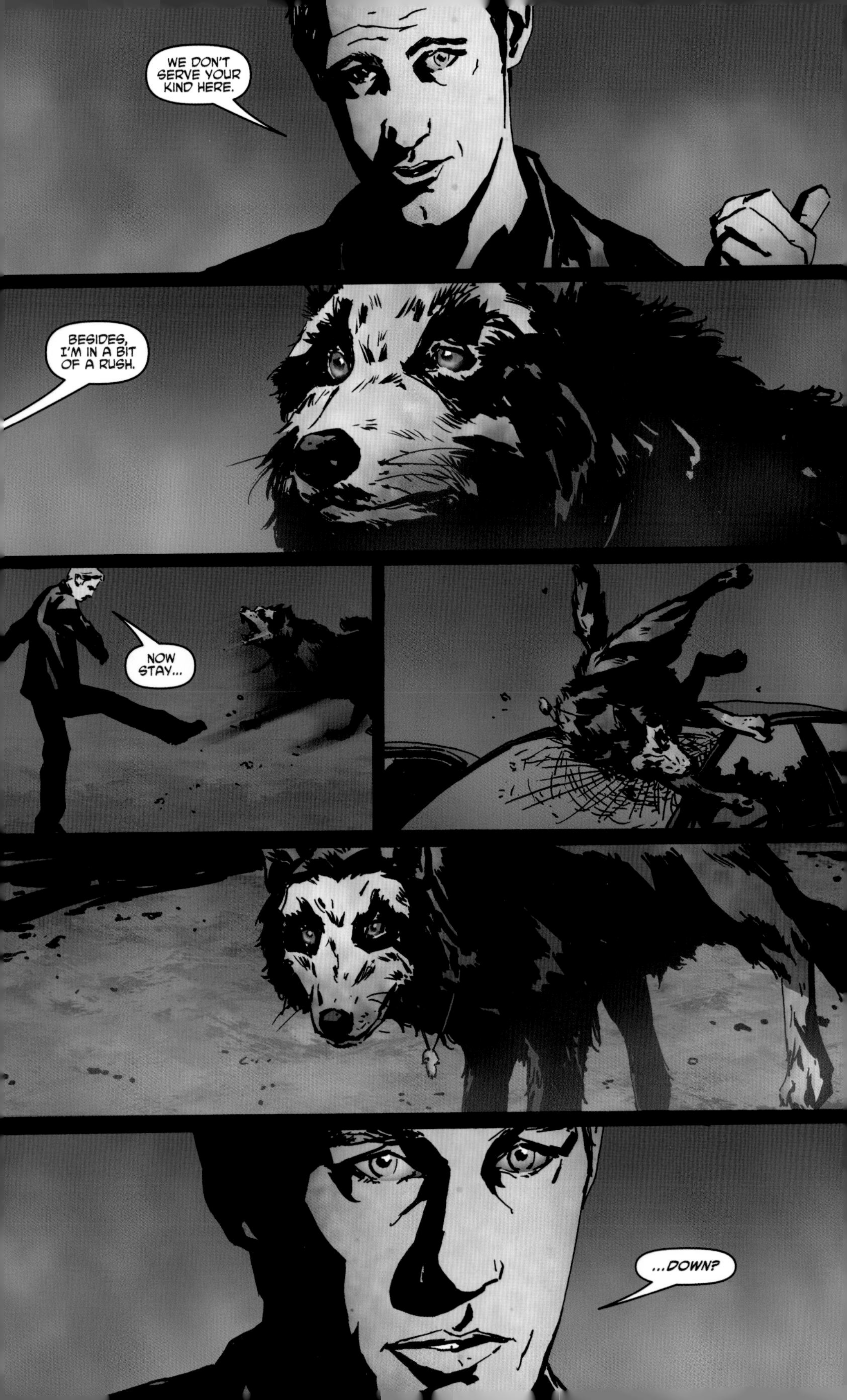
WE DON'T SERVE YOUR KIND HERE.
BESIDES, I'M IN A BIT OF A RUSH.
NOW STAY...
...DOWN?

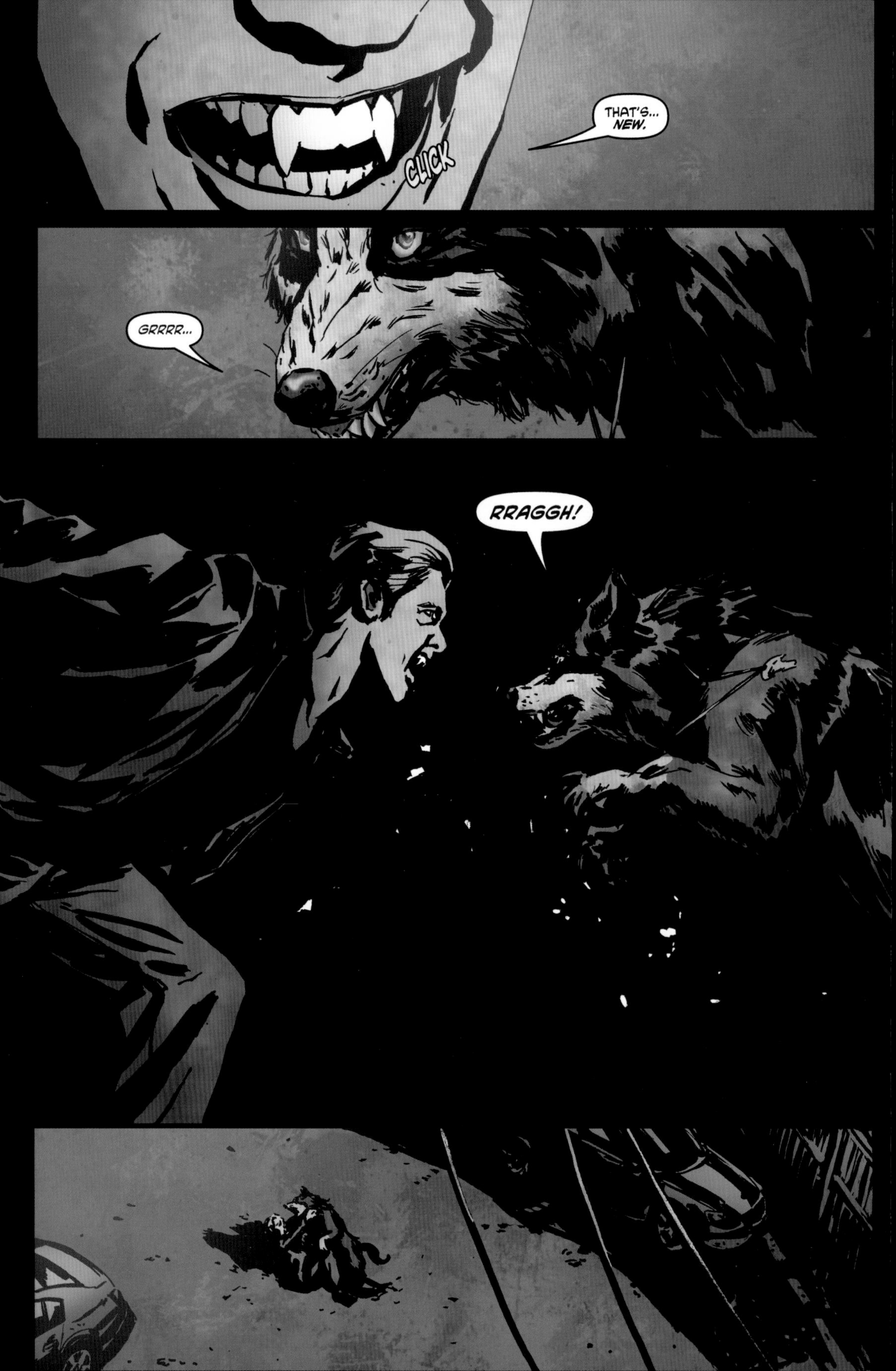
THAT'S... NEW.
CLICK
GRRRR...
RRAGGH!

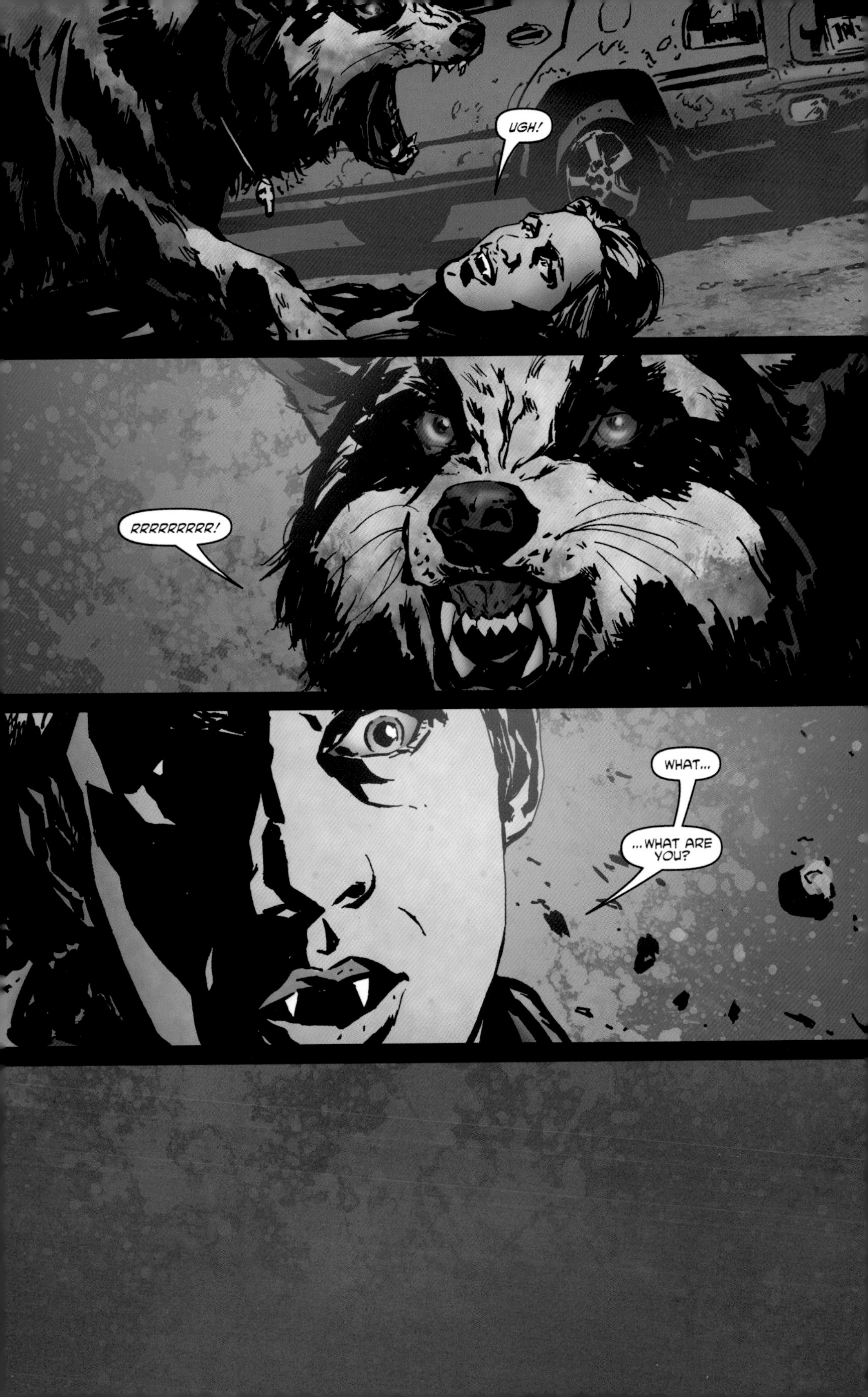
UGH!
RRRRRRRRR!
WHAT...
...WHAT ARE YOU?

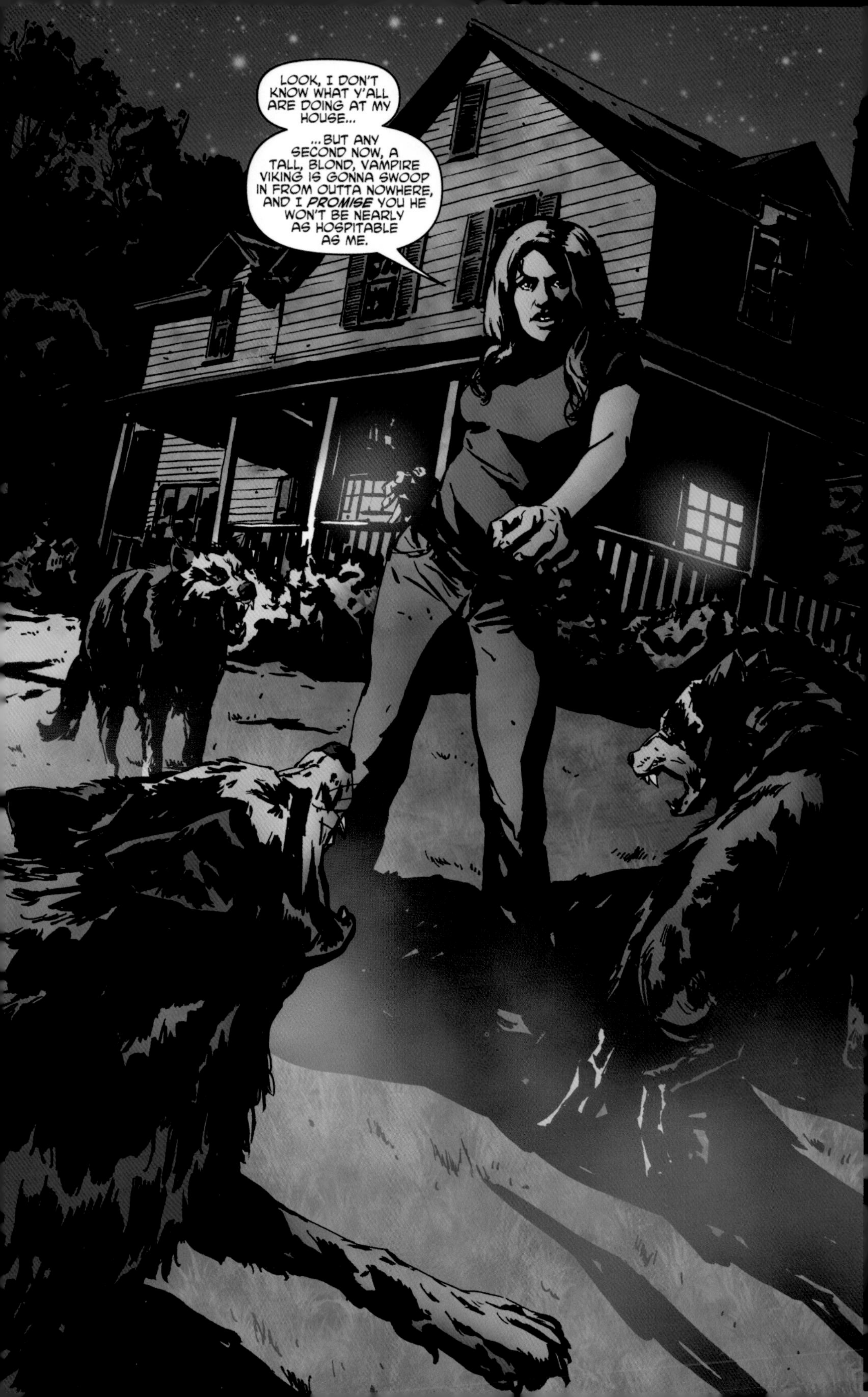
LOOK, I DON'T KNOW WHAT Y'ALL ARE DOING AT MY HOUSE...
...BUT ANY SECOND NOW, A TALL, BLOND, VAMPIRE VIKING IS GONNA SWOOP IN FROM OUTTA NOWHERE, AND I *PROMISE* YOU HE WON'T BE NEARLY AS HOSPITABLE AS ME.

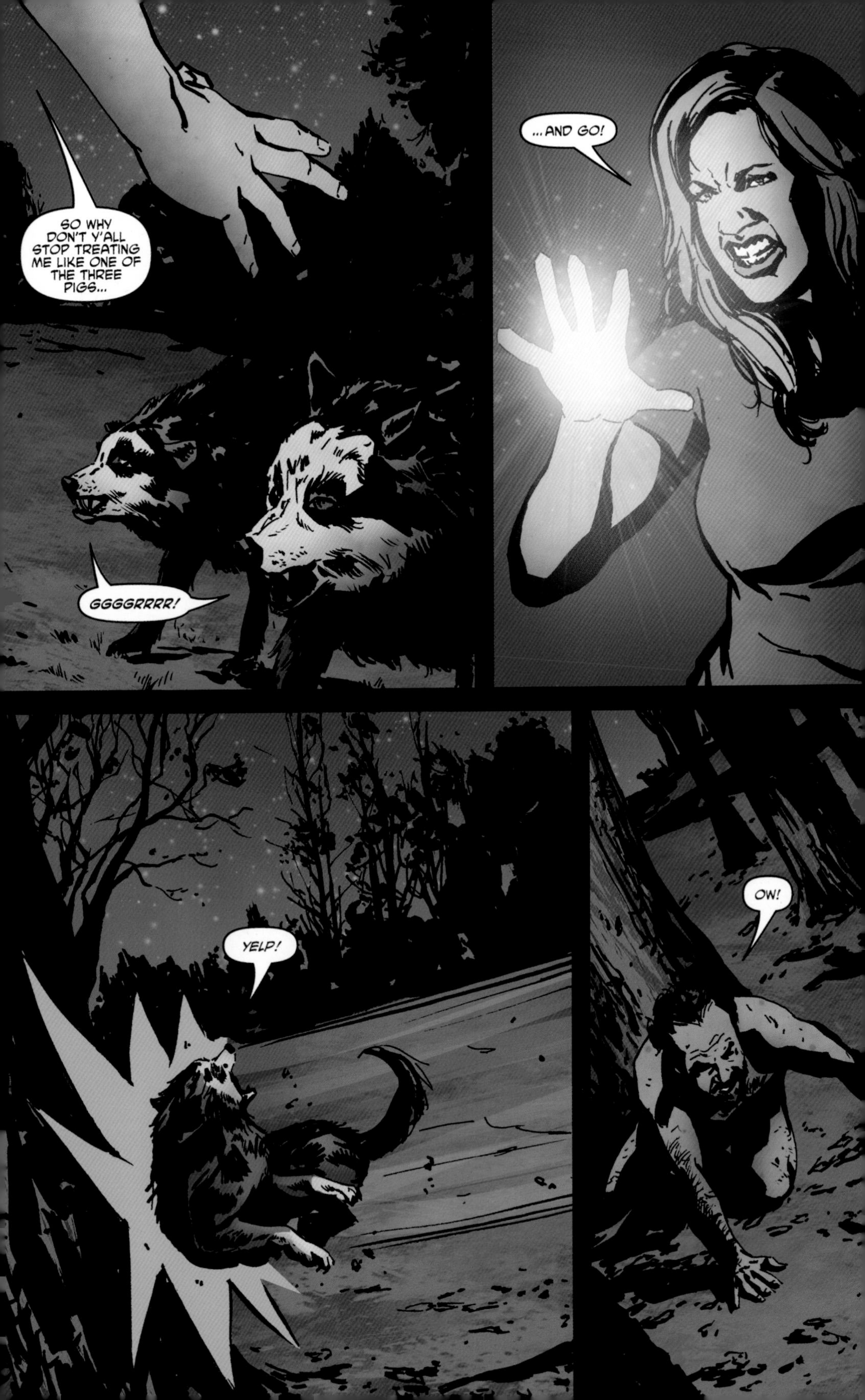
SO WHY DON'T Y'ALL STOP TREATING ME LIKE ONE OF THE THREE PIGS...
GGGGRRRR!
...AND GO!
YELP!
OW!

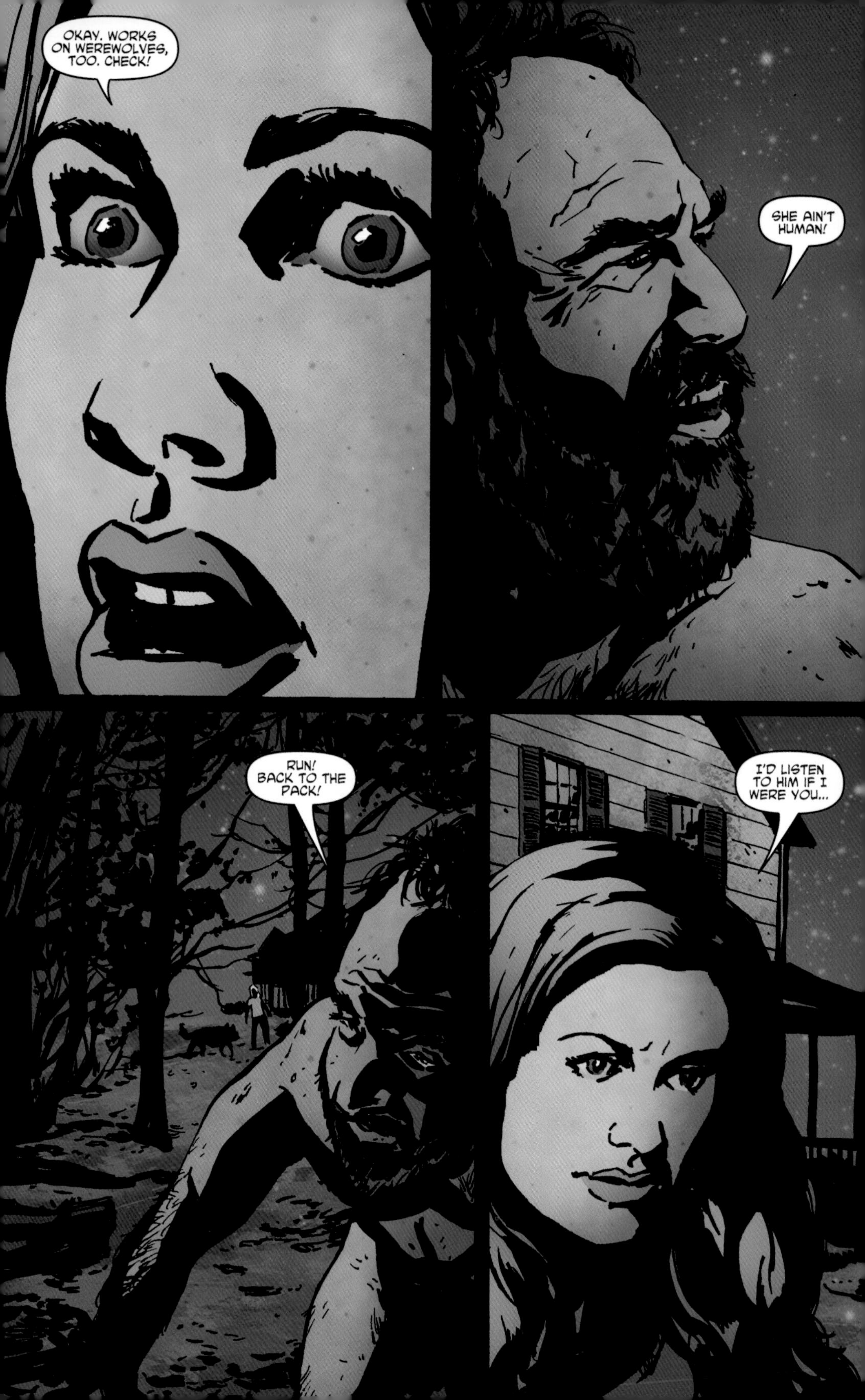
OKAY. WORKS ON WEREWOLVES, TOO. CHECK!
SHE AIN'T HUMAN!
RUN! BACK TO THE PACK!
I'D LISTEN TO HIM IF I WERE YOU...

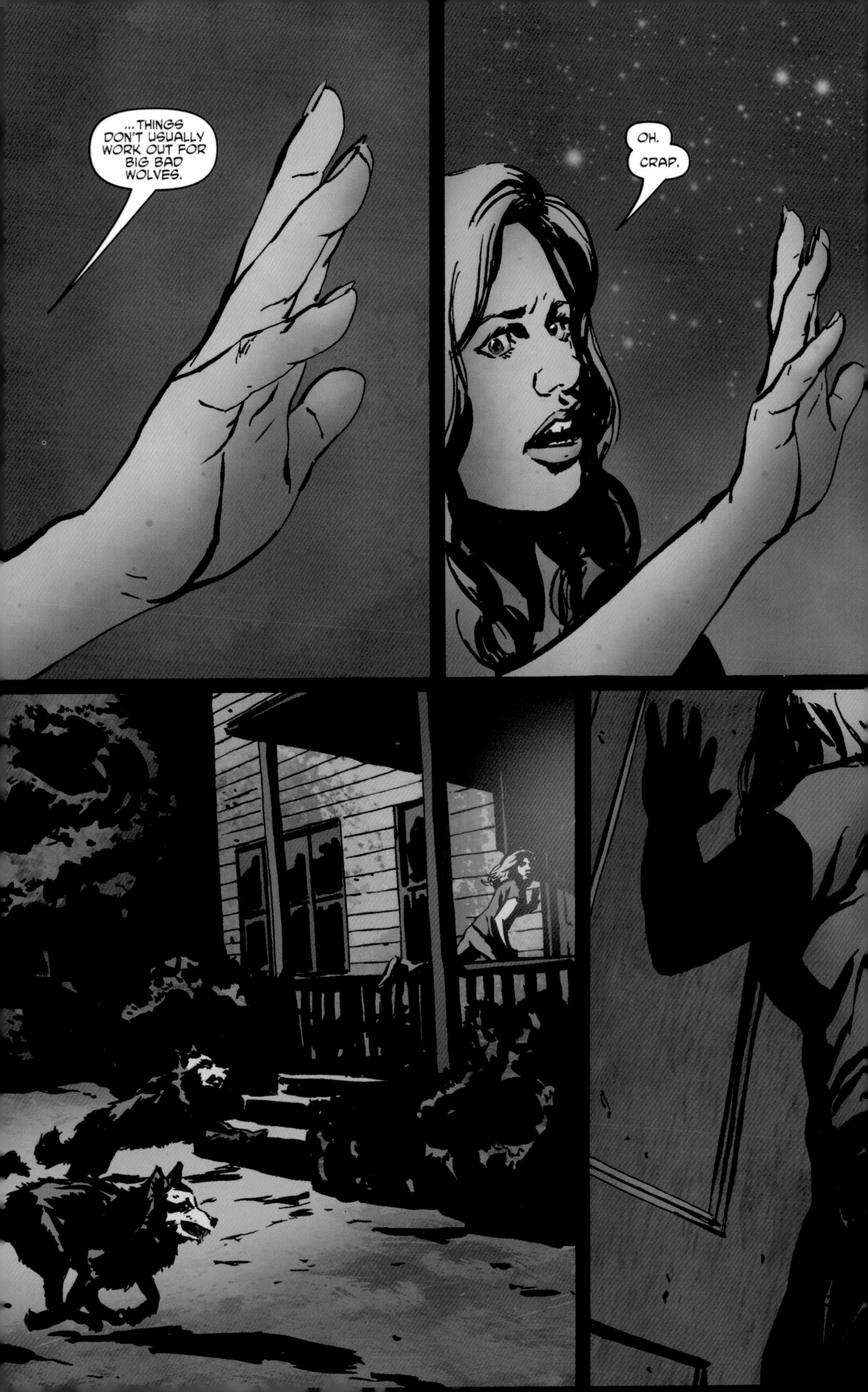
...THINGS DON'T USUALLY WORK OUT FOR BIG BAD WOLVES.
OH.
CRAP.

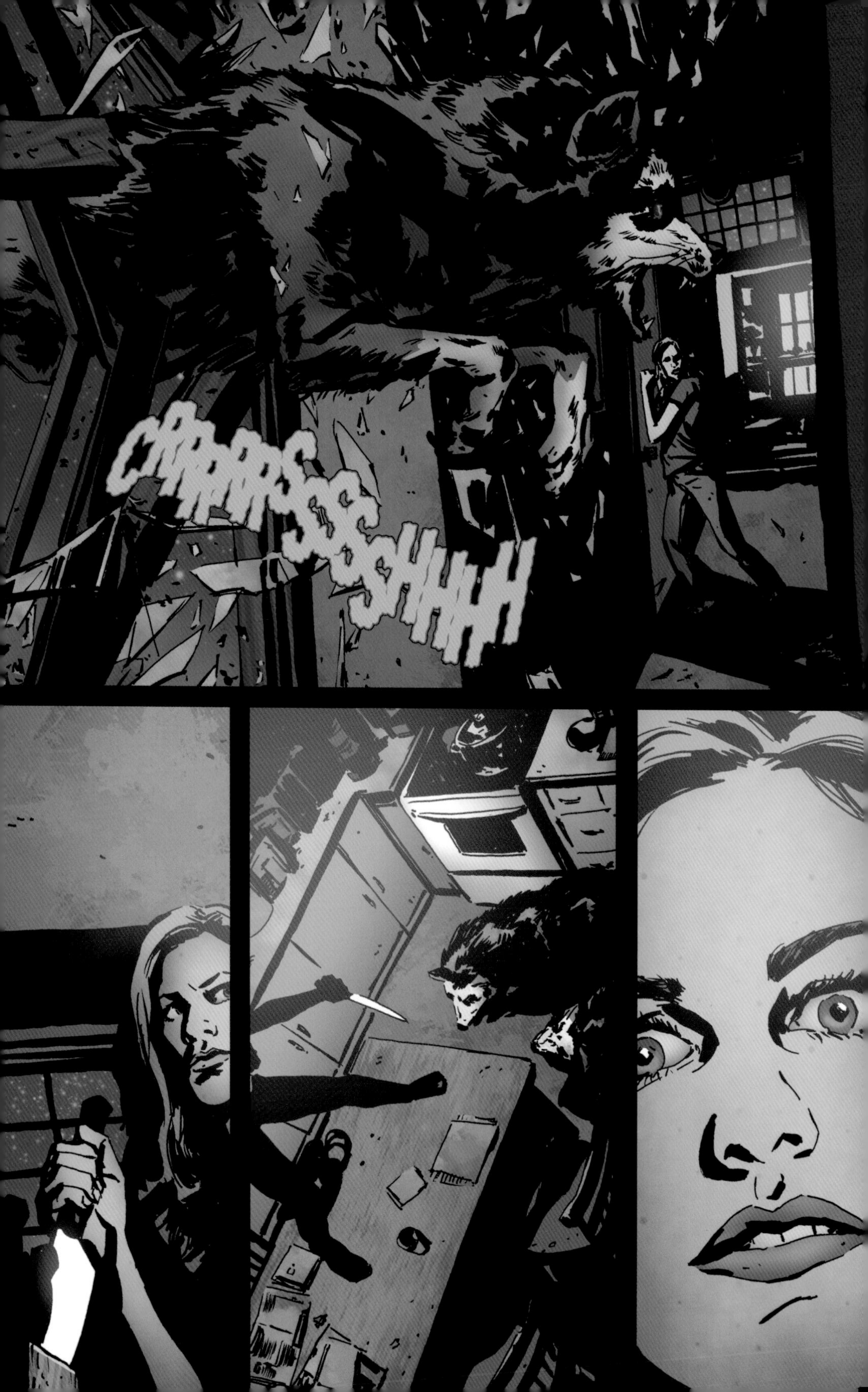
CRRRRSSSHHHH

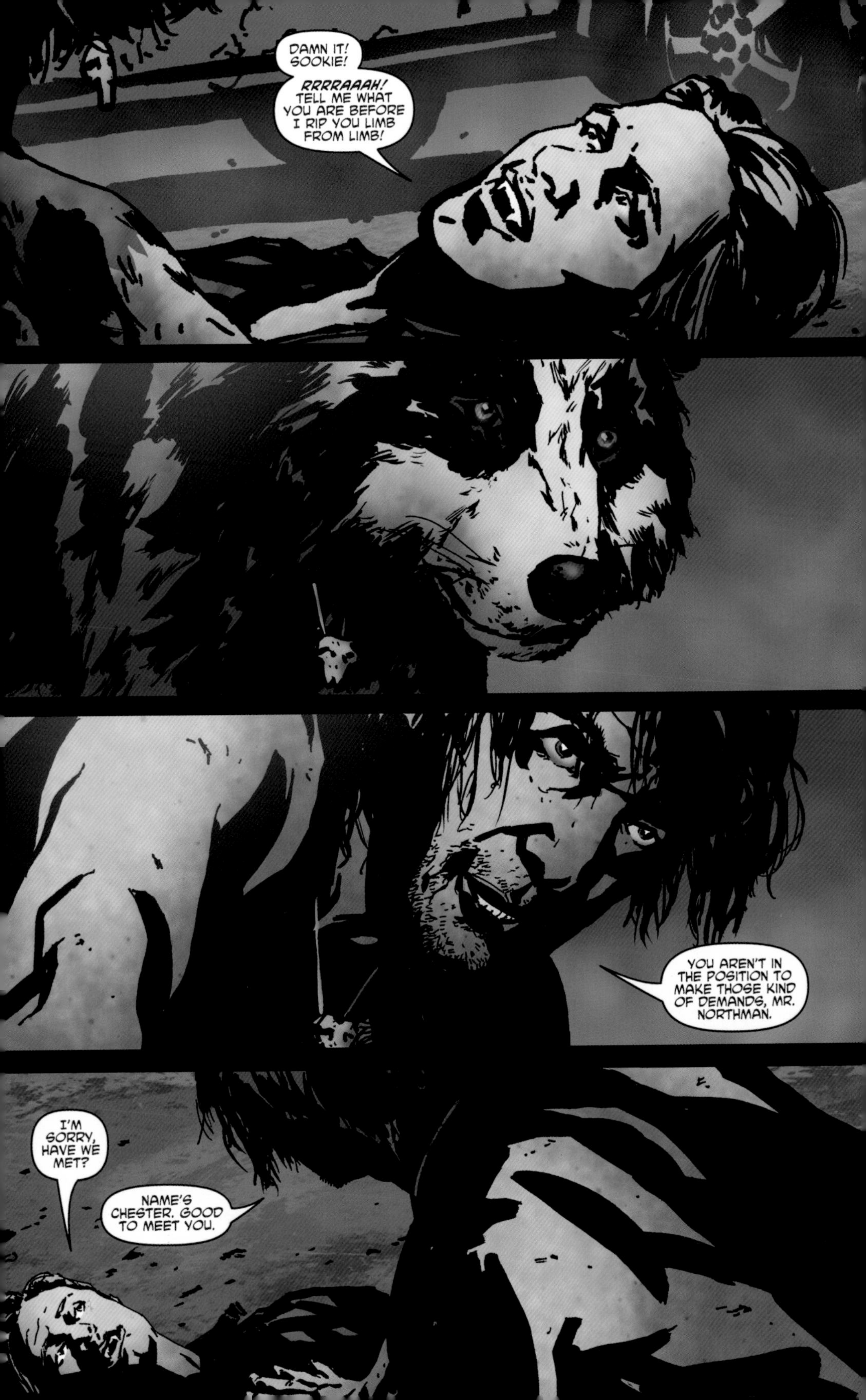
DAMN IT! SOOKIE!
RRRRAAAH! TELL ME WHAT YOU ARE BEFORE I RIP YOU LIMB FROM LIMB!
YOU AREN'T IN THE POSITION TO MAKE THOSE KIND OF DEMANDS, MR. NORTHMAN.
I'M SORRY, HAVE WE MET?
NAME'S CHESTER. GOOD TO MEET YOU.

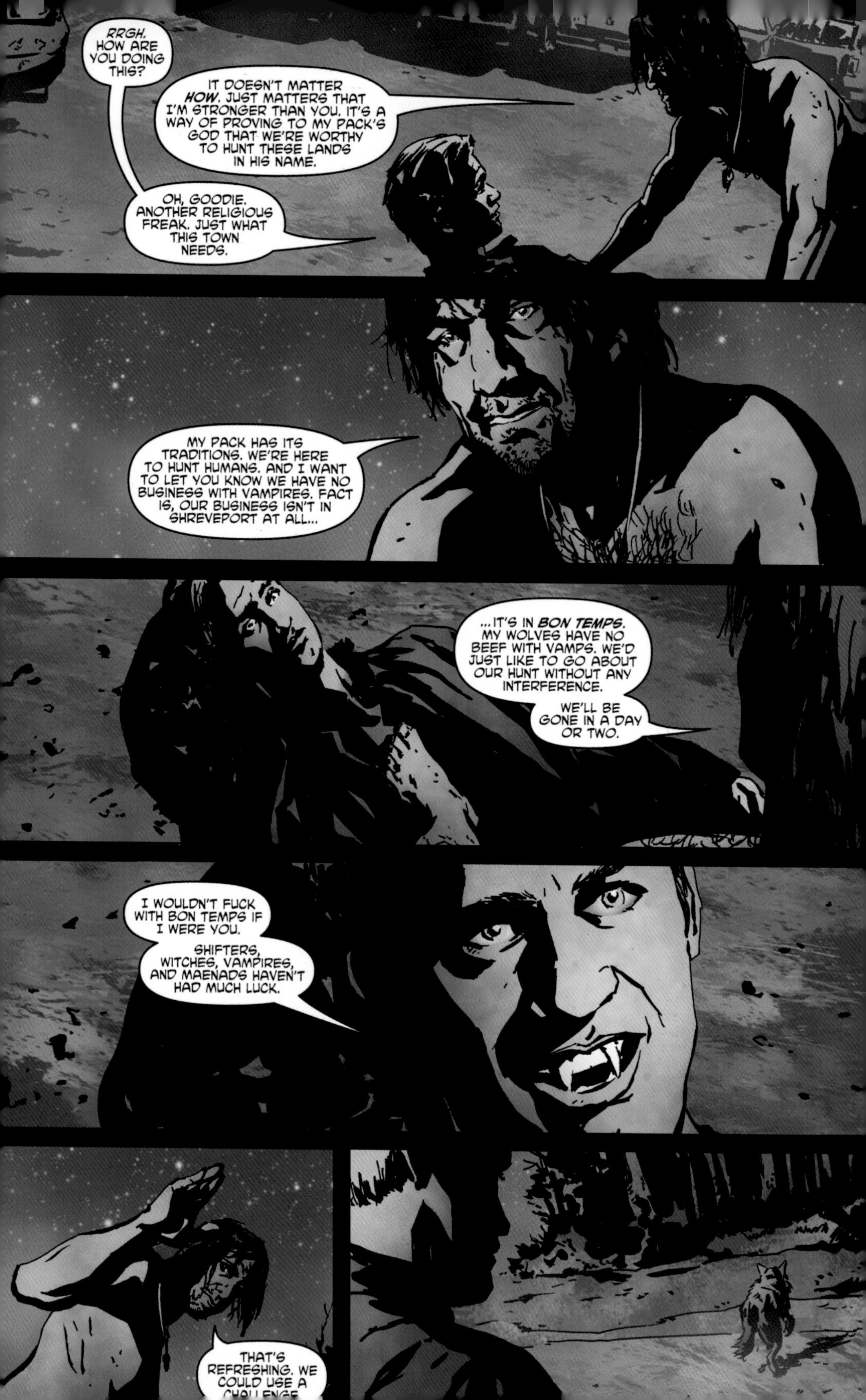
RRGH. HOW ARE YOU DOING THIS?
IT DOESN'T MATTER *HOW*. JUST MATTERS THAT I'M STRONGER THAN YOU. IT'S A WAY OF PROVING TO MY PACK'S GOD THAT WE'RE WORTHY TO HUNT THESE LANDS IN HIS NAME.
OH, GOODIE. ANOTHER RELIGIOUS FREAK. JUST WHAT THIS TOWN NEEDS.
MY PACK HAS ITS TRADITIONS. WE'RE HERE TO HUNT HUMANS. AND I WANT TO LET YOU KNOW WE HAVE NO BUSINESS WITH VAMPIRES. FACT IS, OUR BUSINESS ISN'T IN SHREVEPORT AT ALL...
...IT'S IN *BON TEMPS*. MY WOLVES HAVE NO BEEF WITH VAMPS. WE'D JUST LIKE TO GO ABOUT OUR HUNT WITHOUT ANY INTERFERENCE.
WE'LL BE GONE IN A DAY OR TWO.
I WOULDN'T FUCK WITH BON TEMPS IF I WERE YOU.
SHIFTERS, WITCHES, VAMPIRES, AND MAENADS HAVEN'T HAD MUCH LUCK.
THAT'S REFRESHING. WE COULD USE A

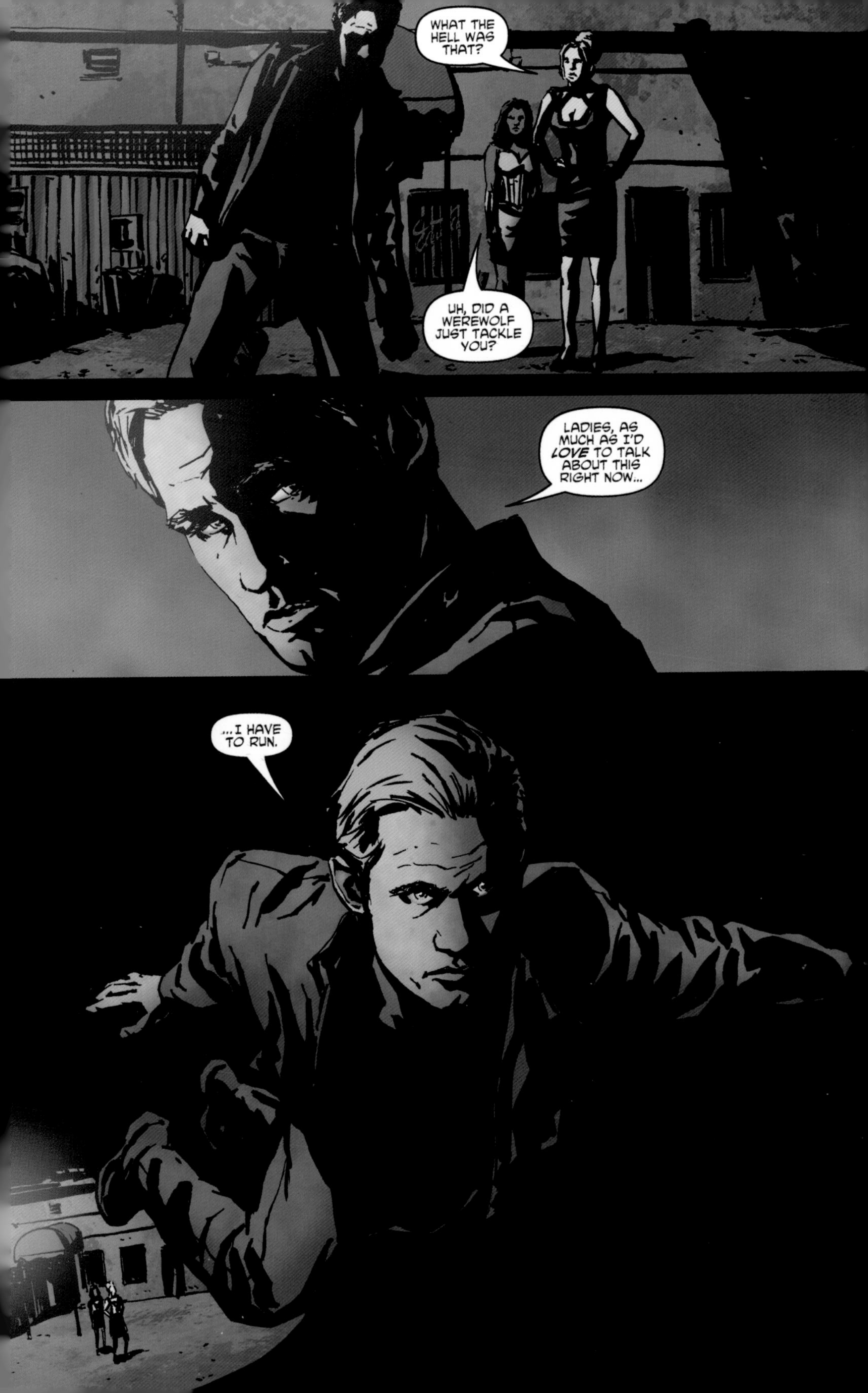
WHAT THE HELL WAS THAT?
UH, DID A WEREWOLF JUST TACKLE YOU?
LADIES, AS MUCH AS I'D *LOVE* TO TALK ABOUT THIS RIGHT NOW...
...I HAVE TO RUN.

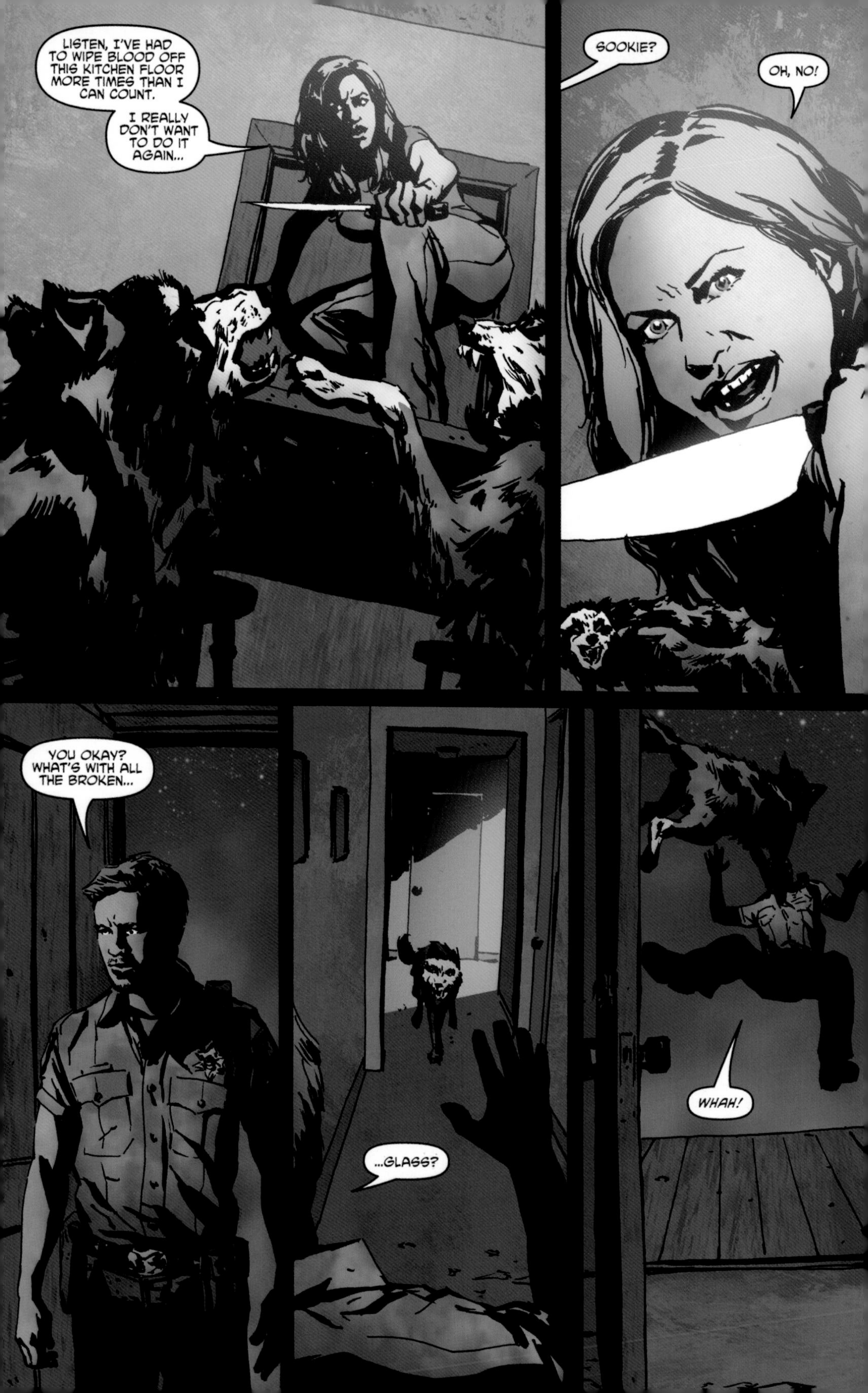
LISTEN, I'VE HAD TO WIPE BLOOD OFF THIS KITCHEN FLOOR MORE TIMES THAN I CAN COUNT.
I REALLY DON'T WANT TO DO IT AGAIN...
SOOKIE?
OH, NO!
YOU OKAY? WHAT'S WITH ALL THE BROKEN...
...GLASS?
WHAH!

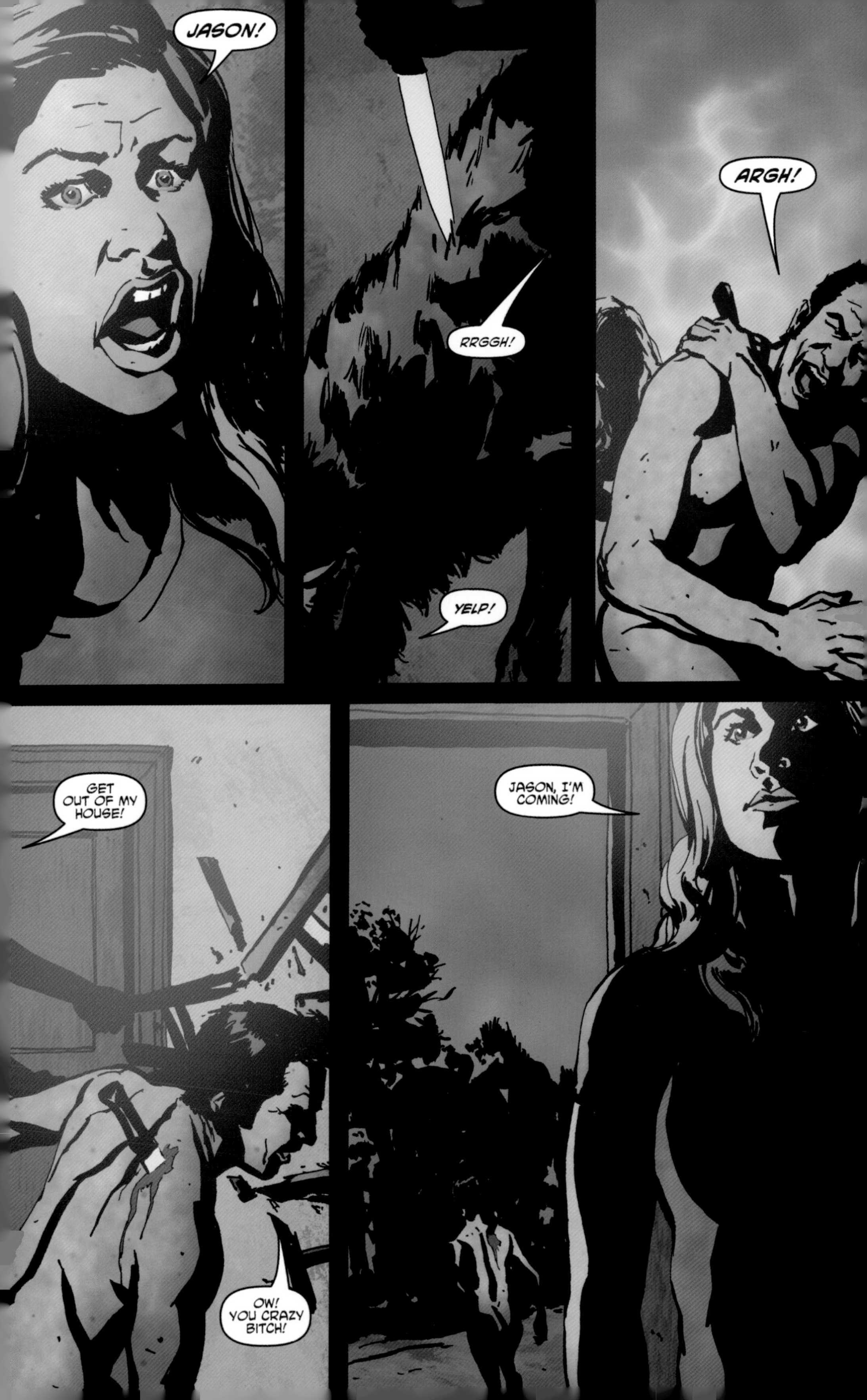
JASON!
RRGGH!
YELP!
ARGH!
GET OUT OF MY HOUSE!
OW! YOU CRAZY BITCH!
JASON, I'M COMING!

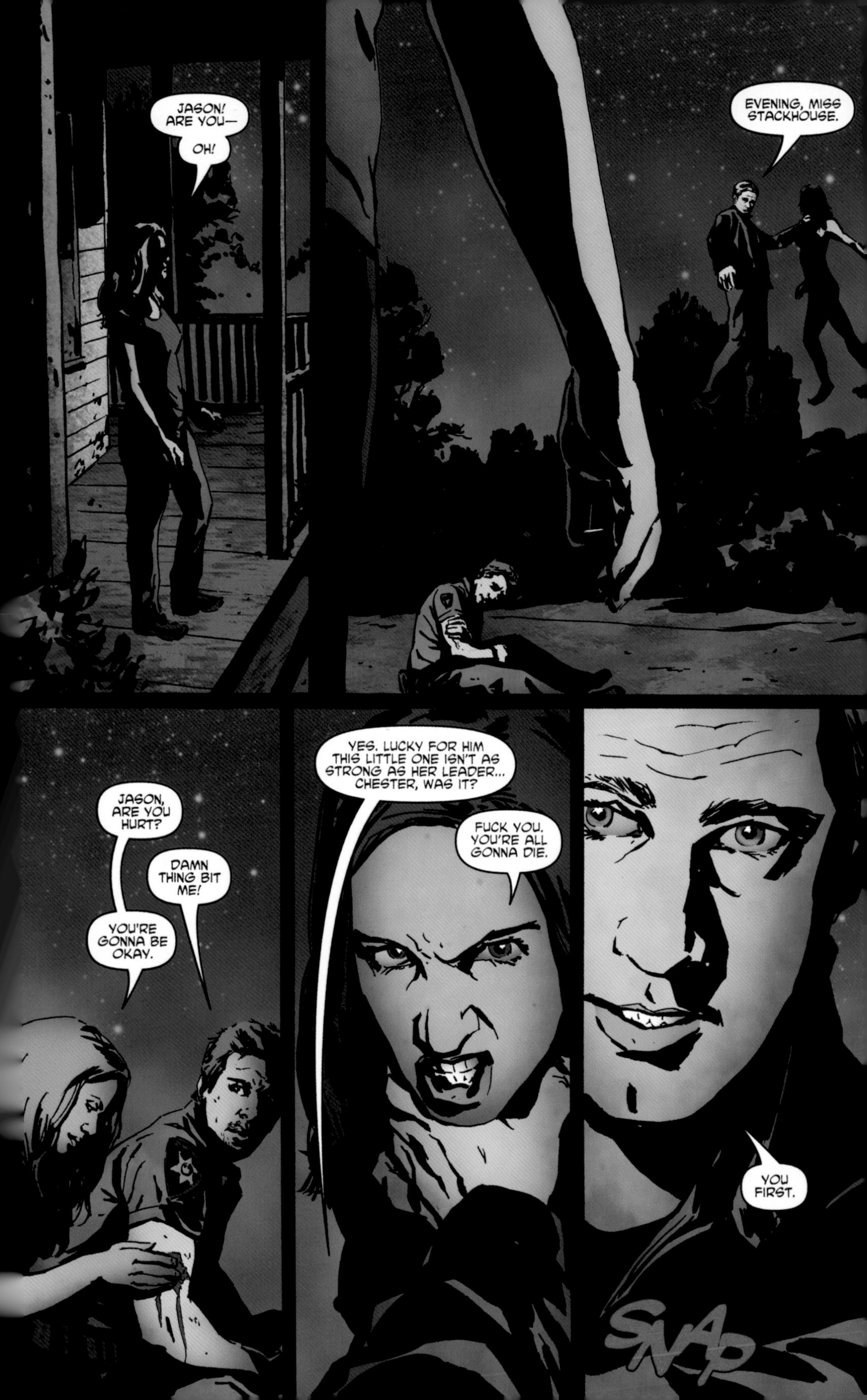
JASON! ARE YOU—
OH!
EVENING, MISS STACKHOUSE.
JASON, ARE YOU HURT?
DAMN THING BIT ME!
YOU'RE GONNA BE OKAY.
YES. LUCKY FOR HIM THIS LITTLE ONE ISN'T AS STRONG AS HER LEADER... CHESTER, WAS IT?
FUCK YOU. YOU'RE ALL GONNA DIE.
YOU FIRST.
SNAP

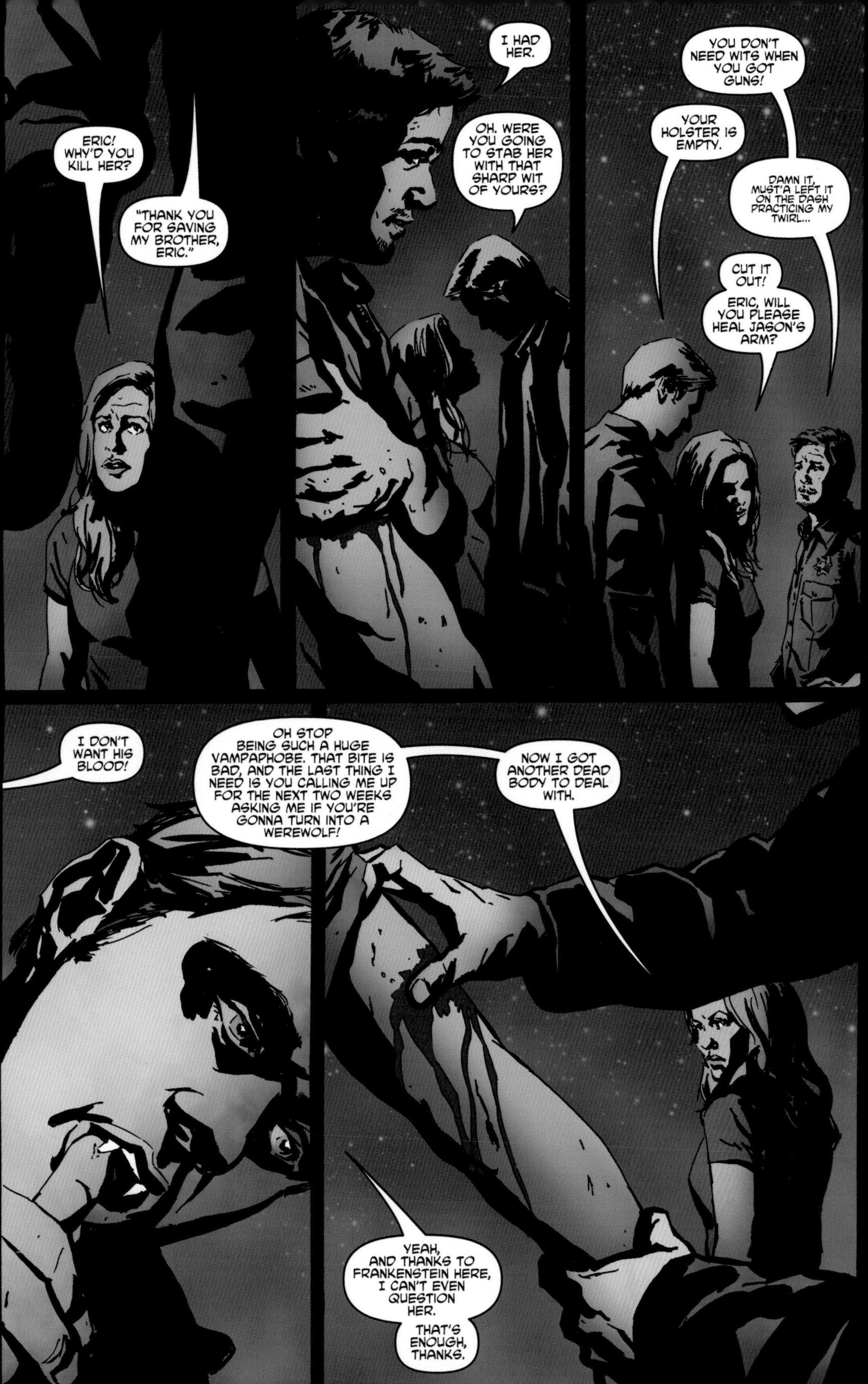
ERIC! WHY'D YOU KILL HER?
"THANK YOU FOR SAVING MY BROTHER, ERIC."
I HAD HER.
OH. WERE YOU GOING TO STAB HER WITH THAT SHARP WIT OF YOURS?
YOU DON'T NEED WITS WHEN YOU GOT GUNS!
YOUR HOLSTER IS EMPTY.
DAMN IT. MUST'A LEFT IT ON THE DASH PRACTICING MY TWIRL...
CUT IT OUT!
ERIC, WILL YOU PLEASE HEAL JASON'S ARM?
I DON'T WANT HIS BLOOD!
OH STOP BEING SUCH A HUGE VAMPAPHOBE. THAT BITE IS BAD, AND THE LAST THING I NEED IS YOU CALLING ME UP FOR THE NEXT TWO WEEKS ASKING ME IF YOU'RE GONNA TURN INTO A WEREWOLF!
NOW I GOT ANOTHER DEAD BODY TO DEAL WITH.
YEAH, AND THANKS TO FRANKENSTEIN HERE, I CAN'T EVEN QUESTION HER.
THAT'S ENOUGH, THANKS.

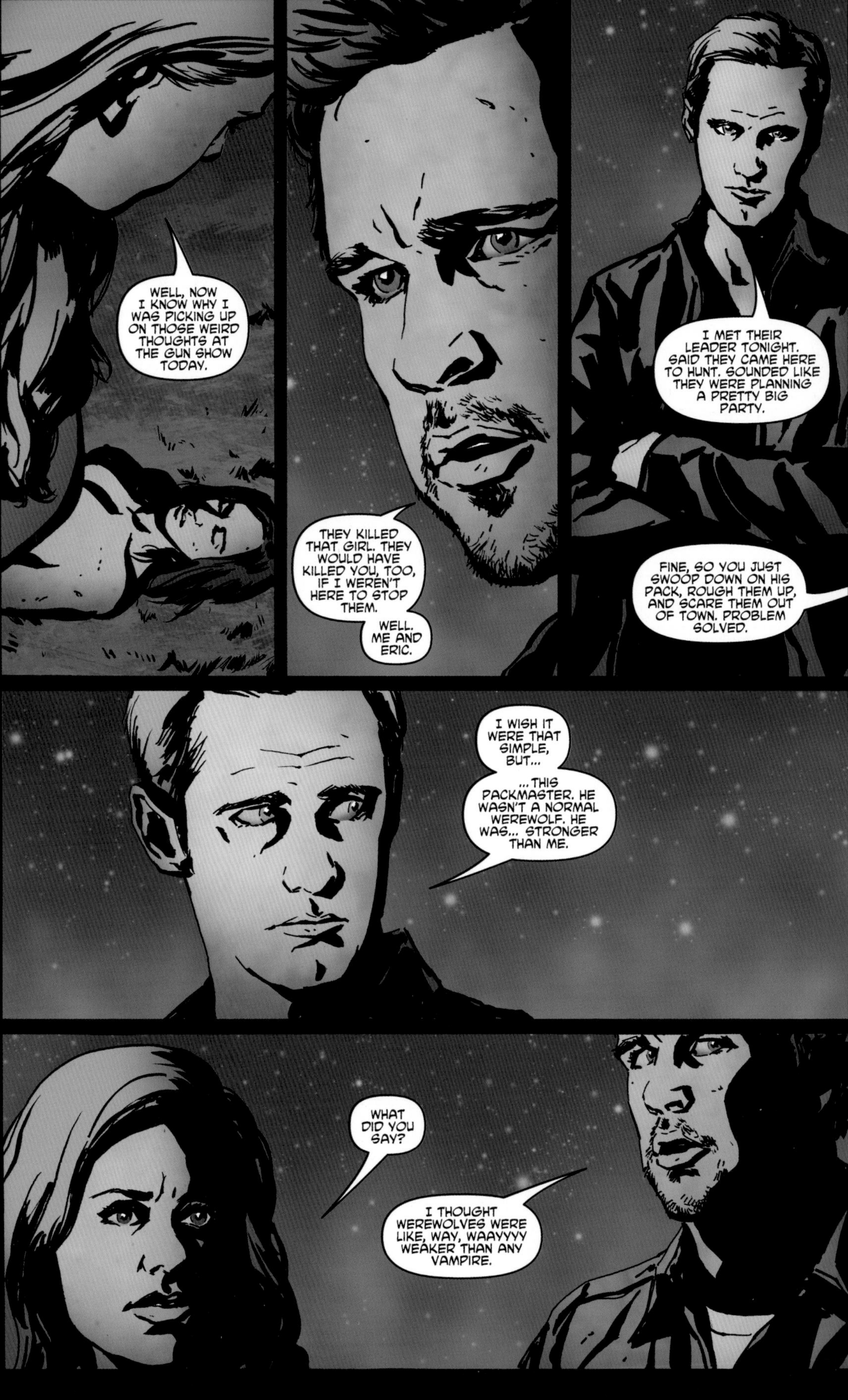
WELL, NOW I KNOW WHY I WAS PICKING UP ON THOSE WEIRD THOUGHTS AT THE GUN SHOW TODAY.
THEY KILLED THAT GIRL. THEY WOULD HAVE KILLED YOU, TOO, IF I WEREN'T HERE TO STOP THEM.
WELL. ME AND ERIC.
I MET THEIR LEADER TONIGHT. SAID THEY CAME HERE TO HUNT. SOUNDED LIKE THEY WERE PLANNING A PRETTY BIG PARTY.
FINE, SO YOU JUST SWOOP DOWN ON HIS PACK, ROUGH THEM UP, AND SCARE THEM OUT OF TOWN. PROBLEM SOLVED.
I WISH IT WERE THAT SIMPLE, BUT...
...THIS PACKMASTER. HE WASN'T A NORMAL WEREWOLF. HE WAS... STRONGER THAN ME.
WHAT DID YOU SAY?
I THOUGHT WEREWOLVES WERE LIKE, WAY, WAAYYYY WEAKER THAN ANY VAMPIRE.

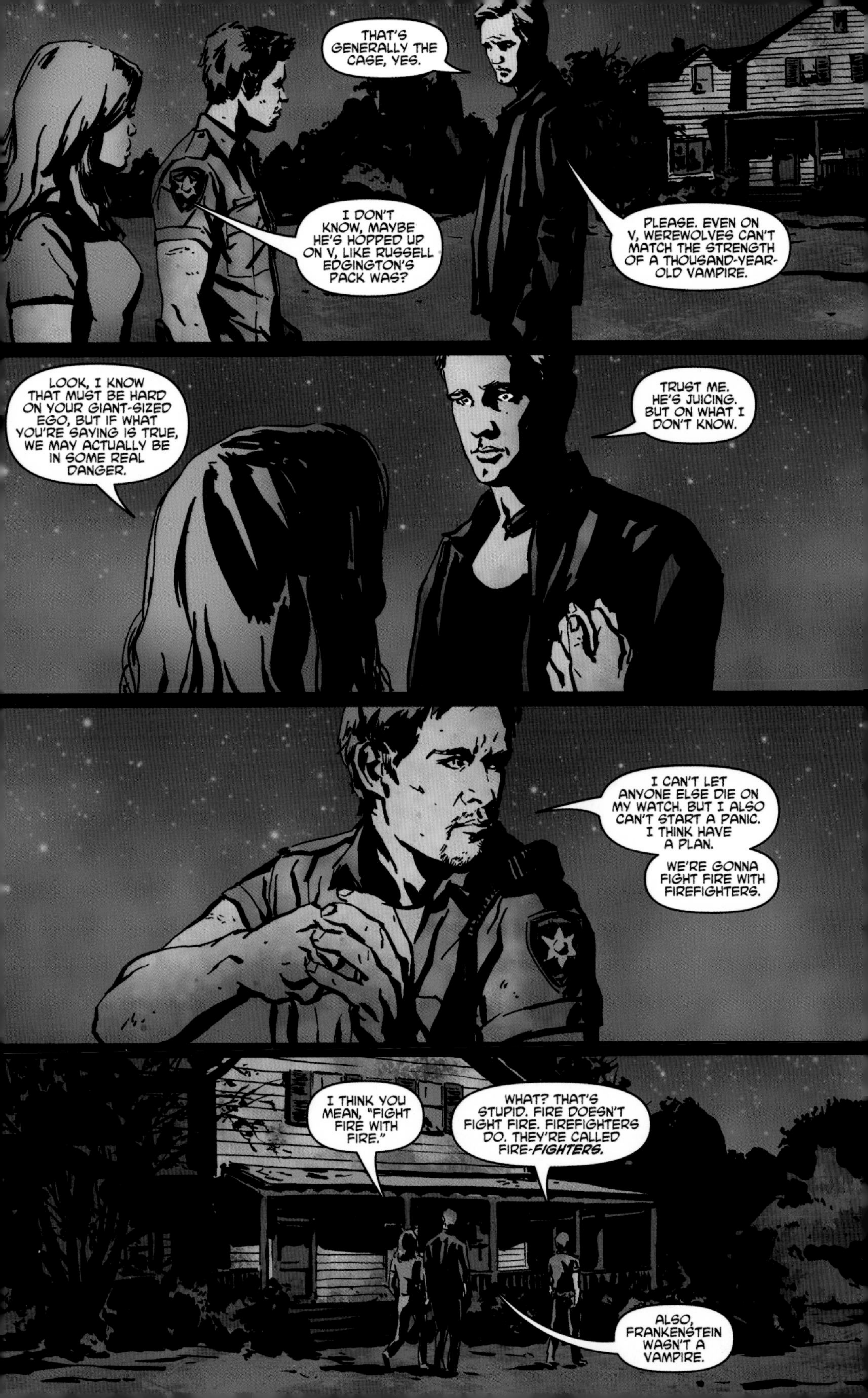
THAT'S GENERALLY THE CASE, YES.
I DON'T KNOW, MAYBE HE'S HOPPED UP ON V, LIKE RUSSELL EDGINGTON'S PACK WAS?
PLEASE. EVEN ON V, WEREWOLVES CAN'T MATCH THE STRENGTH OF A THOUSAND-YEAR-OLD VAMPIRE.
LOOK, I KNOW THAT MUST BE HARD ON YOUR GIANT-SIZED EGO, BUT IF WHAT YOU'RE SAYING IS TRUE, WE MAY ACTUALLY BE IN SOME REAL DANGER.
TRUST ME. HE'S JUICING. BUT ON WHAT I DON'T KNOW.
I CAN'T LET ANYONE ELSE DIE ON MY WATCH. BUT I ALSO CAN'T START A PANIC. I THINK HAVE A PLAN.
WE'RE GONNA FIGHT FIRE WITH FIREFIGHTERS.
I THINK YOU MEAN, "FIGHT FIRE WITH FIRE."
WHAT? THAT'S STUPID. FIRE DOESN'T FIGHT FIRE. FIREFIGHTERS DO. THEY'RE CALLED FIRE-*FIGHTERS*.
ALSO, FRANKENSTEIN WASN'T A VAMPIRE.

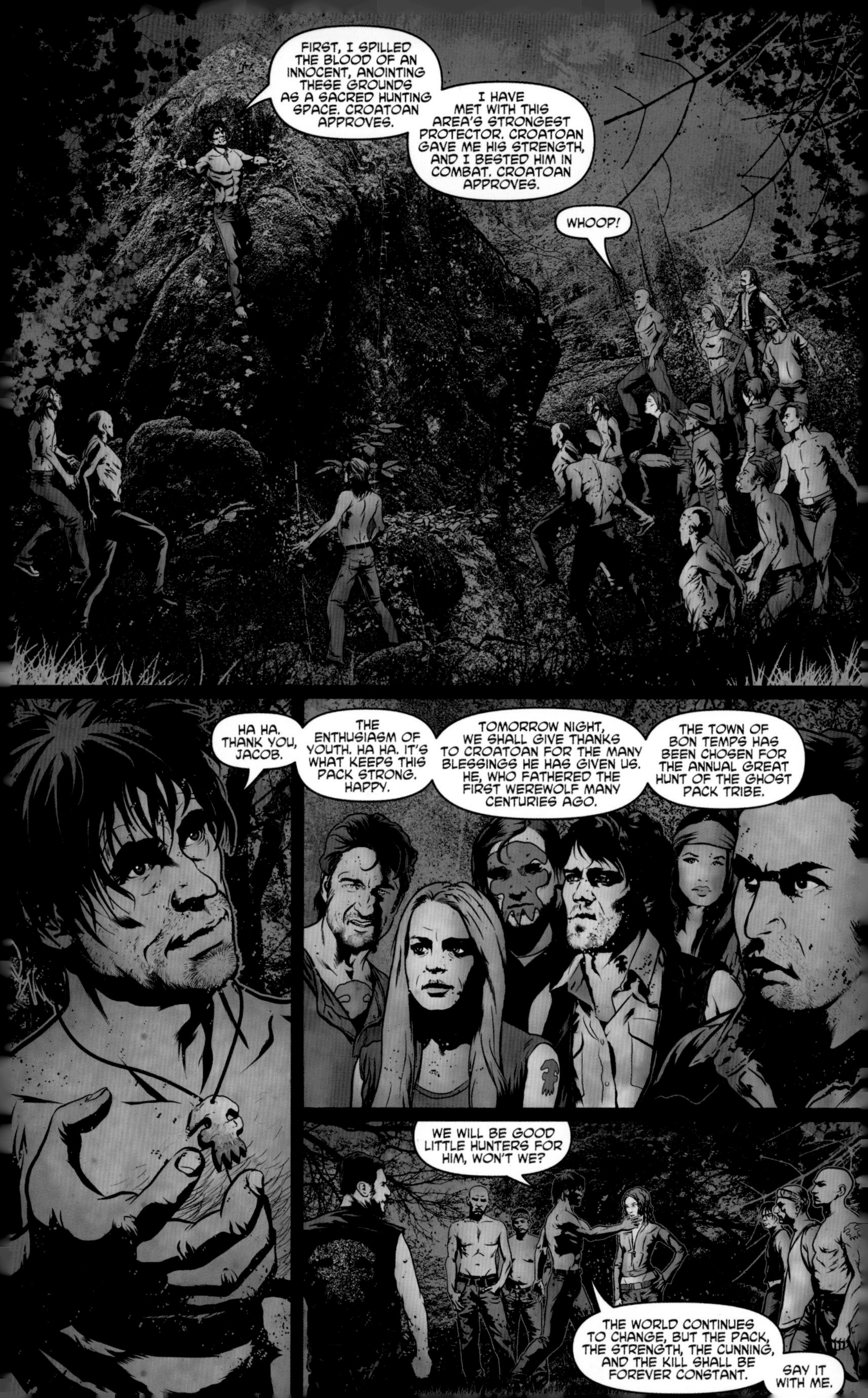
FIRST, I SPILLED THE BLOOD OF AN INNOCENT, ANOINTING THESE GROUNDS AS A SACRED HUNTING SPACE. CROATOAN APPROVES.
I HAVE MET WITH THIS AREA'S STRONGEST PROTECTOR. CROATOAN GAVE ME HIS STRENGTH, AND I BESTED HIM IN COMBAT. CROATOAN APPROVES.
WHOOP!
HA HA. THANK YOU, JACOB.
THE ENTHUSIASM OF YOUTH. HA HA. IT'S WHAT KEEPS THIS PACK STRONG. HAPPY.
TOMORROW NIGHT, WE SHALL GIVE THANKS TO CROATOAN FOR THE MANY BLESSINGS HE HAS GIVEN US. HE, WHO FATHERED THE FIRST WEREWOLF MANY CENTURIES AGO.
THE TOWN OF BON TEMPS HAS BEEN CHOSEN FOR THE ANNUAL GREAT HUNT OF THE GHOST PACK TRIBE.
WE WILL BE GOOD LITTLE HUNTERS FOR HIM, WON'T WE?
THE WORLD CONTINUES TO CHANGE, BUT THE PACK, THE STRENGTH, THE CUNNING, AND THE KILL SHALL BE FOREVER CONSTANT.
SAY IT WITH ME.

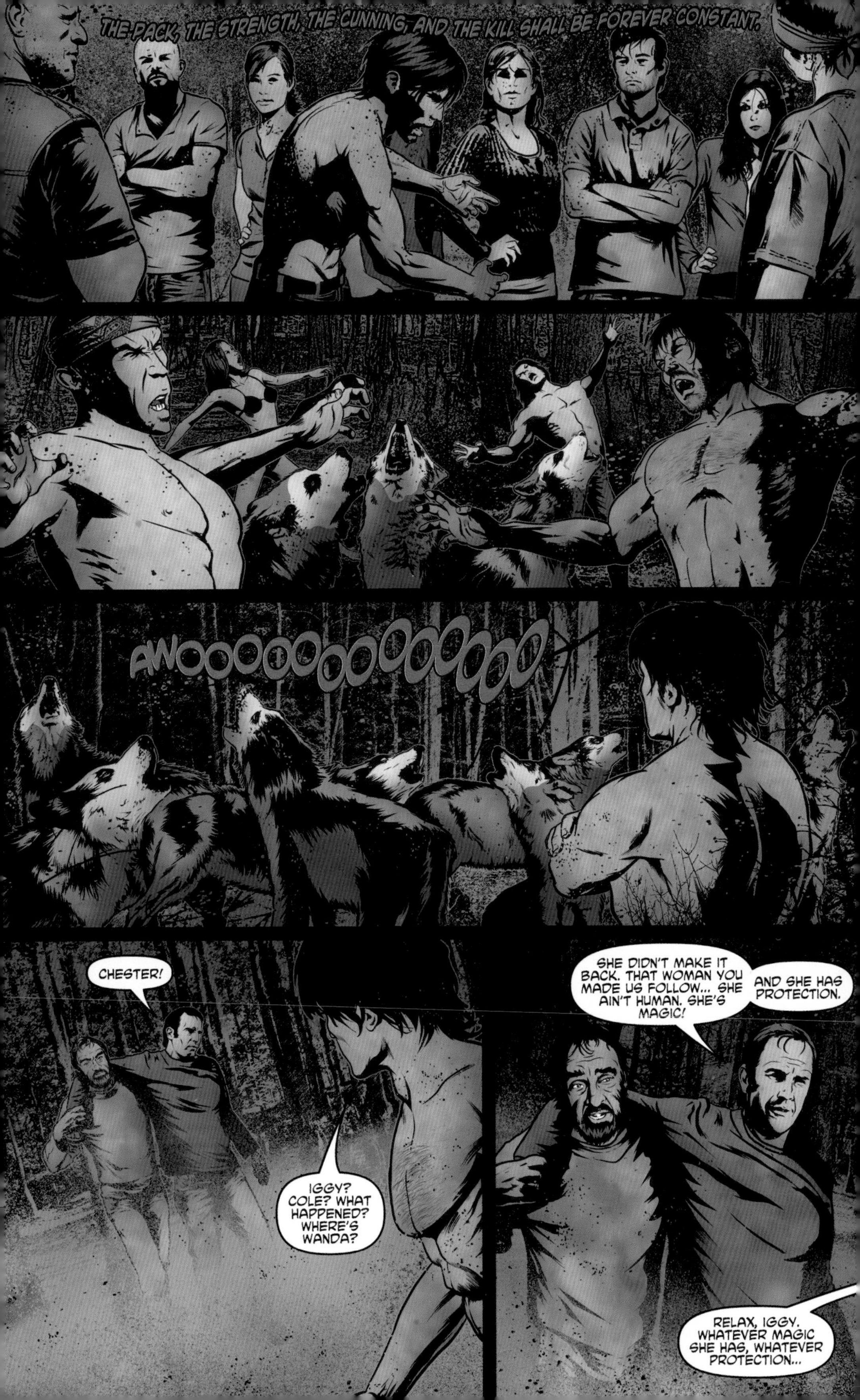
THE PACK, THE STRENGTH, THE CUNNING, AND THE KILL SHALL BE FOREVER CONSTANT.
AWOOOOOOOOOOOOOO
CHESTER!
IGGY? COLE? WHAT HAPPENED? WHERE'S WANDA?
SHE DIDN'T MAKE IT BACK. THAT WOMAN YOU MADE US FOLLOW... SHE AIN'T HUMAN. SHE'S MAGIC!
AND SHE HAS PROTECTION.
RELAX, IGGY. WHATEVER MAGIC SHE HAS, WHATEVER PROTECTION...

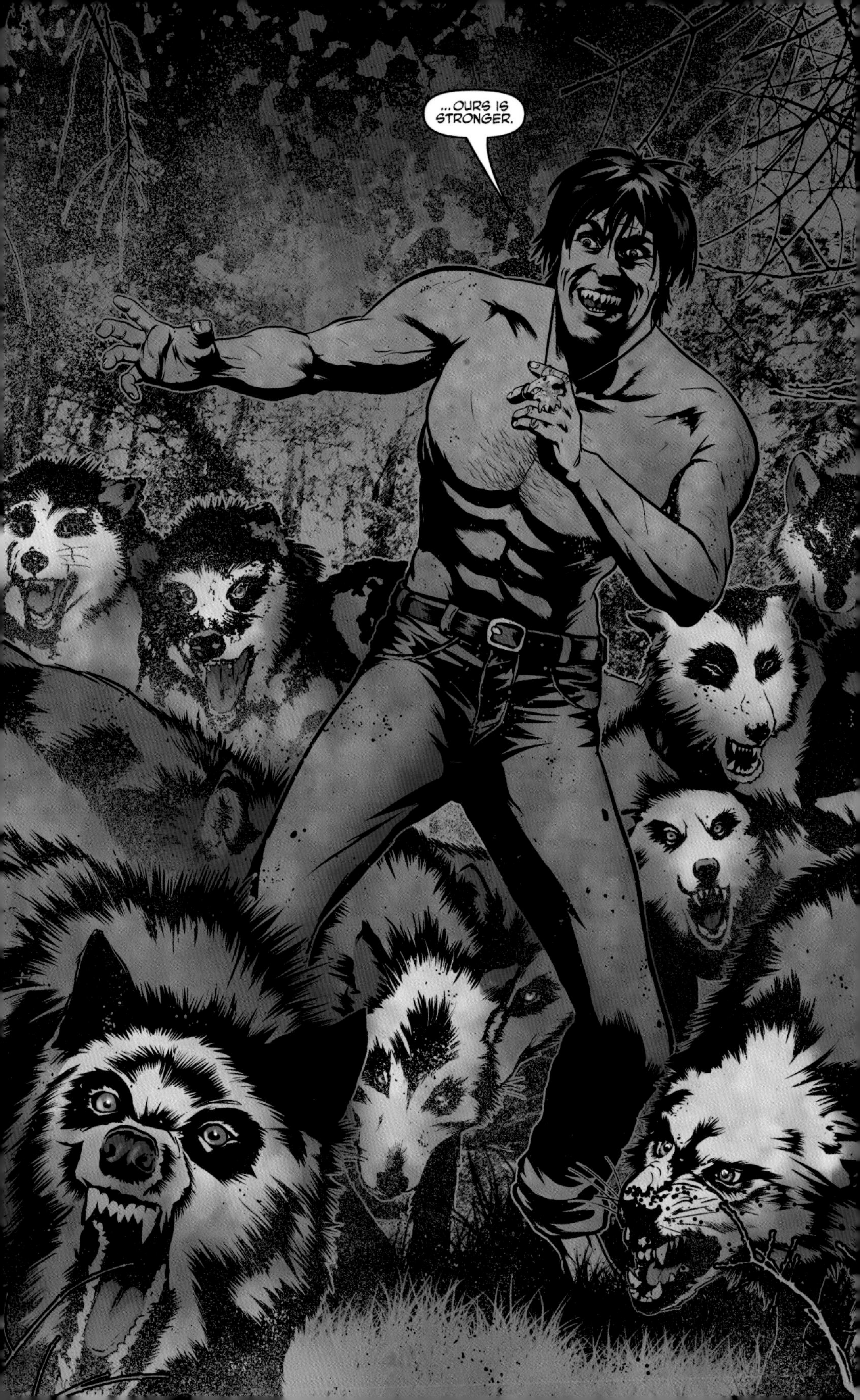
...OURS IS STRONGER.

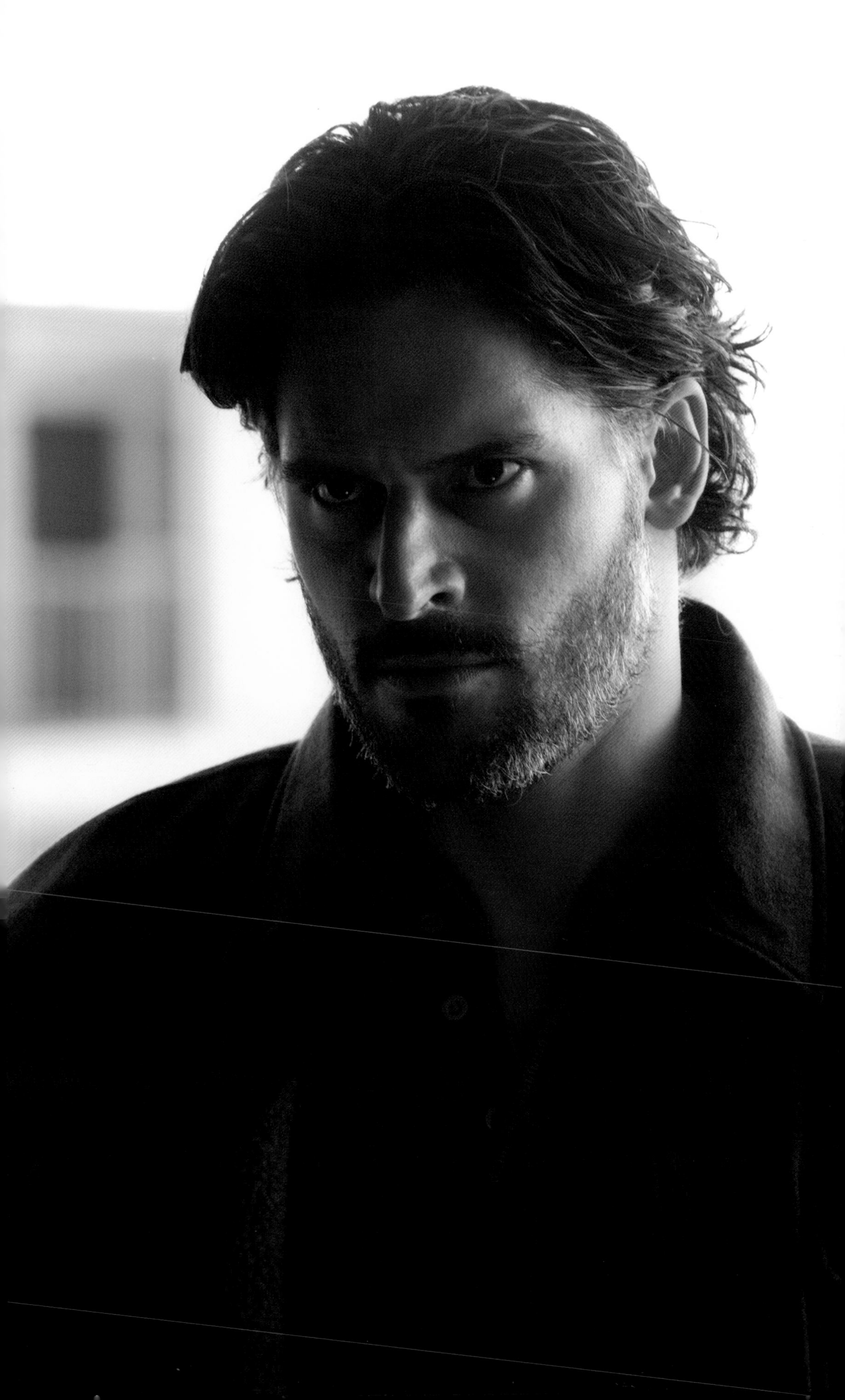

CHAPTER 3

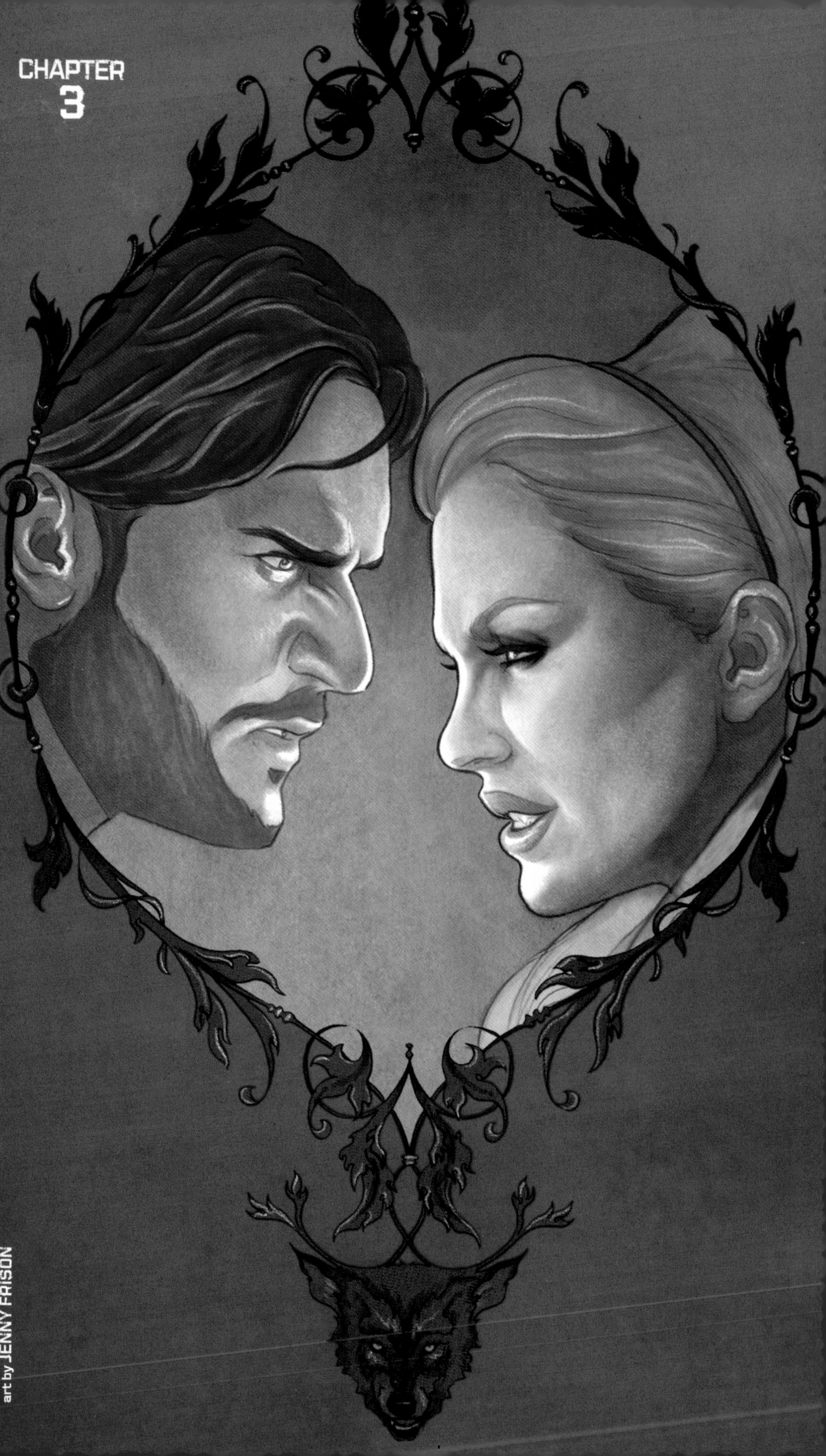

art by JENNY FRISON

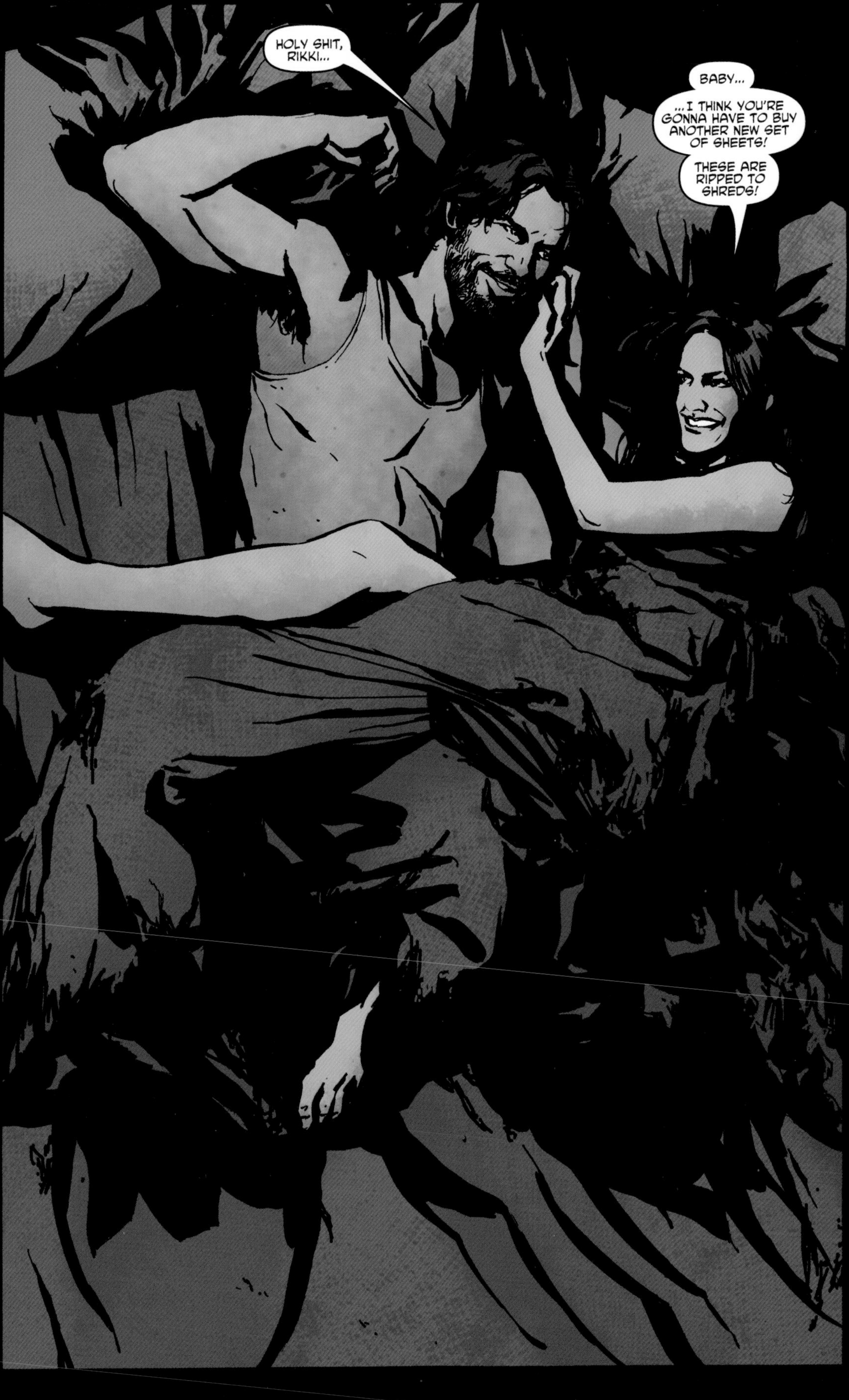
HOLY SHIT, RIKKI...
BABY...
...I THINK YOU'RE GONNA HAVE TO BUY ANOTHER NEW SET OF SHEETS!
THESE ARE RIPPED TO SHREDS!

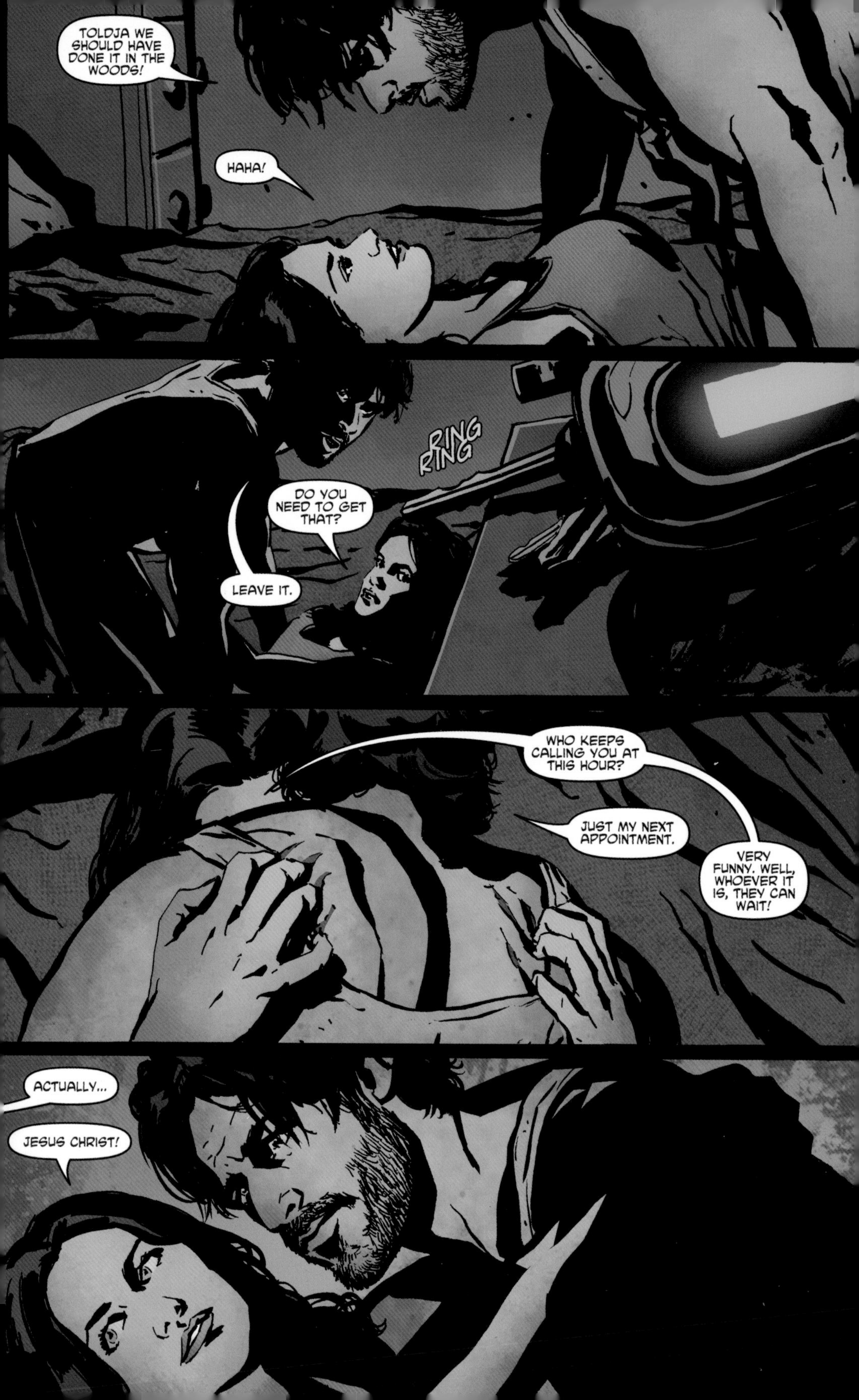
TOLDJA WE SHOULD HAVE DONE IT IN THE WOODS!
HAHA!
RING RING
DO YOU NEED TO GET THAT?
LEAVE IT.
WHO KEEPS CALLING YOU AT THIS HOUR?
JUST MY NEXT APPOINTMENT.
VERY FUNNY. WELL, WHOEVER IT IS, THEY CAN WAIT!
ACTUALLY...
JESUS CHRIST!

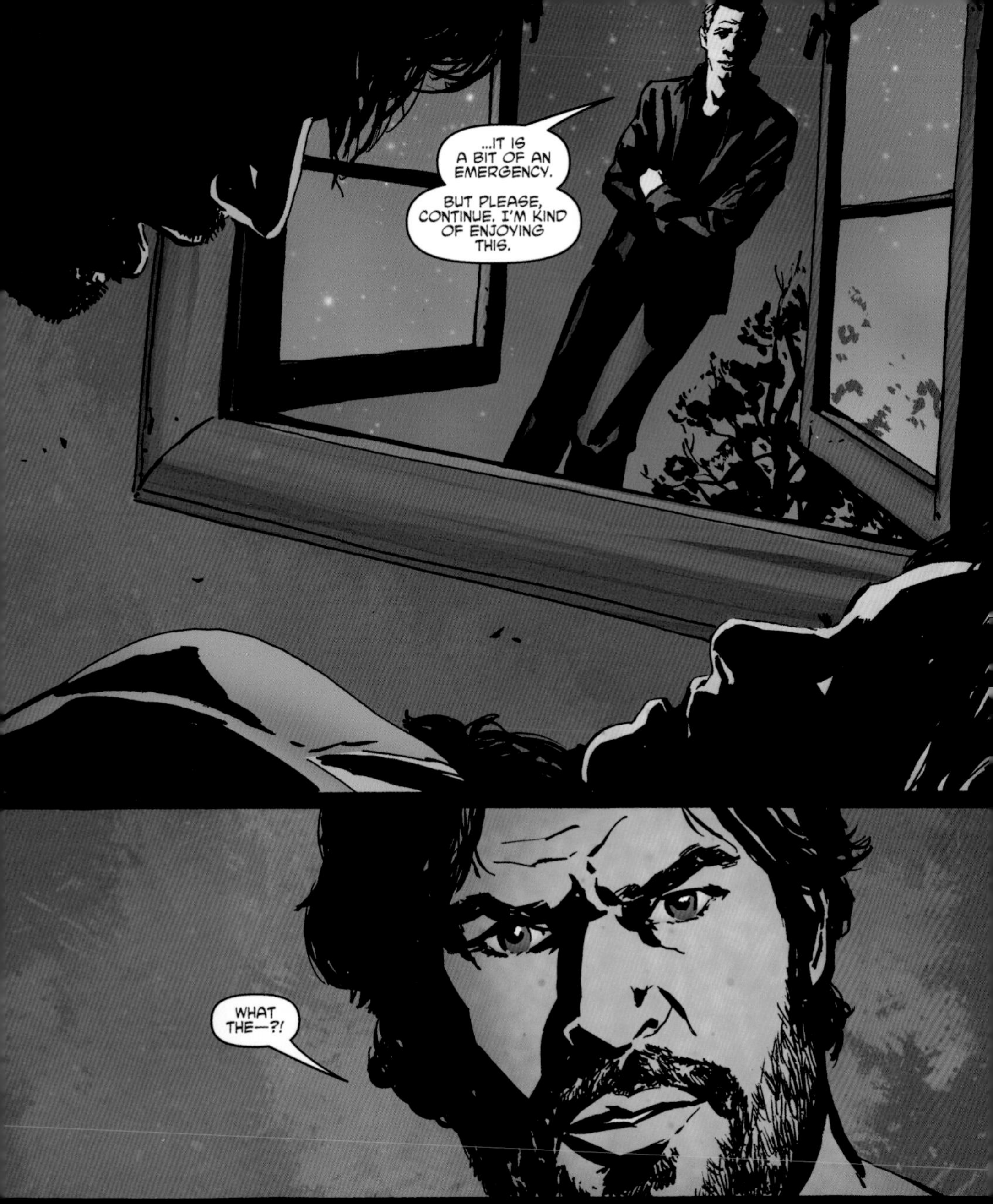
...IT IS A BIT OF AN EMERGENCY.
BUT PLEASE, CONTINUE. I'M KIND OF ENJOYING THIS.
WHAT THE--?!

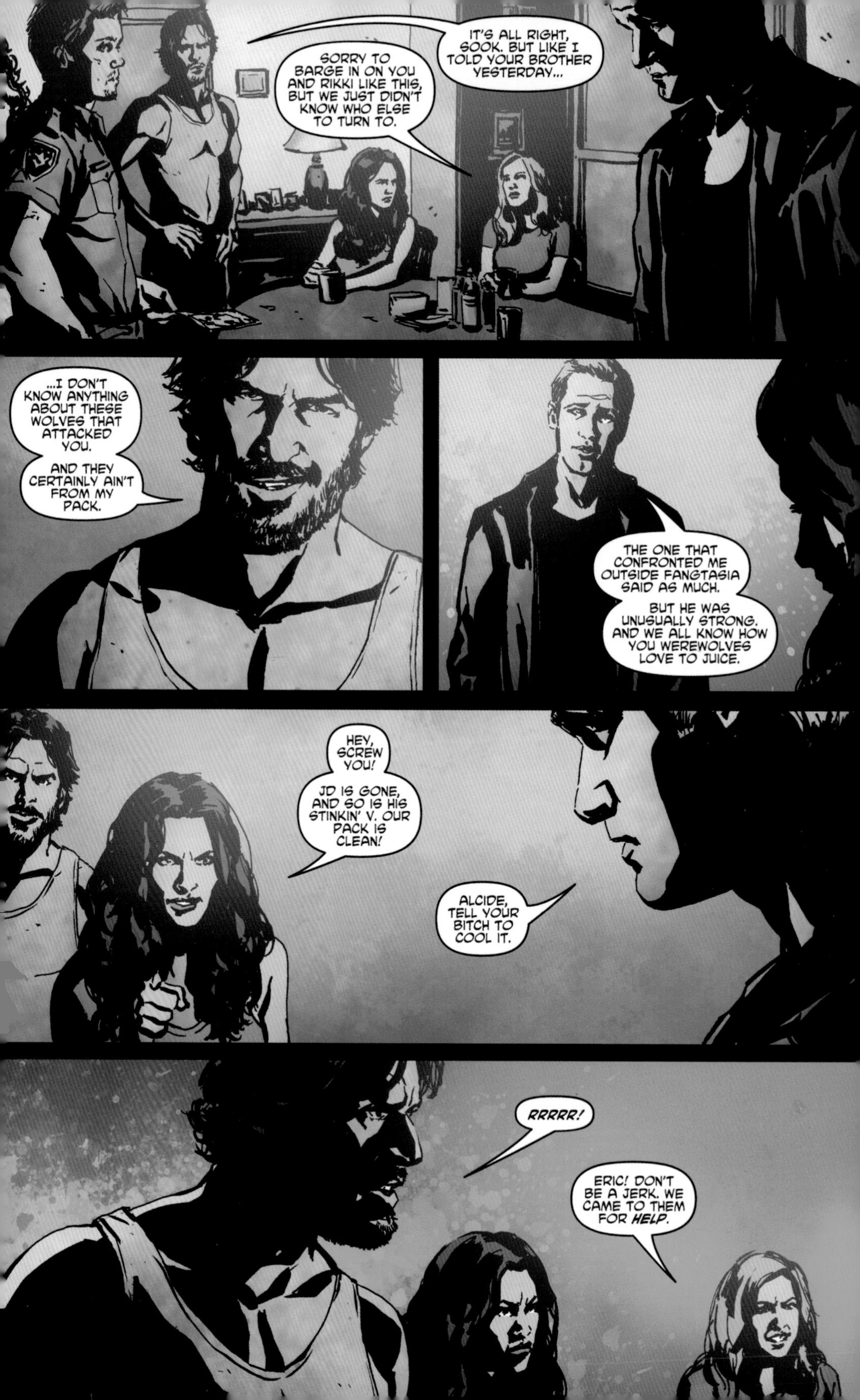

SORRY TO BARGE IN ON YOU AND RIKKI LIKE THIS, BUT WE JUST DIDN'T KNOW WHO ELSE TO TURN TO.
IT'S ALL RIGHT, SOOK. BUT LIKE I TOLD YOUR BROTHER YESTERDAY...
...I DON'T KNOW ANYTHING ABOUT THESE WOLVES THAT ATTACKED YOU.
AND THEY CERTAINLY AIN'T FROM MY PACK.
THE ONE THAT CONFRONTED ME OUTSIDE FANGTASIA SAID AS MUCH.
BUT HE WAS UNUSUALLY STRONG. AND WE ALL KNOW HOW YOU WEREWOLVES LOVE TO JUICE.
HEY, SCREW YOU!
JD IS GONE, AND SO IS HIS STINKIN' V. OUR PACK IS CLEAN!
ALCIDE, TELL YOUR BITCH TO COOL IT.
RRRRR!
ERIC! DON'T BE A JERK. WE CAME TO THEM FOR HELP.

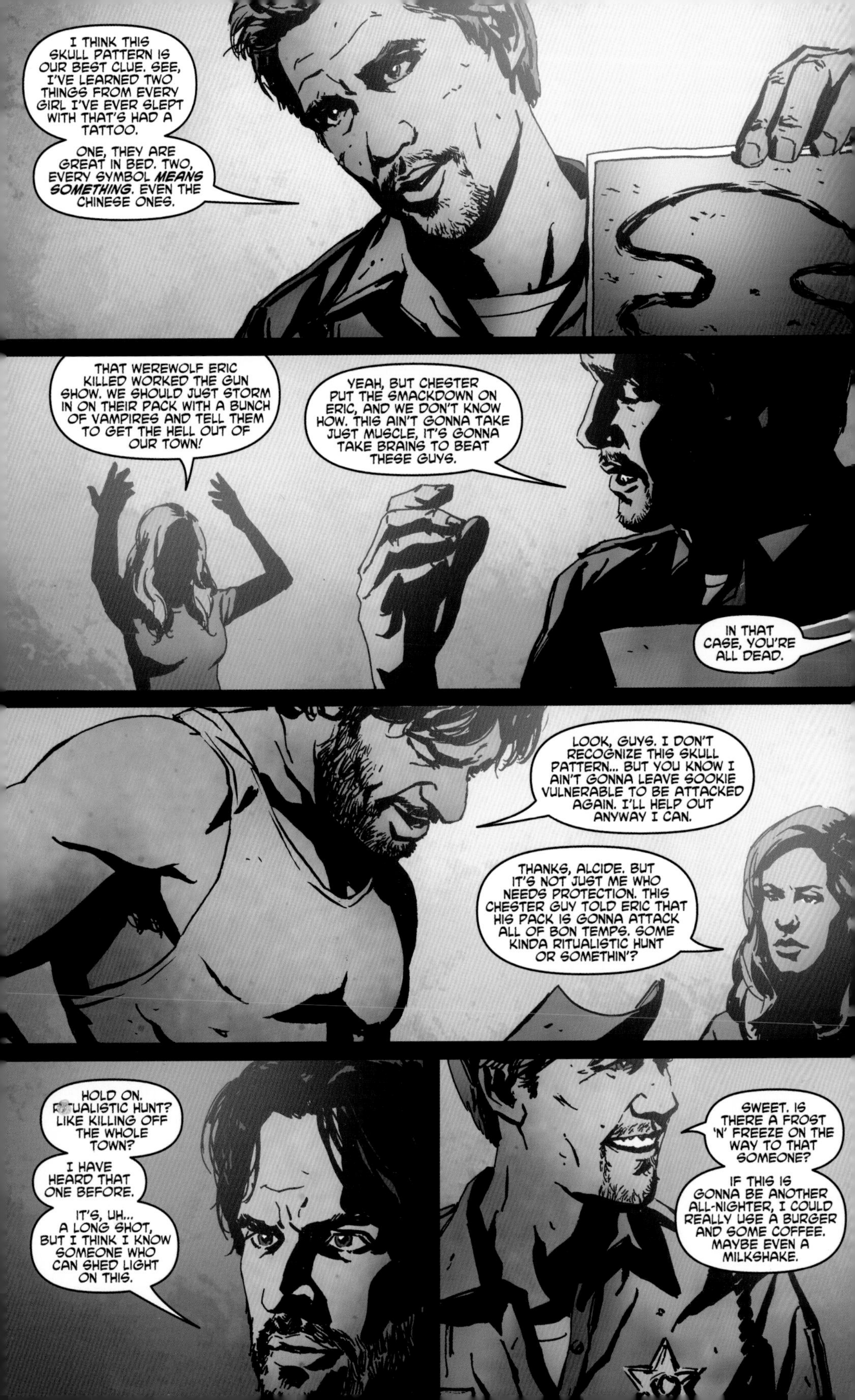
I THINK THIS SKULL PATTERN IS OUR BEST CLUE. SEE, I'VE LEARNED TWO THINGS FROM EVERY GIRL I'VE EVER SLEPT WITH THAT'S HAD A TATTOO.
ONE, THEY ARE GREAT IN BED. TWO, EVERY SYMBOL MEANS SOMETHING. EVEN THE CHINESE ONES.
THAT WEREWOLF ERIC KILLED WORKED THE GUN SHOW. WE SHOULD JUST STORM IN ON THEIR PACK WITH A BUNCH OF VAMPIRES AND TELL THEM TO GET THE HELL OUT OF OUR TOWN!
YEAH, BUT CHESTER PUT THE SMACKDOWN ON ERIC, AND WE DON'T KNOW HOW. THIS AIN'T GONNA TAKE JUST MUSCLE, IT'S GONNA TAKE BRAINS TO BEAT THESE GUYS.
IN THAT CASE, YOU'RE ALL DEAD.
LOOK, GUYS. I DON'T RECOGNIZE THIS SKULL PATTERN... BUT YOU KNOW I AIN'T GONNA LEAVE SOOKIE VULNERABLE TO BE ATTACKED AGAIN. I'LL HELP OUT ANYWAY I CAN.
THANKS, ALCIDE. BUT IT'S NOT JUST ME WHO NEEDS PROTECTION. THIS CHESTER GUY TOLD ERIC THAT HIS PACK IS GONNA ATTACK ALL OF BON TEMPS. SOME KINDA RITUALISTIC HUNT OR SOMETHIN'?
HOLD ON. RITUALISTIC HUNT? LIKE KILLING OFF THE WHOLE TOWN?
I HAVE HEARD THAT ONE BEFORE.
IT'S, UH... A LONG SHOT, BUT I THINK I KNOW SOMEONE WHO CAN SHED LIGHT ON THIS.
SWEET. IS THERE A FROST 'N' FREEZE ON THE WAY TO THAT SOMEONE?
IF THIS IS GONNA BE ANOTHER ALL-NIGHTER, I COULD REALLY USE A BURGER AND SOME COFFEE. MAYBE EVEN A MILKSHAKE.

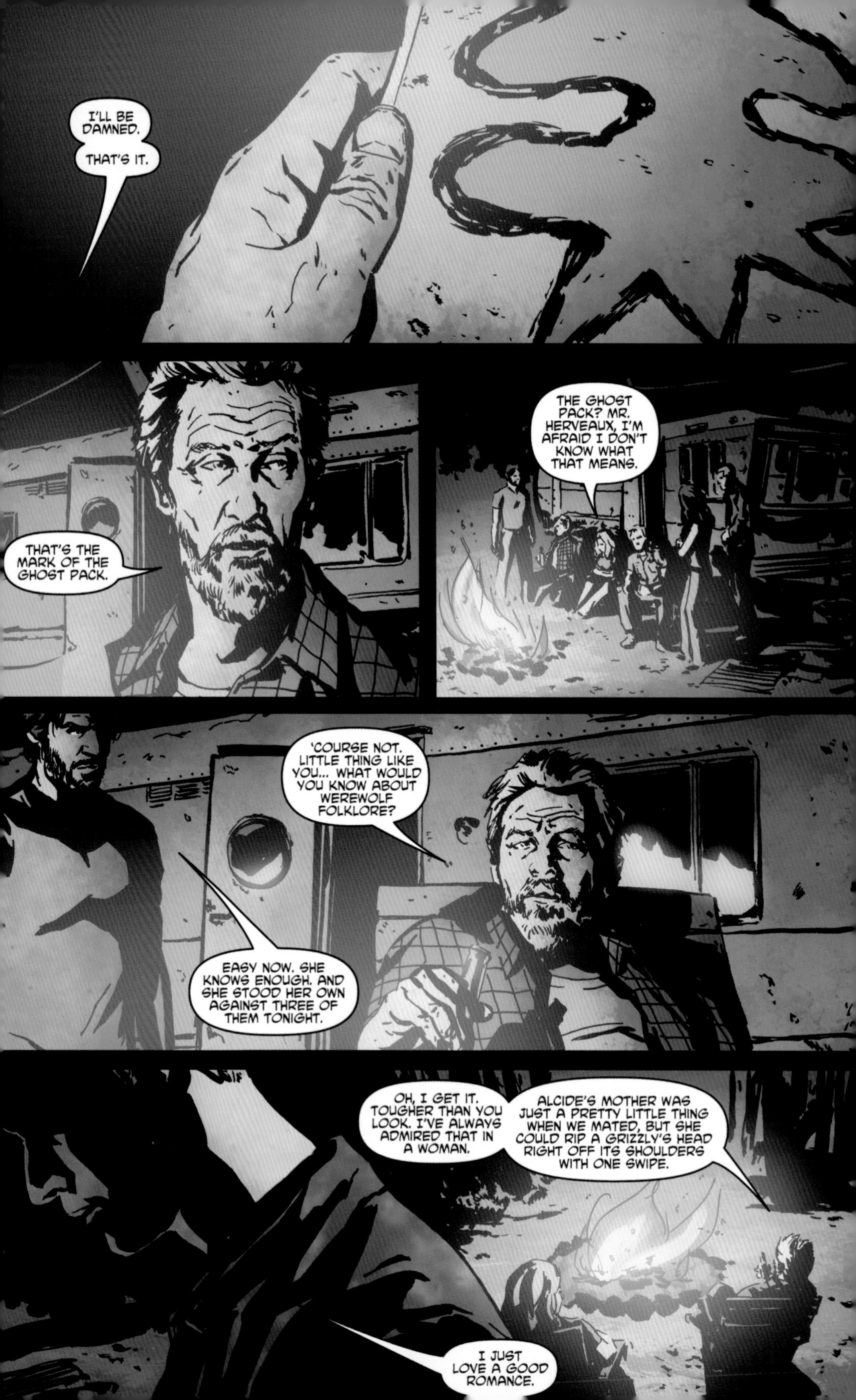
I'LL BE DAMNED.
THAT'S IT.
THAT'S THE MARK OF THE GHOST PACK.
THE GHOST PACK? MR. HERVEAUX, I'M AFRAID I DON'T KNOW WHAT THAT MEANS.
'COURSE NOT. LITTLE THING LIKE YOU... WHAT WOULD YOU KNOW ABOUT WEREWOLF FOLKLORE?
EASY NOW. SHE KNOWS ENOUGH. AND SHE STOOD HER OWN AGAINST THREE OF THEM TONIGHT.
OH, I GET IT. TOUGHER THAN YOU LOOK. I'VE ALWAYS ADMIRED THAT IN A WOMAN.
ALCIDE'S MOTHER WAS JUST A PRETTY LITTLE THING WHEN WE MATED, BUT SHE COULD RIP A GRIZZLY'S HEAD RIGHT OFF ITS SHOULDERS WITH ONE SWIPE.
I JUST LOVE A GOOD ROMANCE.

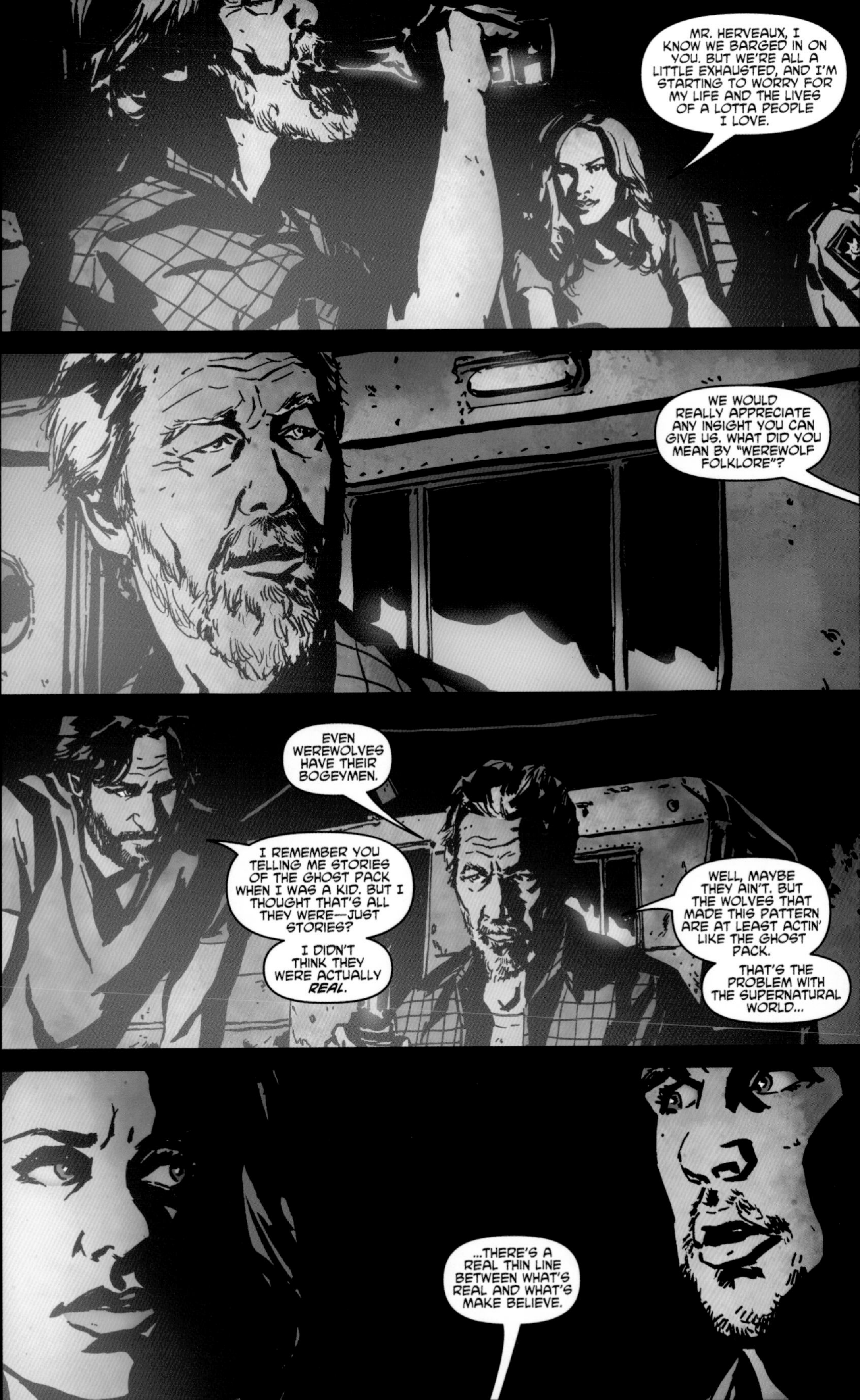
MR. HERVEAUX, I KNOW WE BARGED IN ON YOU. BUT WE'RE ALL A LITTLE EXHAUSTED, AND I'M STARTING TO WORRY FOR MY LIFE AND THE LIVES OF A LOTTA PEOPLE I LOVE.
WE WOULD REALLY APPRECIATE ANY INSIGHT YOU CAN GIVE US. WHAT DID YOU MEAN BY "WEREWOLF FOLKLORE"?
EVEN WEREWOLVES HAVE THEIR BOGEYMEN.
I REMEMBER YOU TELLING ME STORIES OF THE GHOST PACK WHEN I WAS A KID. BUT I THOUGHT THAT'S ALL THEY WERE—JUST STORIES?
I DIDN'T THINK THEY WERE ACTUALLY *REAL*.
WELL, MAYBE THEY AIN'T. BUT THE WOLVES THAT MADE THIS PATTERN ARE AT LEAST ACTIN' LIKE THE GHOST PACK.
THAT'S THE PROBLEM WITH THE SUPERNATURAL WORLD...
...THERE'S A REAL THIN LINE BETWEEN WHAT'S REAL AND WHAT'S MAKE BELIEVE.

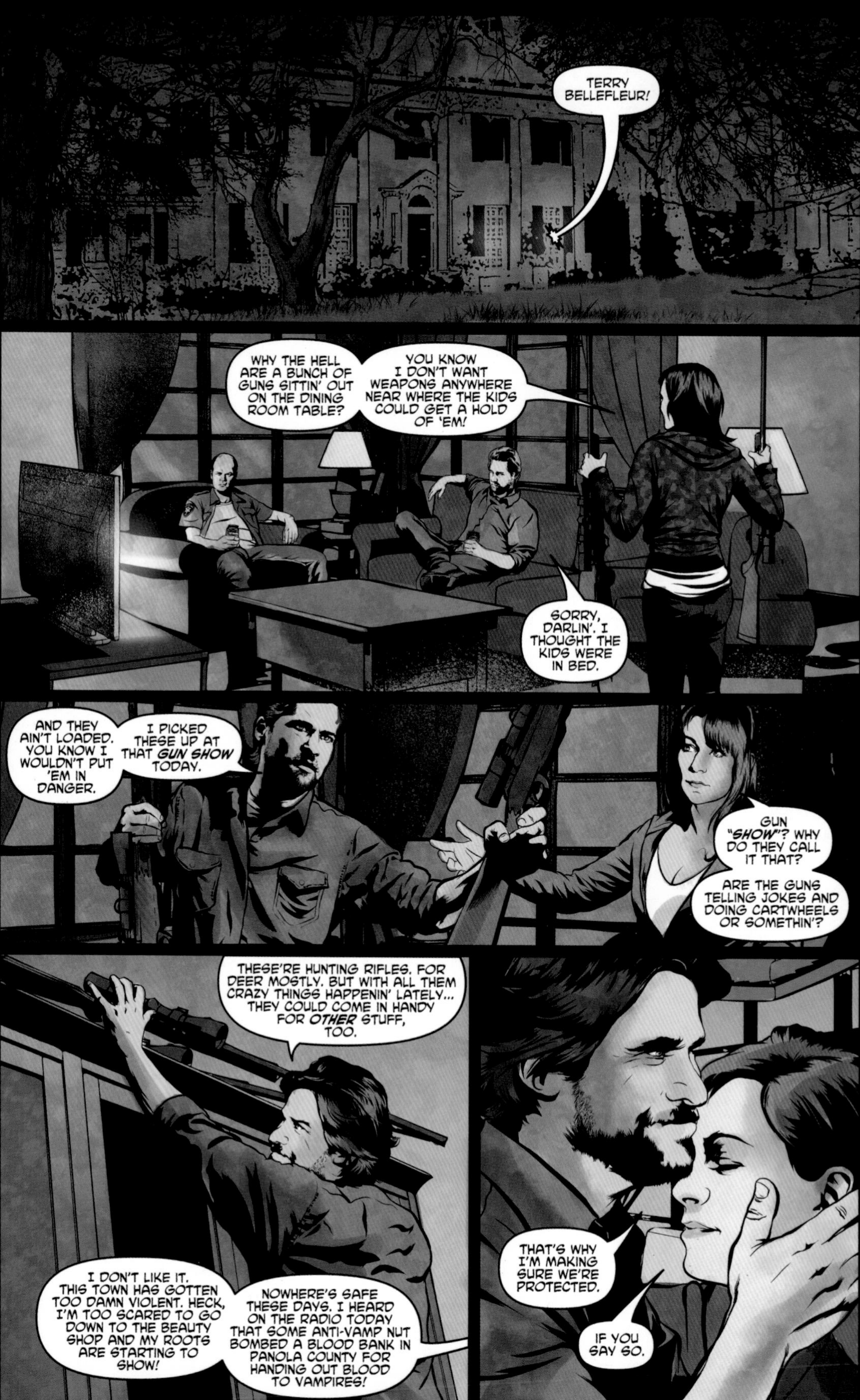
TERRY BELLEFLEUR!
WHY THE HELL ARE A BUNCH OF GUNS SITTIN' OUT ON THE DINING ROOM TABLE?
YOU KNOW I DON'T WANT WEAPONS ANYWHERE NEAR WHERE THE KIDS COULD GET A HOLD OF 'EM!
SORRY, DARLIN'. I THOUGHT THE KIDS WERE IN BED.
AND THEY AIN'T LOADED. YOU KNOW I WOULDN'T PUT 'EM IN DANGER.
I PICKED THESE UP AT THAT GUN SHOW TODAY.
GUN "SHOW"? WHY DO THEY CALL IT THAT?
ARE THE GUNS TELLING JOKES AND DOING CARTWHEELS OR SOMETHIN'?
THESE'RE HUNTING RIFLES. FOR DEER MOSTLY. BUT WITH ALL THEM CRAZY THINGS HAPPENIN' LATELY... THEY COULD COME IN HANDY FOR OTHER STUFF, TOO.
I DON'T LIKE IT. THIS TOWN HAS GOTTEN TOO DAMN VIOLENT. HECK, I'M TOO SCARED TO GO DOWN TO THE BEAUTY SHOP AND MY ROOTS ARE STARTING TO SHOW!
NOWHERE'S SAFE THESE DAYS. I HEARD ON THE RADIO TODAY THAT SOME ANTI-VAMP NUT BOMBED A BLOOD BANK IN PANOLA COUNTY FOR HANDING OUT BLOOD TO VAMPIRES!
THAT'S WHY I'M MAKING SURE WE'RE PROTECTED.
IF YOU SAY SO.

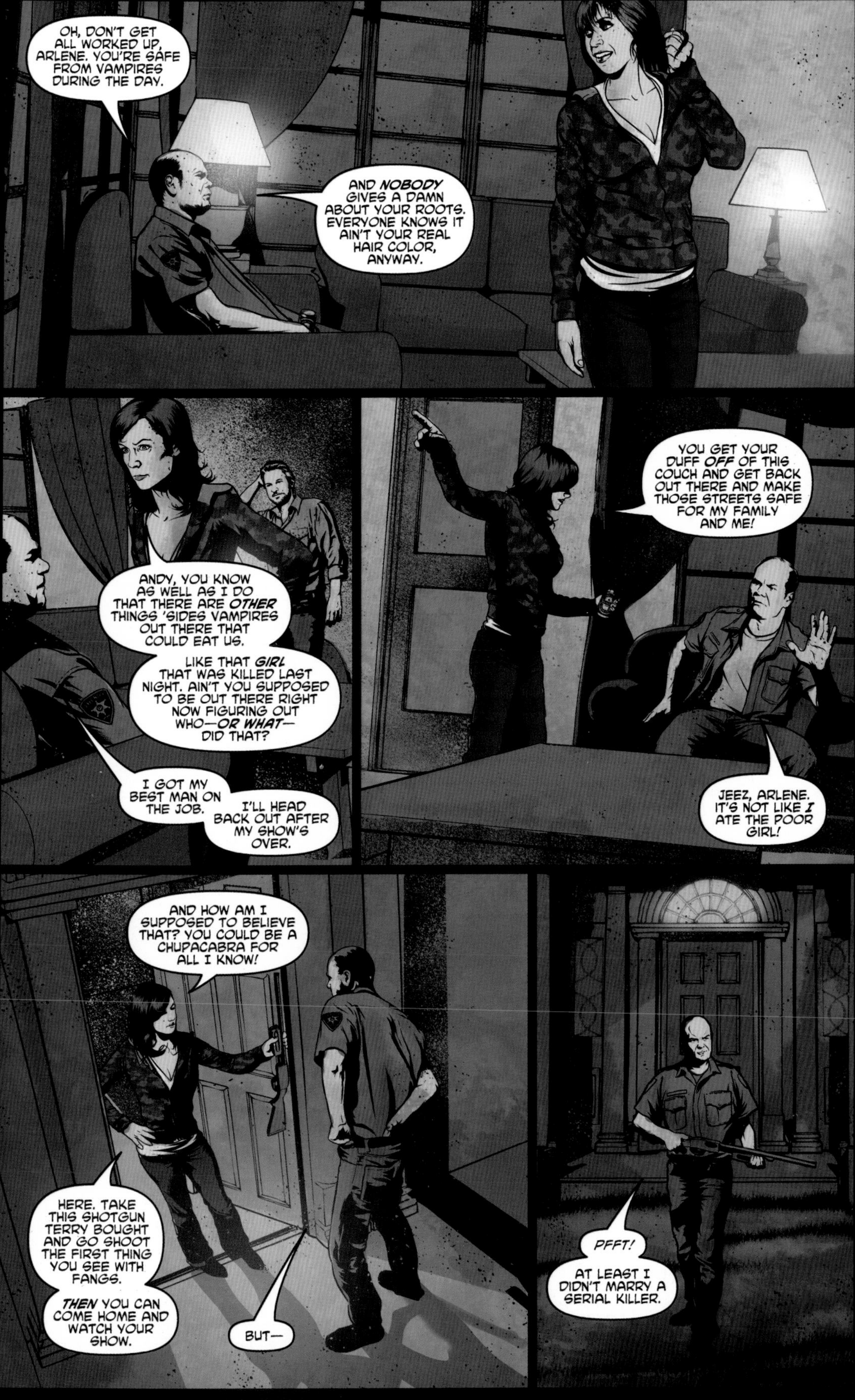
OH, DON'T GET ALL WORKED UP, ARLENE. YOU'RE SAFE FROM VAMPIRES DURING THE DAY.
AND NOBODY GIVES A DAMN ABOUT YOUR ROOTS. EVERYONE KNOWS IT AIN'T YOUR REAL HAIR COLOR, ANYWAY.
ANDY, YOU KNOW AS WELL AS I DO THAT THERE ARE OTHER THINGS 'SIDES VAMPIRES OUT THERE THAT COULD EAT US.
LIKE THAT GIRL THAT WAS KILLED LAST NIGHT. AIN'T YOU SUPPOSED TO BE OUT THERE RIGHT NOW FIGURING OUT WHO—OR WHAT—DID THAT?
I GOT MY BEST MAN ON THE JOB.
I'LL HEAD BACK OUT AFTER MY SHOW'S OVER.
YOU GET YOUR DUFF OFF OF THIS COUCH AND GET BACK OUT THERE AND MAKE THOSE STREETS SAFE FOR MY FAMILY AND ME!
JEEZ, ARLENE. IT'S NOT LIKE I ATE THE POOR GIRL!
AND HOW AM I SUPPOSED TO BELIEVE THAT? YOU COULD BE A CHUPACABRA FOR ALL I KNOW!
HERE. TAKE THIS SHOTGUN TERRY BOUGHT AND GO SHOOT THE FIRST THING YOU SEE WITH FANGS.
THEN YOU CAN COME HOME AND WATCH YOUR SHOW.
BUT—
PFFT!
AT LEAST I DIDN'T MARRY A SERIAL KILLER.

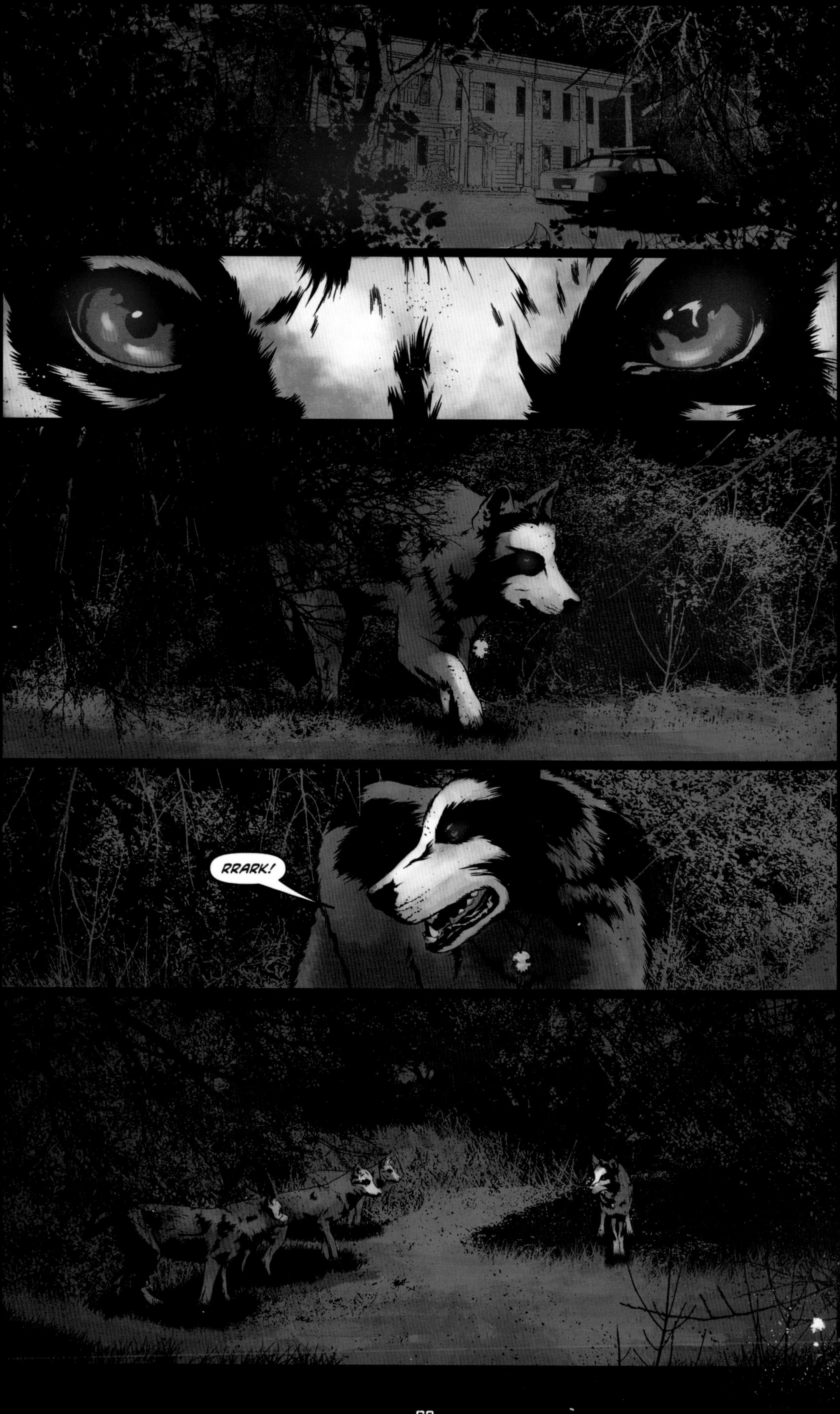
RRARK!

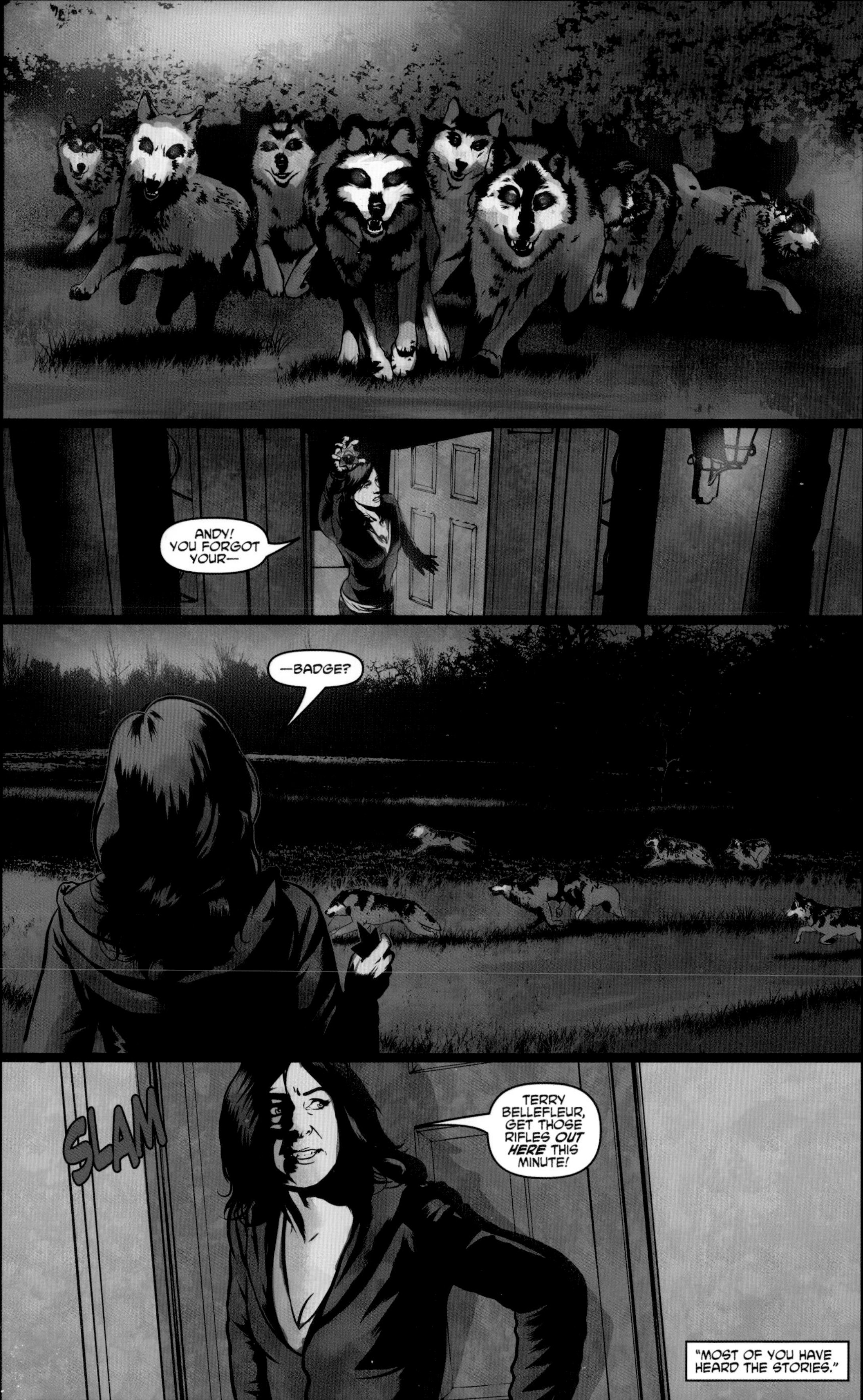
ANDY! YOU FORGOT YOUR—
—BADGE?
SLAM
TERRY BELLEFLEUR, GET THOSE RIFLES OUT HERE THIS MINUTE!
"MOST OF YOU HAVE HEARD THE STORIES."

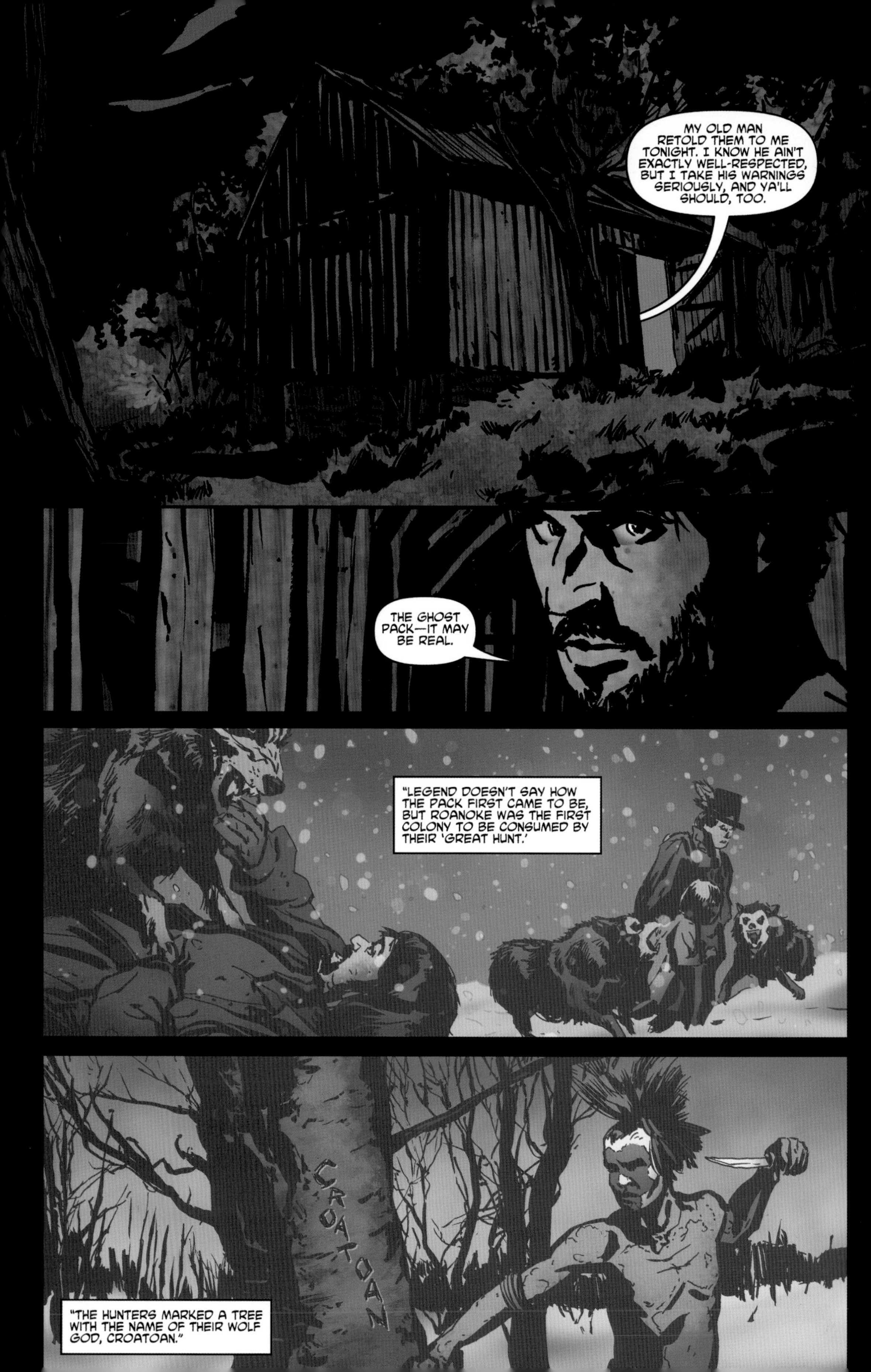
MY OLD MAN RETOLD THEM TO ME TONIGHT. I KNOW HE AIN'T EXACTLY WELL-RESPECTED, BUT I TAKE HIS WARNINGS SERIOUSLY, AND YA'LL SHOULD, TOO.
THE GHOST PACK—IT MAY BE REAL.
"LEGEND DOESN'T SAY HOW THE PACK FIRST CAME TO BE, BUT ROANOKE WAS THE FIRST COLONY TO BE CONSUMED BY THEIR 'GREAT HUNT.'
CROATOAN
"THE HUNTERS MARKED A TREE WITH THE NAME OF THEIR WOLF GOD, CROATOAN."

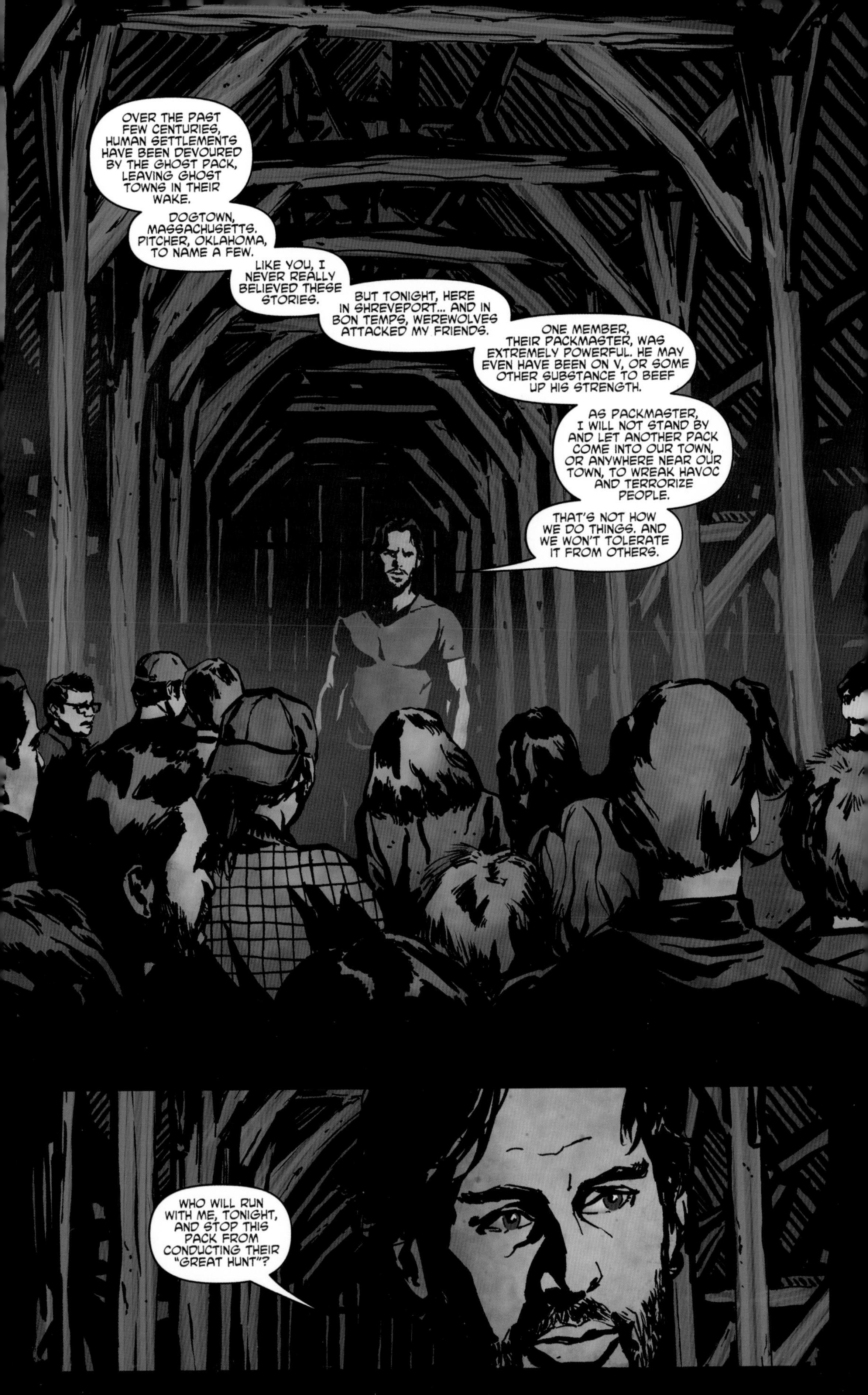
OVER THE PAST FEW CENTURIES, HUMAN SETTLEMENTS HAVE BEEN DEVOURED BY THE GHOST PACK, LEAVING GHOST TOWNS IN THEIR WAKE.
DOGTOWN, MASSACHUSETTS. PITCHER, OKLAHOMA, TO NAME A FEW.
LIKE YOU, I NEVER REALLY BELIEVED THESE STORIES.
BUT TONIGHT, HERE IN SHREVEPORT... AND IN BON TEMPS, WEREWOLVES ATTACKED MY FRIENDS.
ONE MEMBER, THEIR PACKMASTER, WAS EXTREMELY POWERFUL. HE MAY EVEN HAVE BEEN ON V, OR SOME OTHER SUBSTANCE TO BEEF UP HIS STRENGTH.
AS PACKMASTER, I WILL NOT STAND BY AND LET ANOTHER PACK COME INTO OUR TOWN, OR ANYWHERE NEAR OUR TOWN, TO WREAK HAVOC AND TERRORIZE PEOPLE.
THAT'S NOT HOW WE DO THINGS. AND WE WON'T TOLERATE IT FROM OTHERS.
WHO WILL RUN WITH ME, TONIGHT, AND STOP THIS PACK FROM CONDUCTING THEIR "GREAT HUNT"?

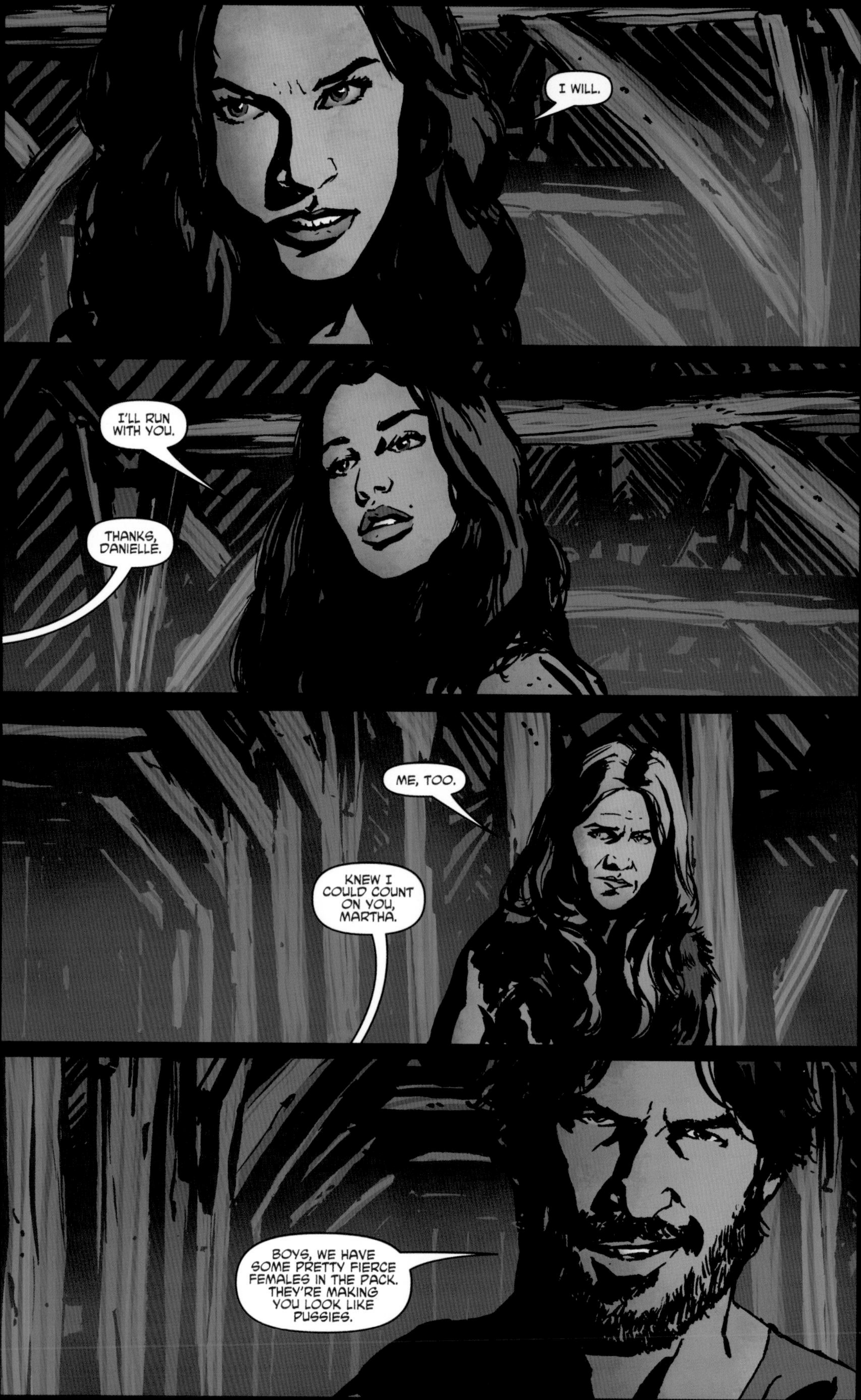
I WILL.
I'LL RUN WITH YOU.
THANKS, DANIELLE.
ME, TOO.
KNEW I COULD COUNT ON YOU, MARTHA.
BOYS, WE HAVE SOME PRETTY FIERCE FEMALES IN THE PACK. THEY'RE MAKING YOU LOOK LIKE PUSSIES.

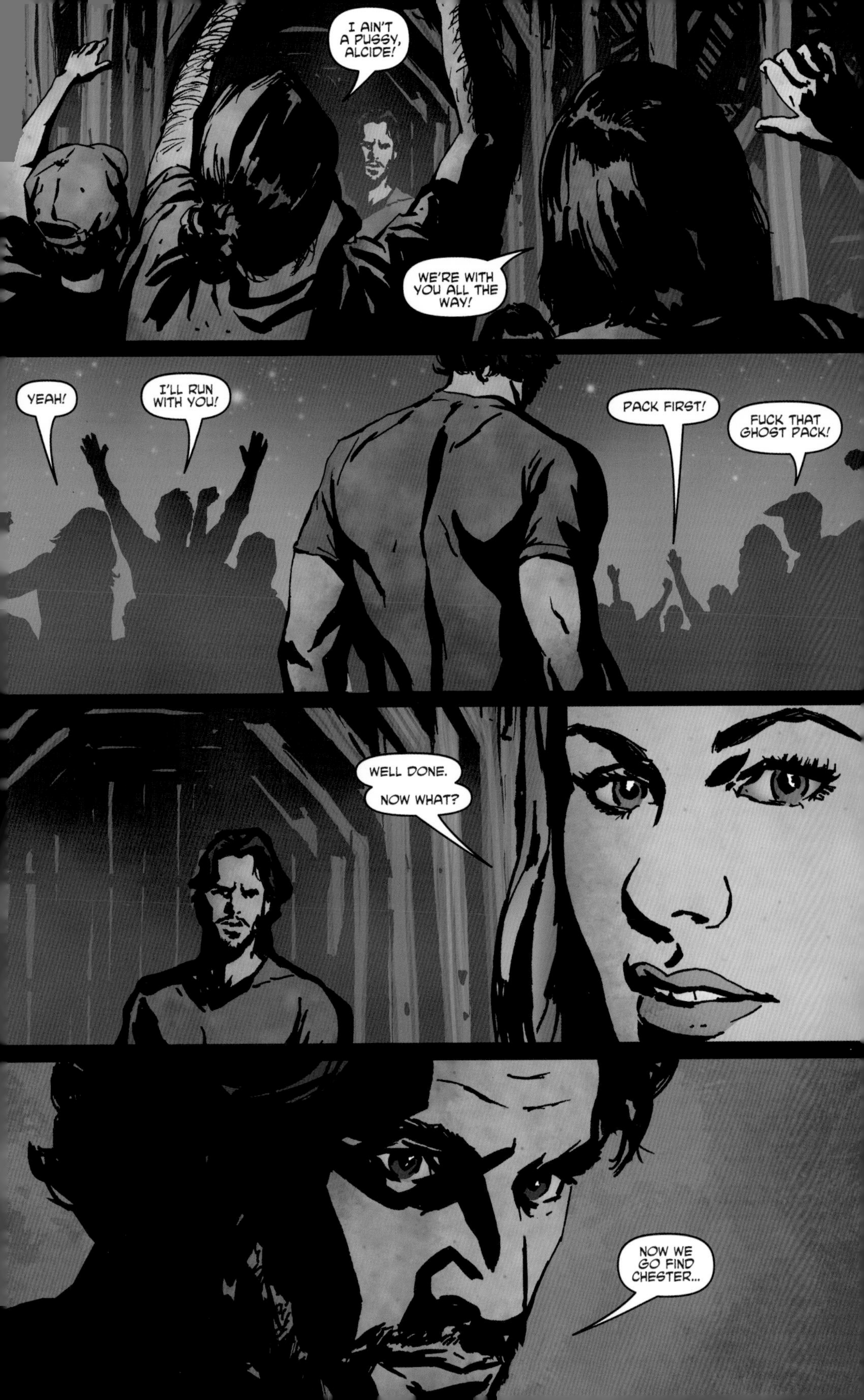
I AIN'T A PUSSY, ALCIDE!
WE'RE WITH YOU ALL THE WAY!
YEAH!
I'LL RUN WITH YOU!
PACK FIRST!
FUCK THAT GHOST PACK!
WELL DONE.
NOW WHAT?
NOW WE GO FIND CHESTER...

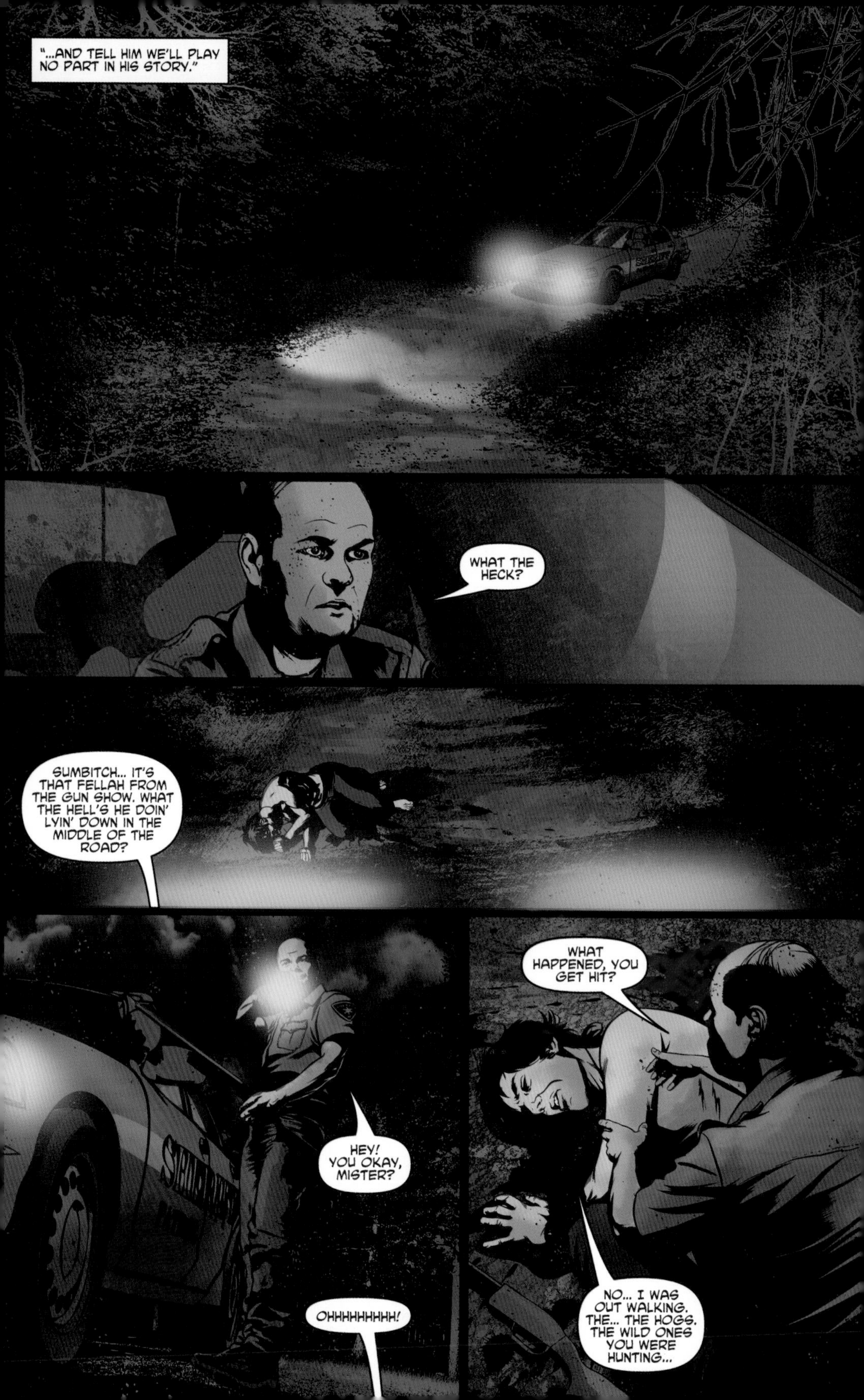
"...AND TELL HIM WE'LL PLAY NO PART IN HIS STORY."
WHAT THE HECK?
SUMBITCH... IT'S THAT FELLAH FROM THE GUN SHOW. WHAT THE HELL'S HE DOIN' LYIN' DOWN IN THE MIDDLE OF THE ROAD?
HEY! YOU OKAY, MISTER?
OHHHHHHHHH!
WHAT HAPPENED, YOU GET HIT?
NO... I WAS OUT WALKING. THE... THE HOGS. THE WILD ONES YOU WERE HUNTING...

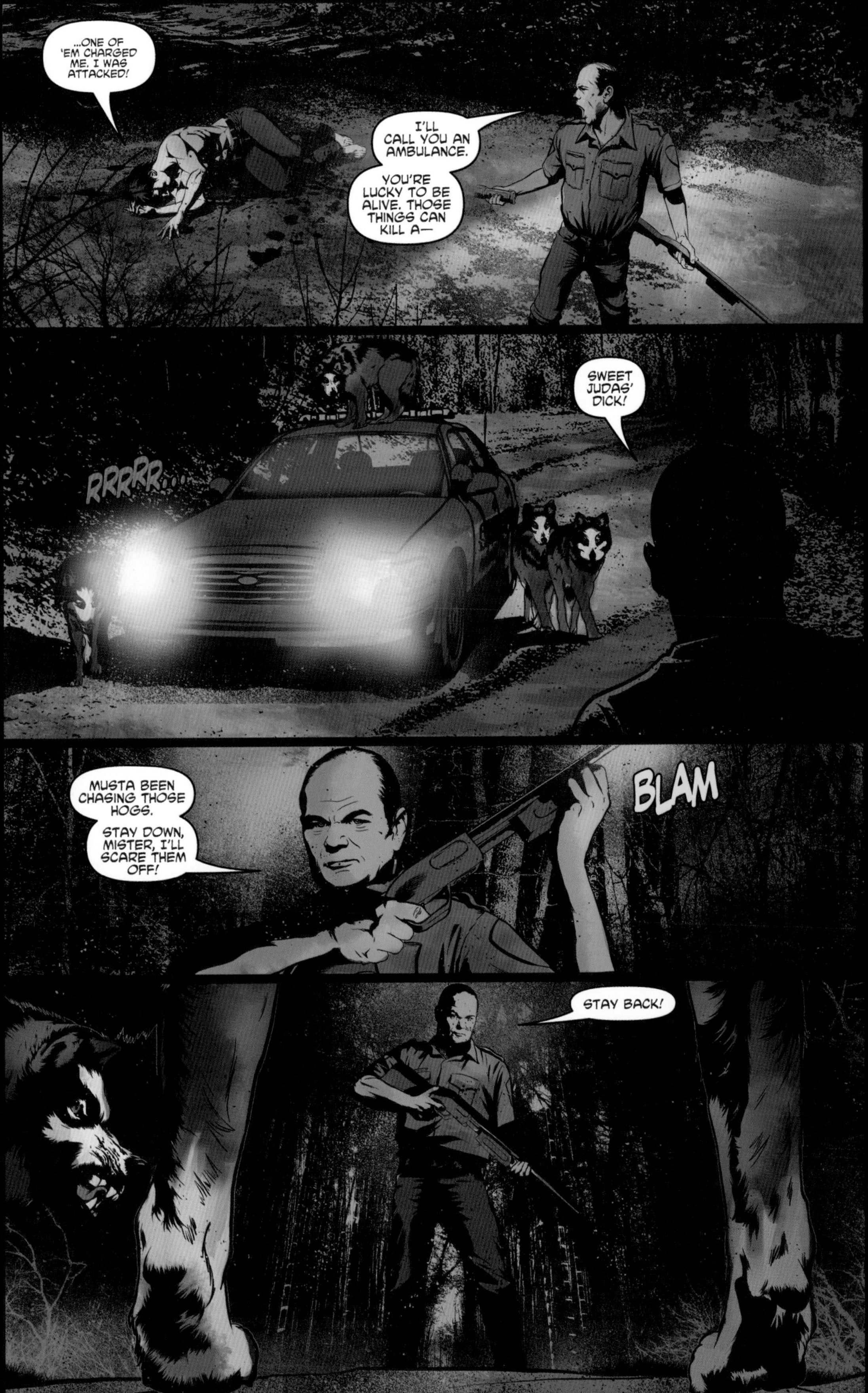
...ONE OF 'EM CHARGED ME. I WAS ATTACKED!
I'LL CALL YOU AN AMBULANCE.
YOU'RE LUCKY TO BE ALIVE. THOSE THINGS CAN KILL A—
SWEET JUDAS' DICK!
RRRRR...
MUSTA BEEN CHASING THOSE HOGS.
STAY DOWN, MISTER, I'LL SCARE THEM OFF!
BLAM
STAY BACK!

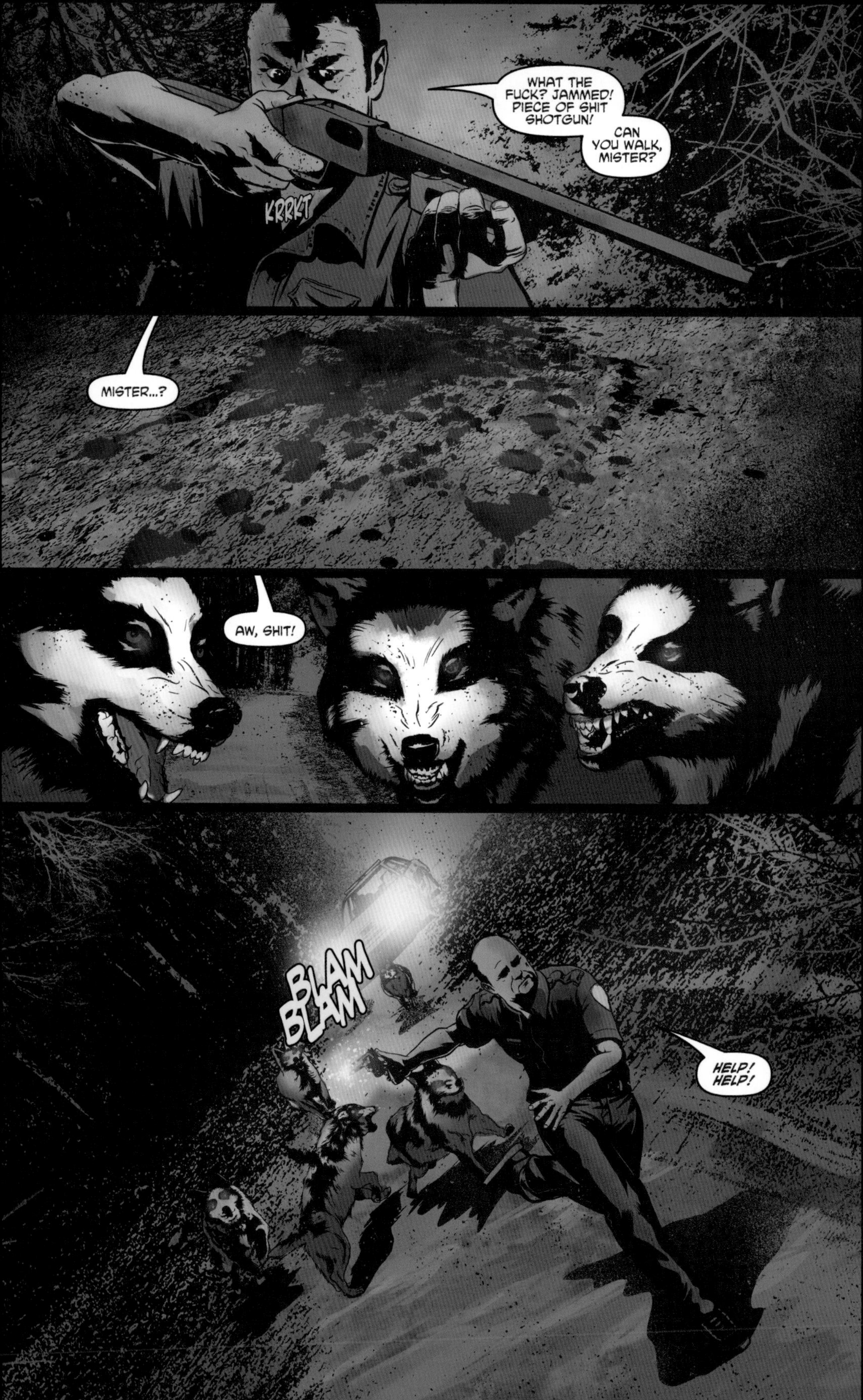
WHAT THE FUCK? JAMMED! PIECE OF SHIT SHOTGUN!
CAN YOU WALK, MISTER?
KRRKT
MISTER...?
AW, SHIT!
BLAM
BLAM
HELP! HELP!

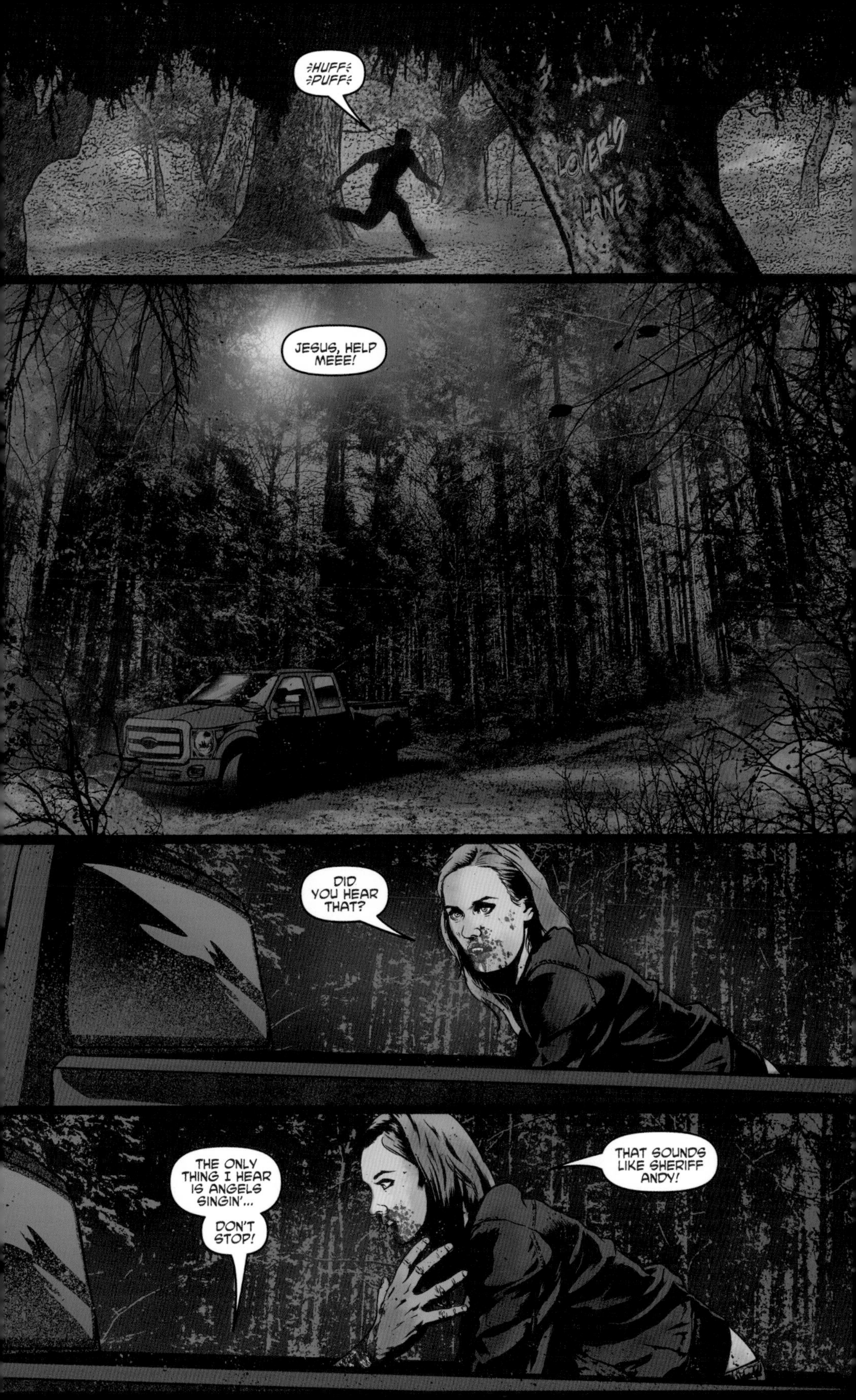

HUFF PUFF
LOVER'S LANE
JESUS, HELP MEEE!
DID YOU HEAR THAT?
THE ONLY THING I HEAR IS ANGELS SINGIN'...
DON'T STOP!
THAT SOUNDS LIKE SHERIFF ANDY!

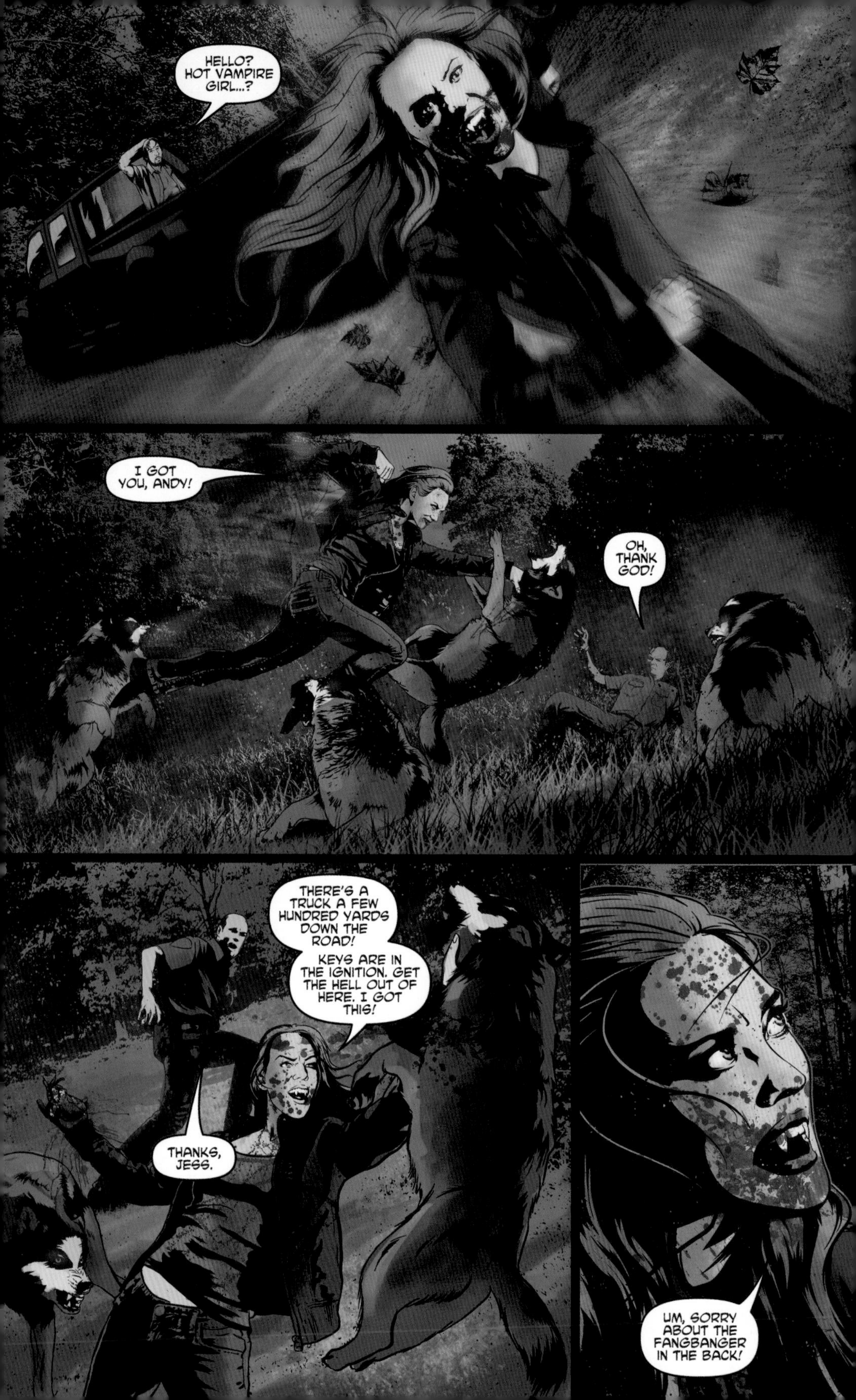
HELLO? HOT VAMPIRE GIRL...?
I GOT YOU, ANDY!
OH, THANK GOD!
THERE'S A TRUCK A FEW HUNDRED YARDS DOWN THE ROAD!
KEYS ARE IN THE IGNITION. GET THE HELL OUT OF HERE. I GOT THIS!
THANKS, JESS.
UM, SORRY ABOUT THE FANGBANGER IN THE BACK!

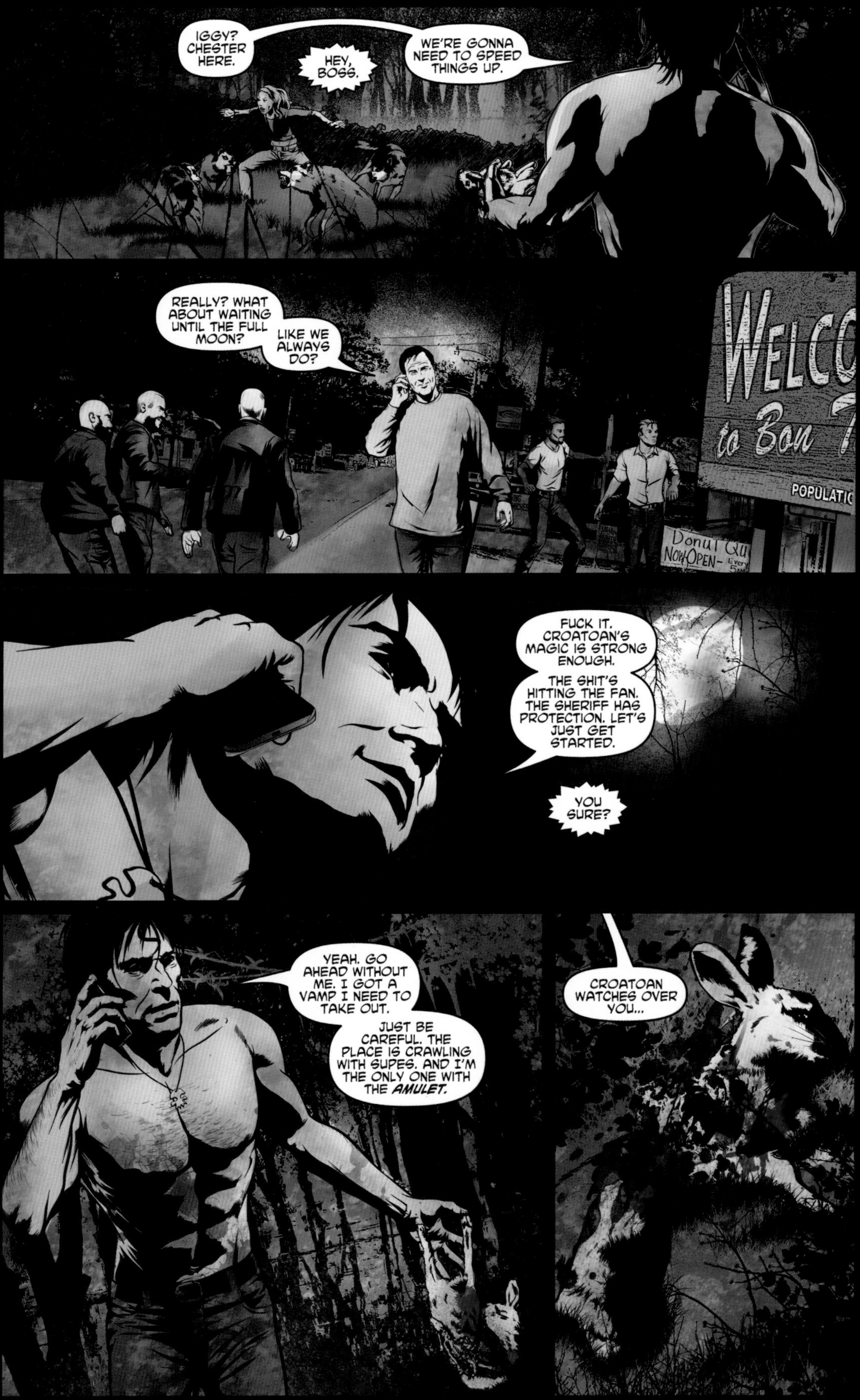
IGGY? CHESTER HERE.
HEY, BOSS.
WE'RE GONNA NEED TO SPEED THINGS UP.
REALLY? WHAT ABOUT WAITING UNTIL THE FULL MOON?
LIKE WE ALWAYS DO?
WELCO
to Bon
POPULATIO
Donut Qu
NOW OPEN-
FUCK IT. CROATOAN'S MAGIC IS STRONG ENOUGH.
THE SHIT'S HITTING THE FAN. THE SHERIFF HAS PROTECTION. LET'S JUST GET STARTED.
YOU SURE?
YEAH. GO AHEAD WITHOUT ME. I GOT A VAMP I NEED TO TAKE OUT.
JUST BE CAREFUL. THE PLACE IS CRAWLING WITH SUPES. AND I'M THE ONLY ONE WITH THE AMULET.
CROATOAN WATCHES OVER YOU...

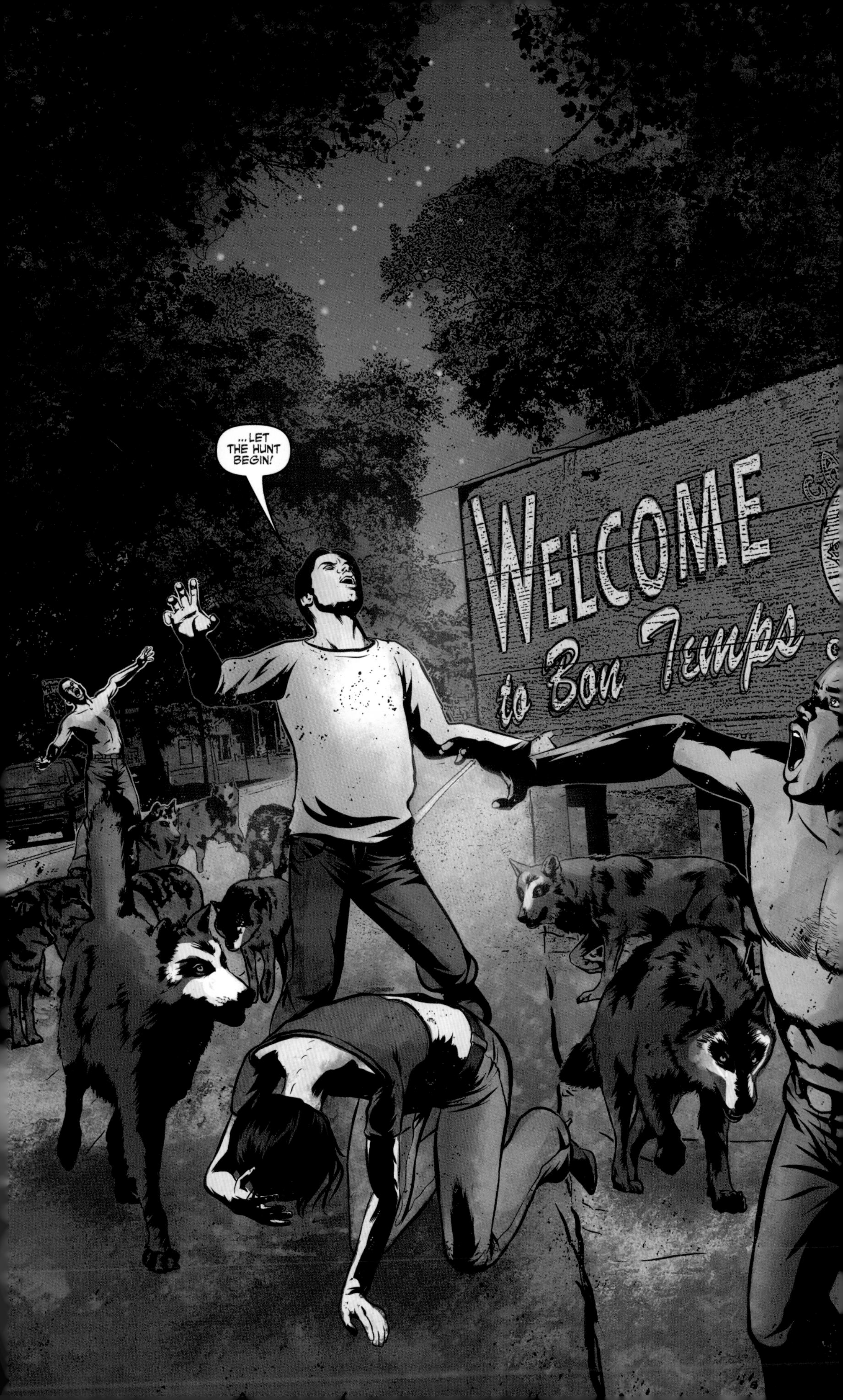
...LET THE HUNT BEGIN!
WELCOME to Bon Temps

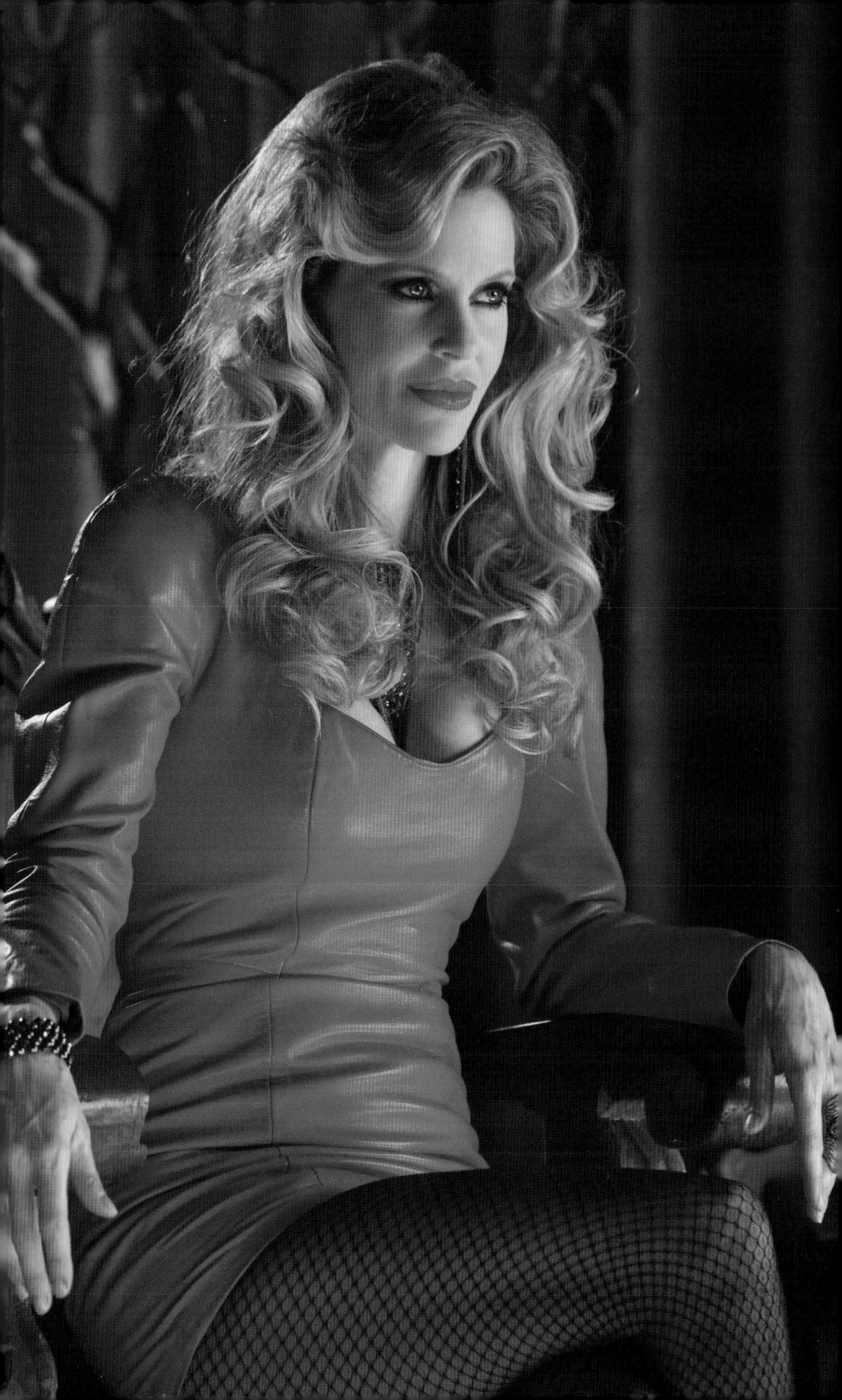

CHAPTER 4

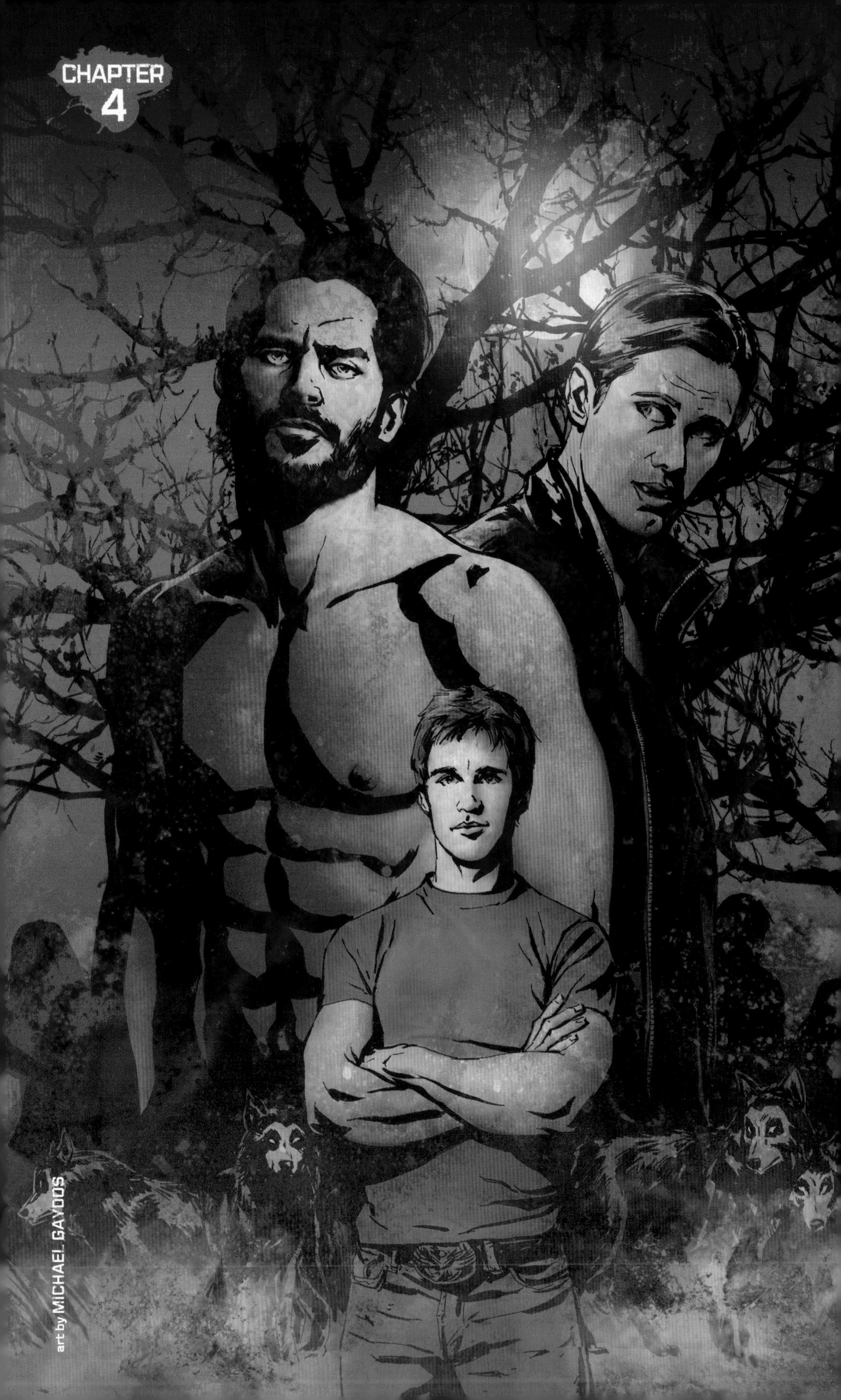
art by MICHAEL GAYDOS

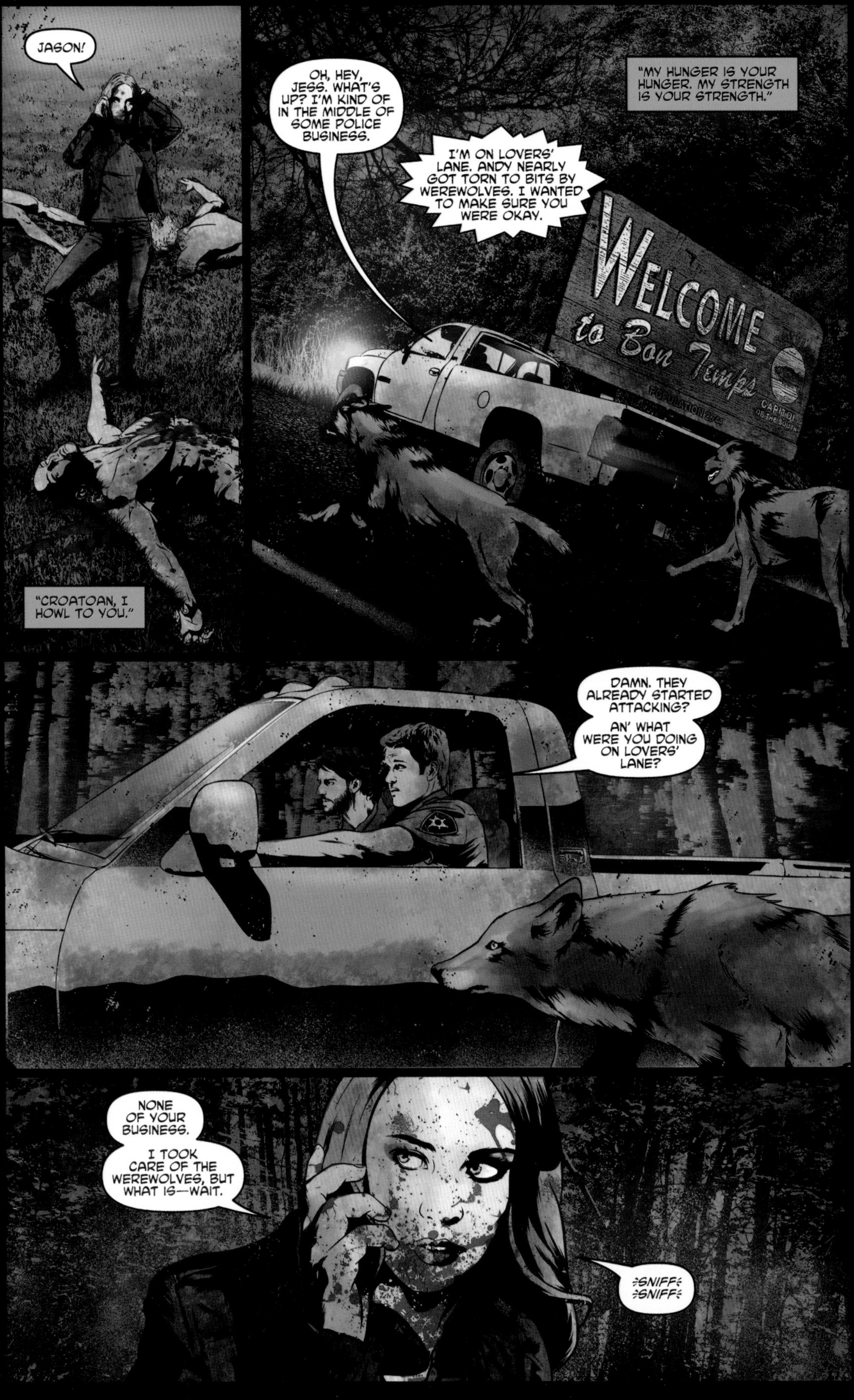
JASON!
"CROATOAN, I HOWL TO YOU."
OH, HEY, JESS. WHAT'S UP? I'M KIND OF IN THE MIDDLE OF SOME POLICE BUSINESS.
I'M ON LOVERS' LANE. ANDY NEARLY GOT TORN TO BITS BY WEREWOLVES. I WANTED TO MAKE SURE YOU WERE OKAY.
"MY HUNGER IS YOUR HUNGER. MY STRENGTH IS YOUR STRENGTH."
WELCOME to Bon Temps
DAMN. THEY ALREADY STARTED ATTACKING?
AN' WHAT WERE YOU DOING ON LOVERS' LANE?
NONE OF YOUR BUSINESS.
I TOOK CARE OF THE WEREWOLVES, BUT WHAT IS—WAIT.
≠SNIFF≠
≠SNIFF≠

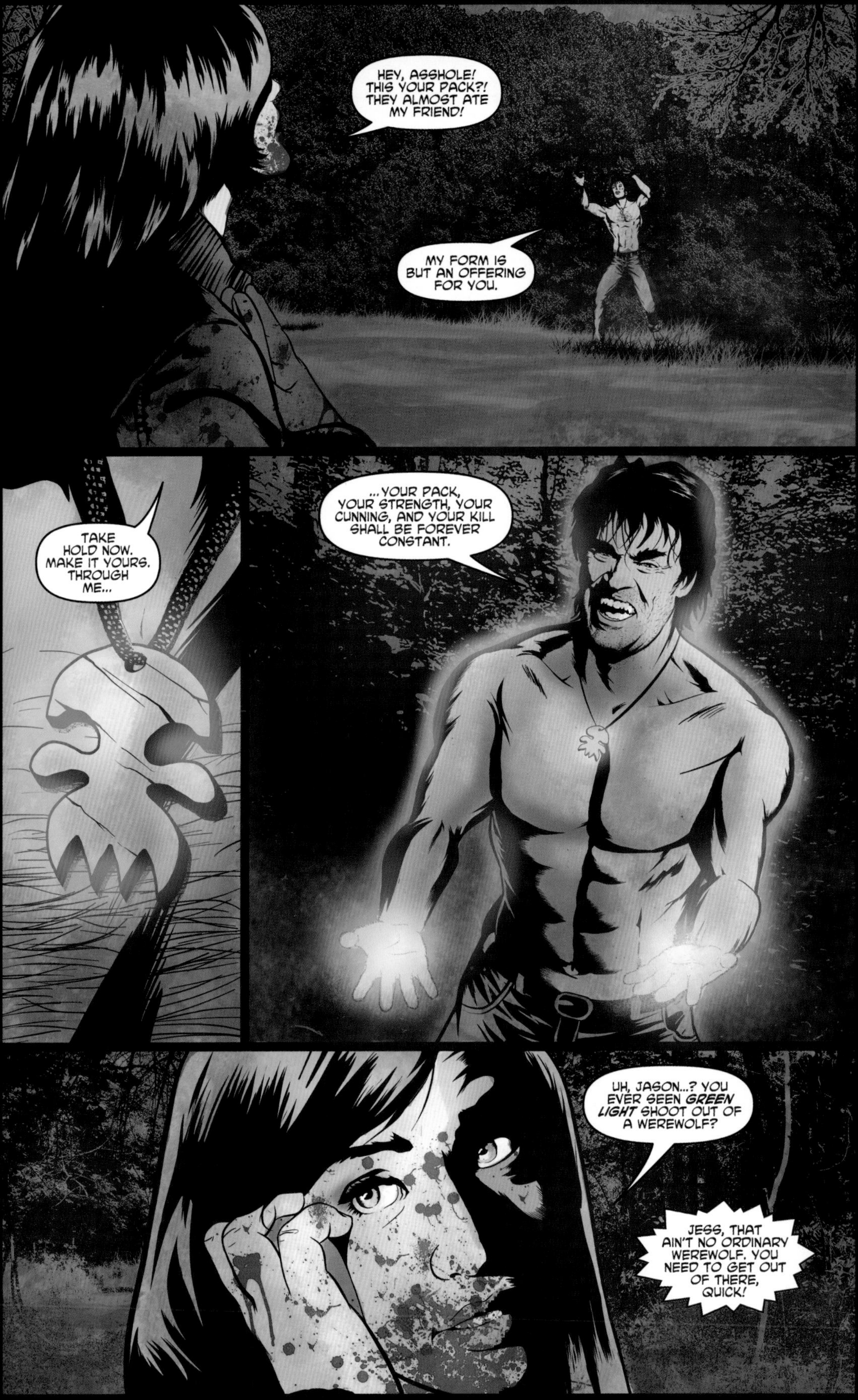
HEY, ASSHOLE! THIS YOUR PACK?! THEY ALMOST ATE MY FRIEND!
MY FORM IS BUT AN OFFERING FOR YOU.
TAKE HOLD NOW. MAKE IT YOURS. THROUGH ME...
...YOUR PACK, YOUR STRENGTH, YOUR CUNNING, AND YOUR KILL SHALL BE FOREVER CONSTANT.
UH, JASON...? YOU EVER SEEN GREEN LIGHT SHOOT OUT OF A WEREWOLF?
JESS, THAT AIN'T NO ORDINARY WEREWOLF. YOU NEED TO GET OUT OF THERE, QUICK!

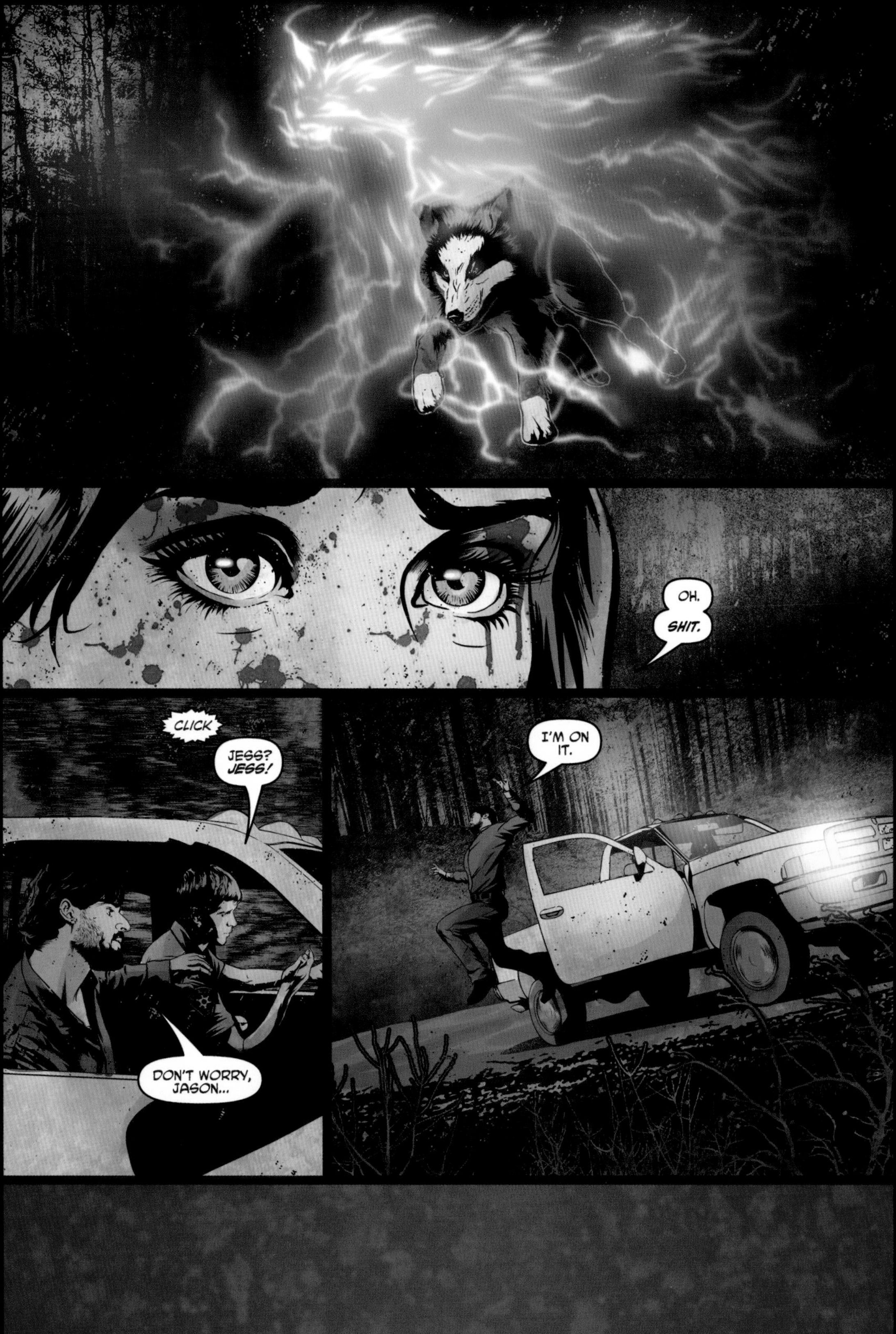
OH.
SHIT.
CLICK
JESS? JESS!
DON'T WORRY, JASON...
I'M ON IT.

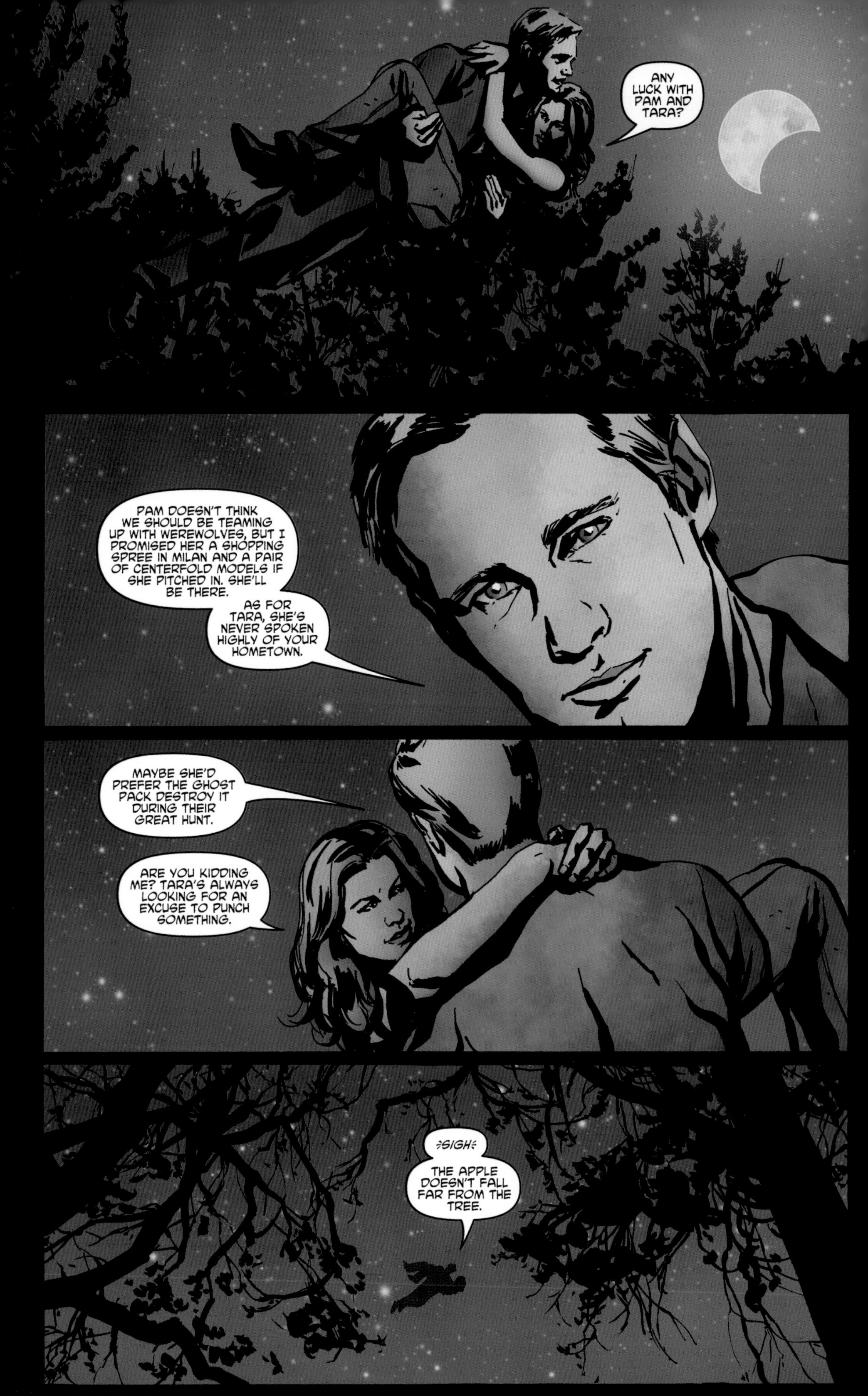
ANY LUCK WITH PAM AND TARA?
PAM DOESN'T THINK WE SHOULD BE TEAMING UP WITH WEREWOLVES, BUT I PROMISED HER A SHOPPING SPREE IN MILAN AND A PAIR OF CENTERFOLD MODELS IF SHE PITCHED IN. SHE'LL BE THERE.
AS FOR TARA, SHE'S NEVER SPOKEN HIGHLY OF YOUR HOMETOWN.
MAYBE SHE'D PREFER THE GHOST PACK DESTROY IT DURING THEIR GREAT HUNT.
ARE YOU KIDDING ME? TARA'S ALWAYS LOOKING FOR AN EXCUSE TO PUNCH SOMETHING.
SIGH
THE APPLE DOESN'T FALL FAR FROM THE TREE.

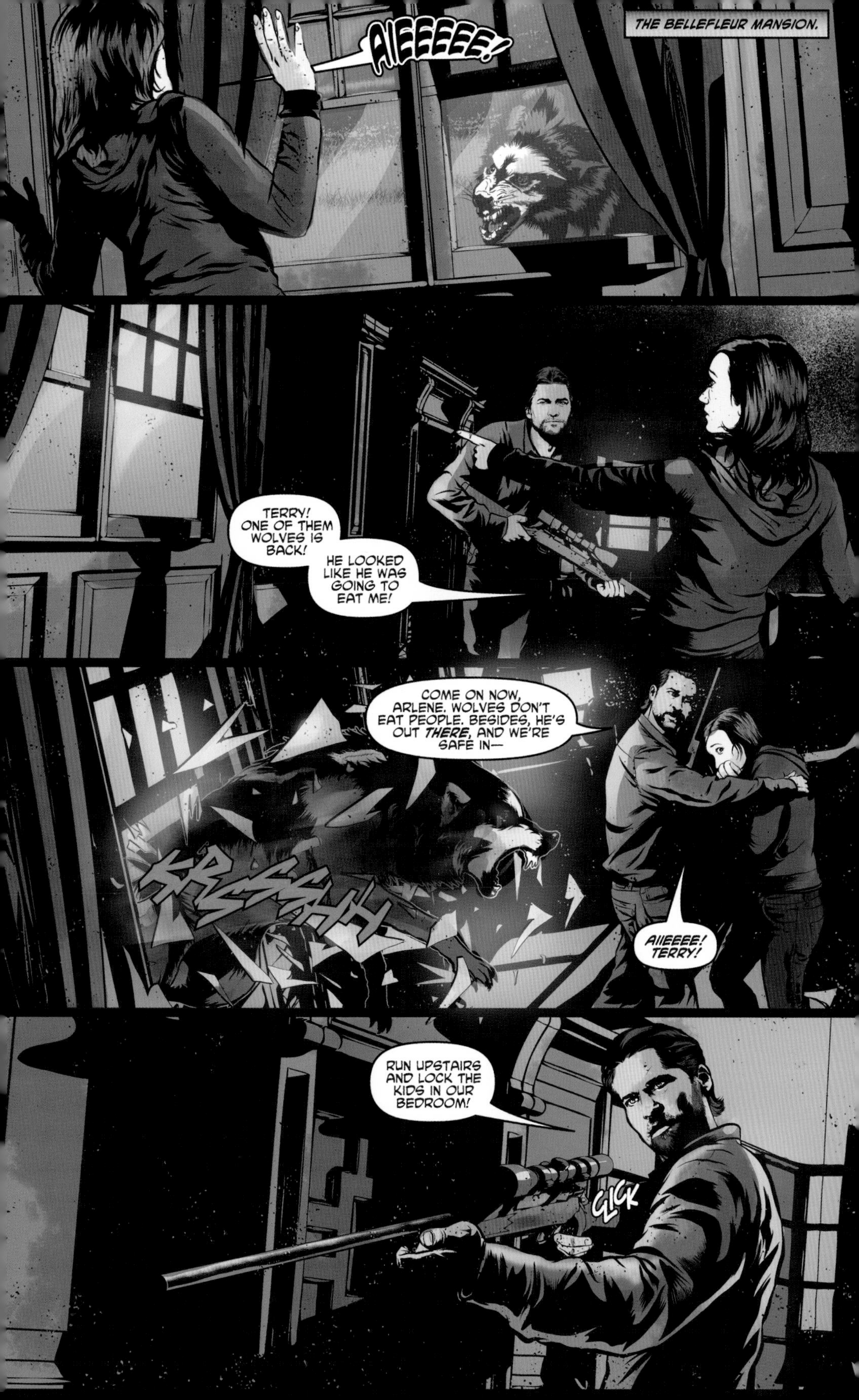
THE BELLEFLEUR MANSION.
AIEEEEE!
TERRY! ONE OF THEM WOLVES IS BACK!
HE LOOKED LIKE HE WAS GOING TO EAT ME!
COME ON NOW, ARLENE. WOLVES DON'T EAT PEOPLE. BESIDES, HE'S OUT THERE, AND WE'RE SAFE IN—
KRSSHH
AIIEEEE! TERRY!
RUN UPSTAIRS AND LOCK THE KIDS IN OUR BEDROOM!
CLICK

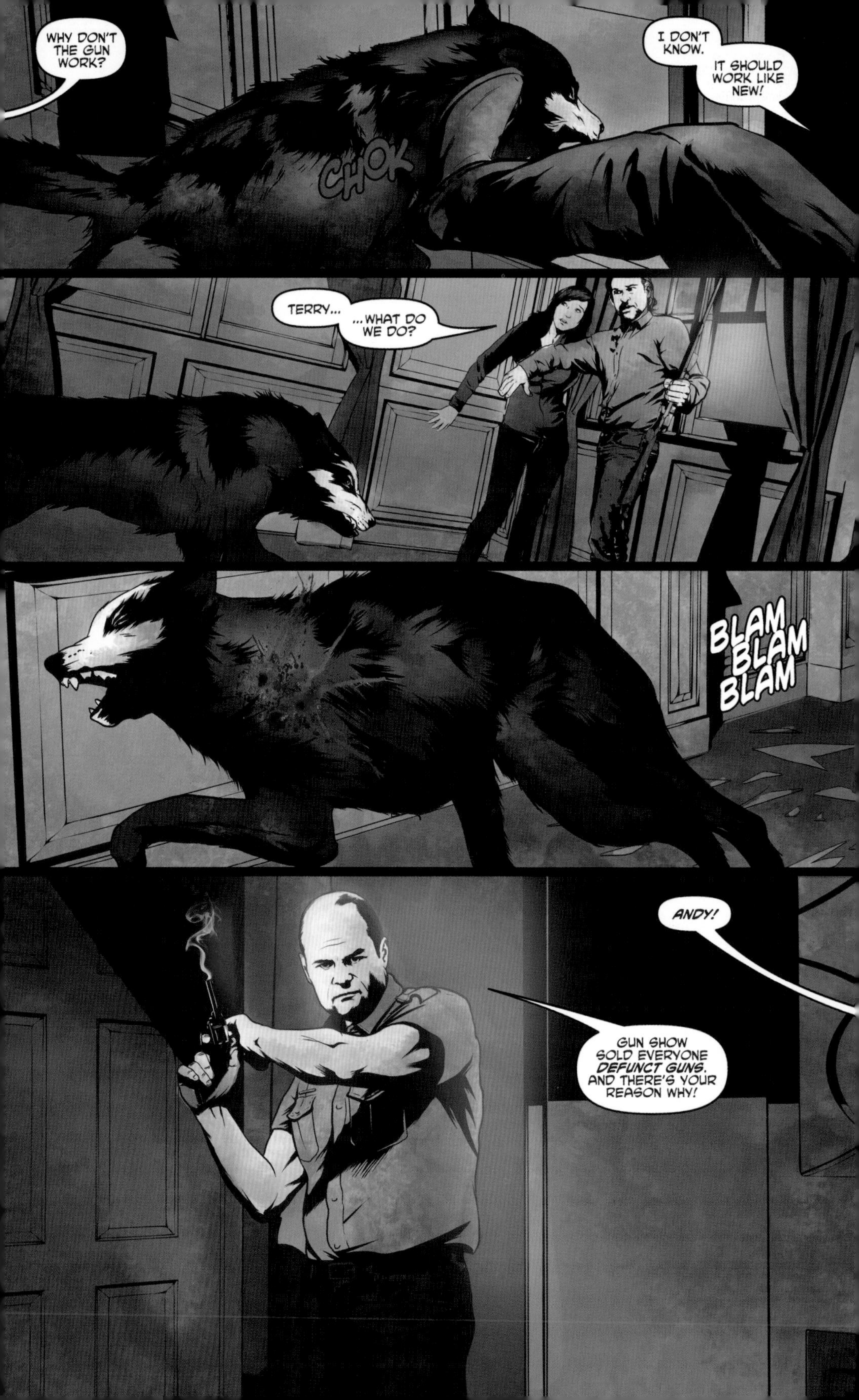

WHY DON'T THE GUN WORK?
I DON'T KNOW.
IT SHOULD WORK LIKE NEW!
CHOK
TERRY...
...WHAT DO WE DO?
BLAM
BLAM
BLAM
ANDY!
GUN SHOW SOLD EVERYONE DEFUNCT GUNS. AND THERE'S YOUR REASON WHY!

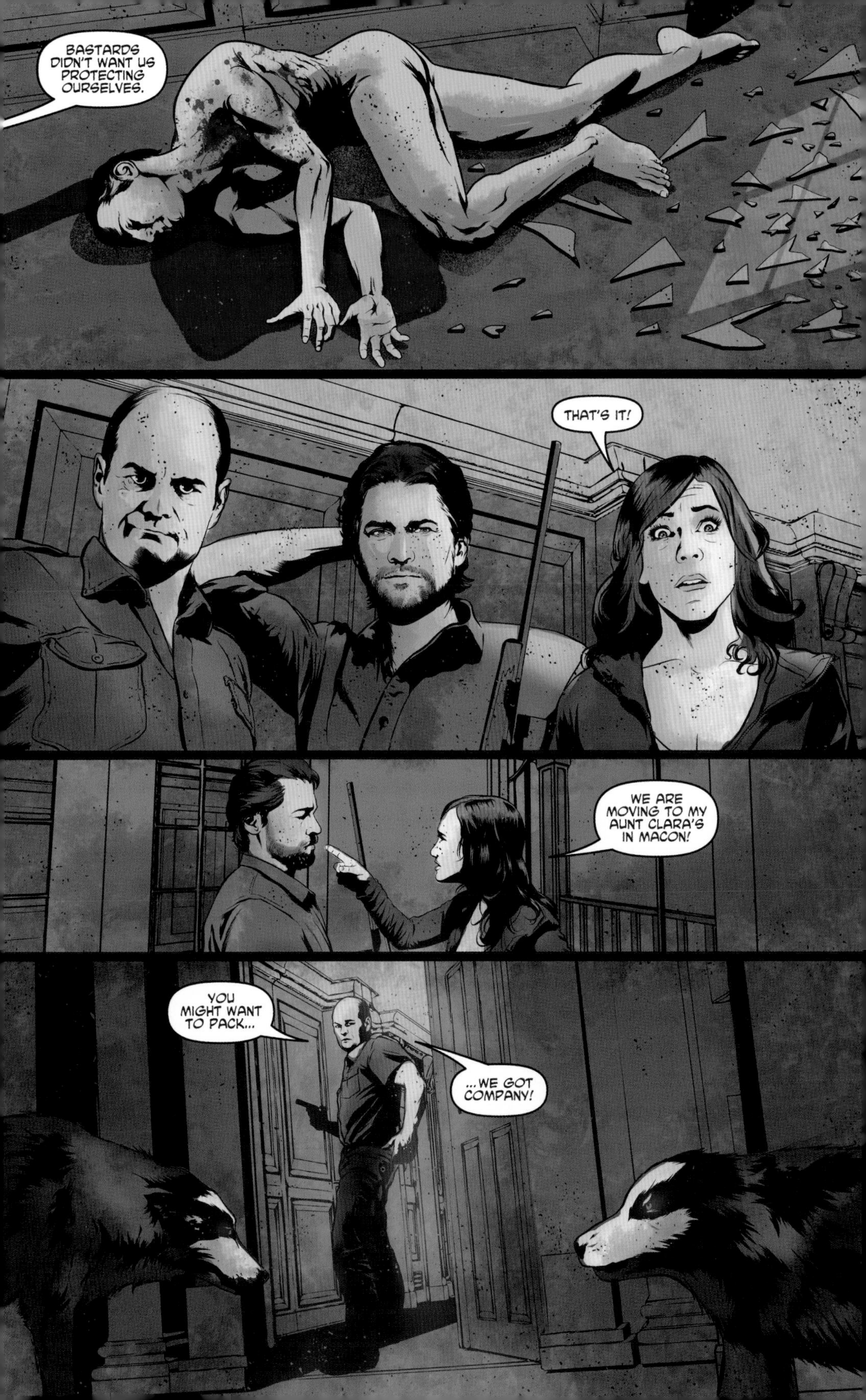
BASTARDS DIDN'T WANT US PROTECTING OURSELVES.
THAT'S IT!
WE ARE MOVING TO MY AUNT CLARA'S IN MACON!
YOU MIGHT WANT TO PACK...
...WE GOT COMPANY!

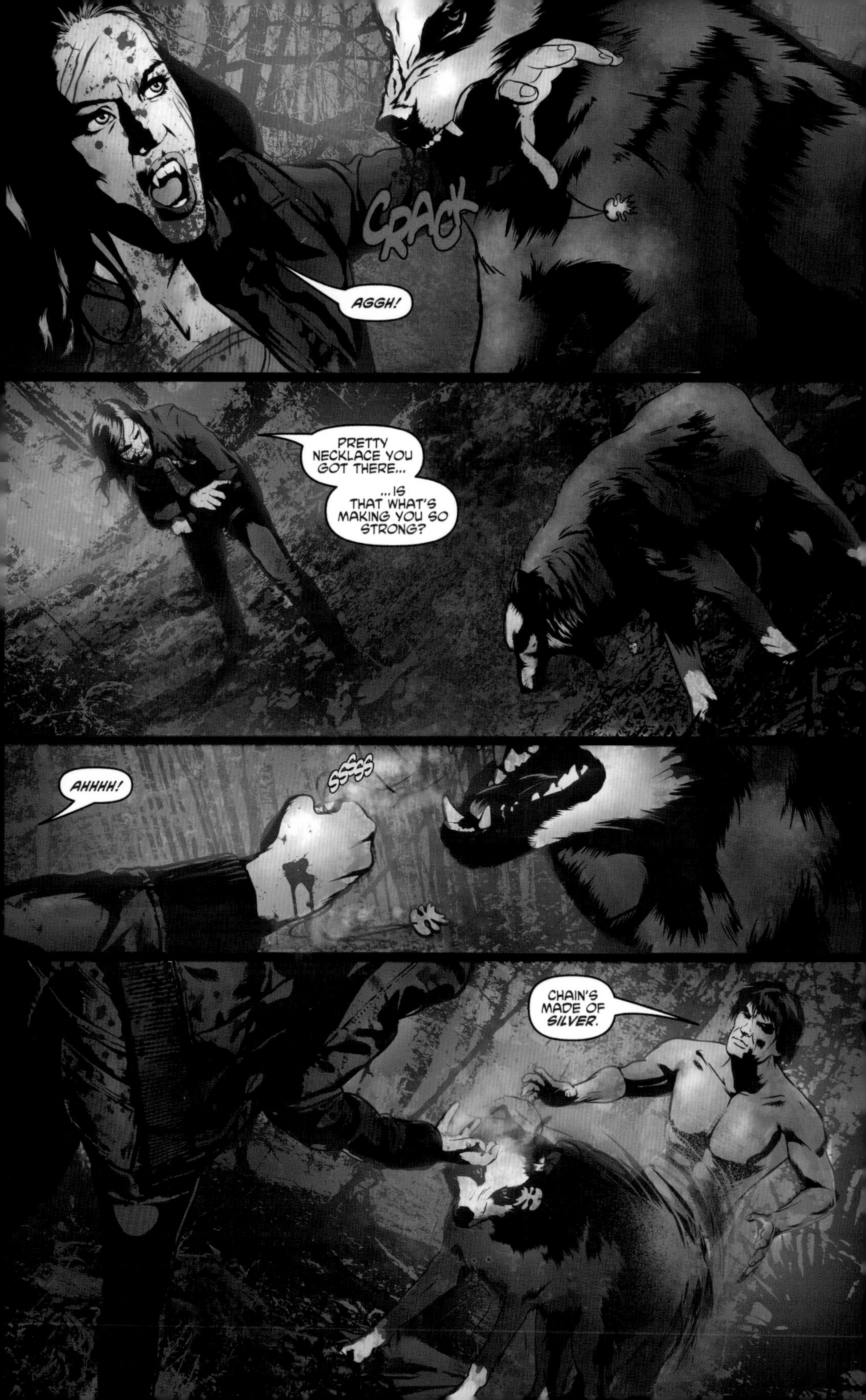
CRACK
AGGH!
PRETTY NECKLACE YOU GOT THERE...
...IS THAT WHAT'S MAKING YOU SO STRONG?
AHHHH!
SSSSS
CHAIN'S MADE OF *SILVER*.

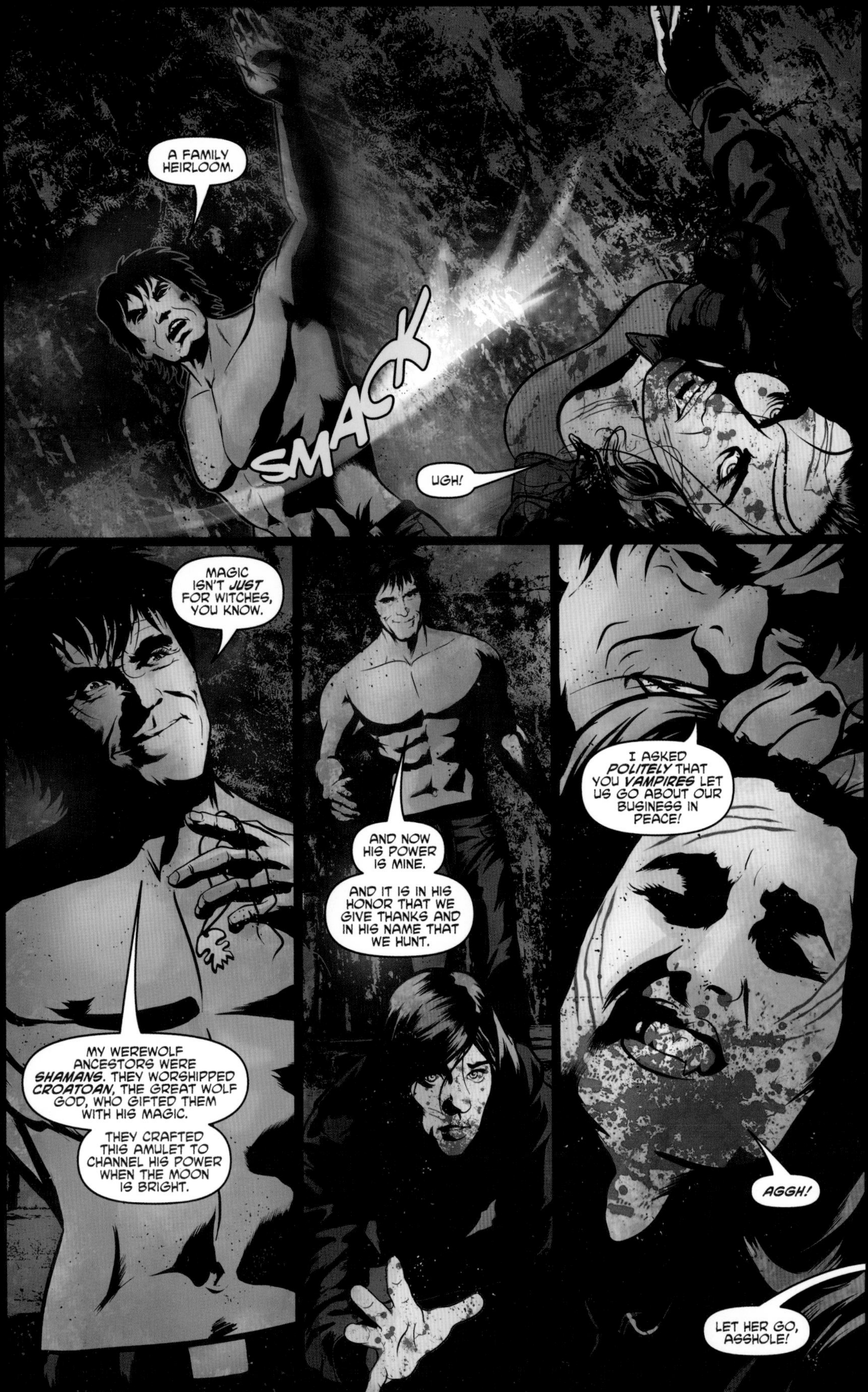
A FAMILY HEIRLOOM.
SMACK
UGH!
MAGIC ISN'T *JUST* FOR WITCHES, YOU KNOW.
MY WEREWOLF ANCESTORS WERE *SHAMANS*. THEY WORSHIPPED *CROATOAN*, THE GREAT WOLF GOD, WHO GIFTED THEM WITH HIS MAGIC.
THEY CRAFTED THIS AMULET TO CHANNEL HIS POWER WHEN THE MOON IS BRIGHT.
AND NOW HIS POWER IS MINE.
AND IT IS IN HIS HONOR THAT WE GIVE THANKS AND IN HIS NAME THAT WE HUNT.
I ASKED *POLITELY* THAT YOU *VAMPIRES* LET US GO ABOUT OUR BUSINESS IN PEACE!
AGGH!
LET HER GO, ASSHOLE!

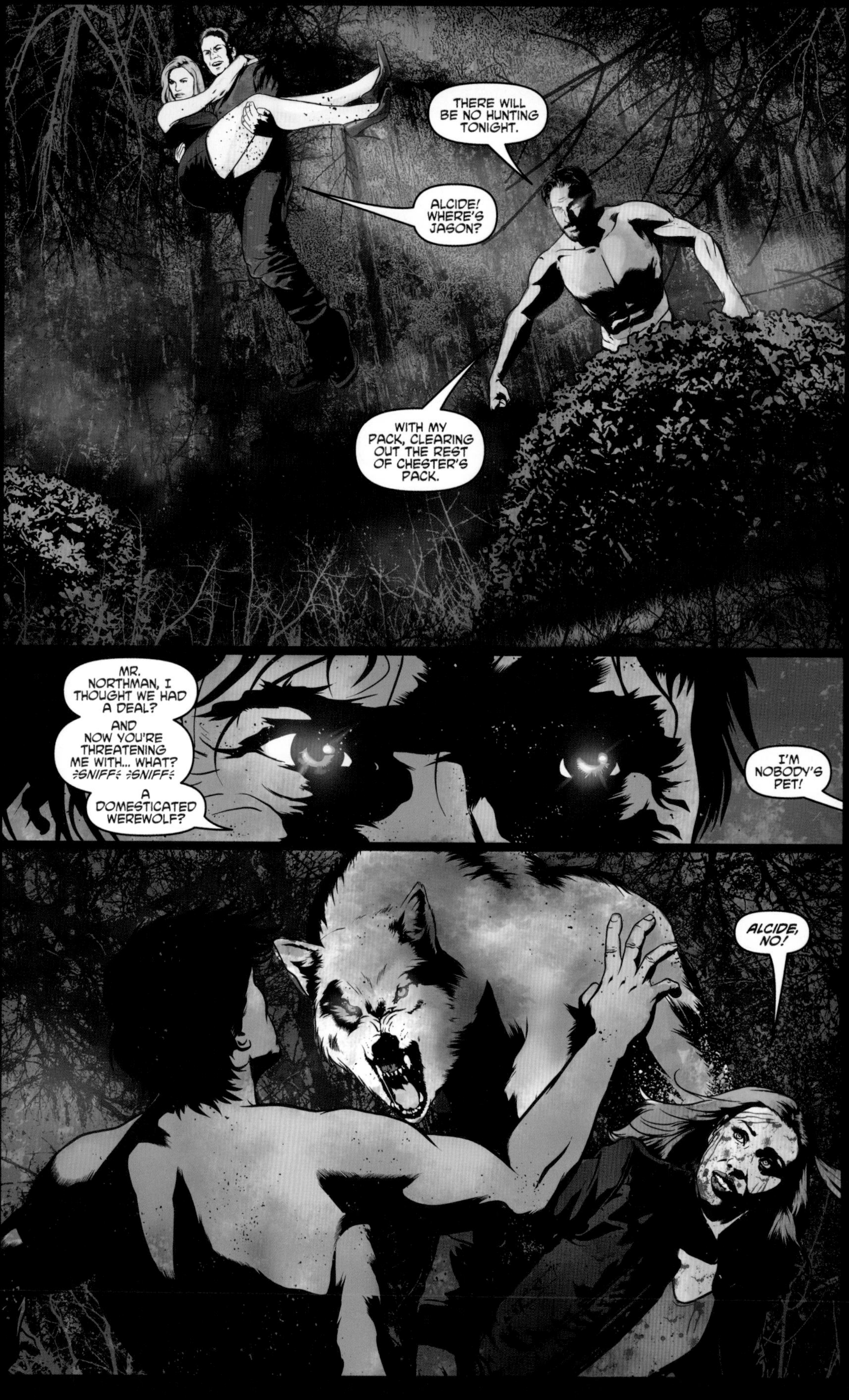
THERE WILL BE NO HUNTING TONIGHT.
ALCIDE! WHERE'S JASON?
WITH MY PACK, CLEARING OUT THE REST OF CHESTER'S PACK.
MR. NORTHMAN, I THOUGHT WE HAD A DEAL?
AND NOW YOU'RE THREATENING ME WITH... WHAT? *SNIFF* *SNIFF*
A DOMESTICATED WEREWOLF?
I'M NOBODY'S PET!
ALCIDE, NO!

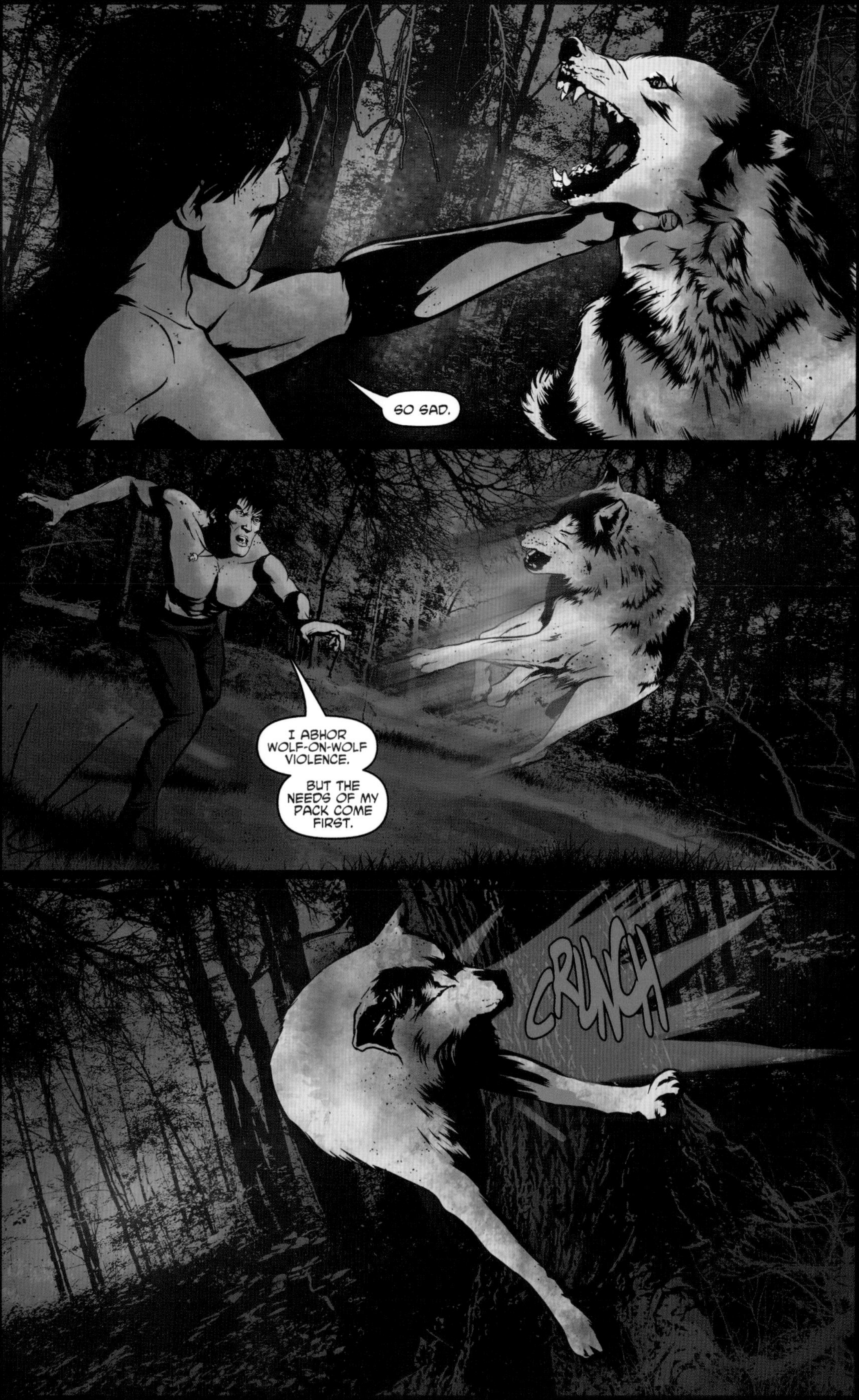
SO SAD.
I ABHOR WOLF-ON-WOLF VIOLENCE.
BUT THE NEEDS OF MY PACK COME FIRST.
CRUNCH

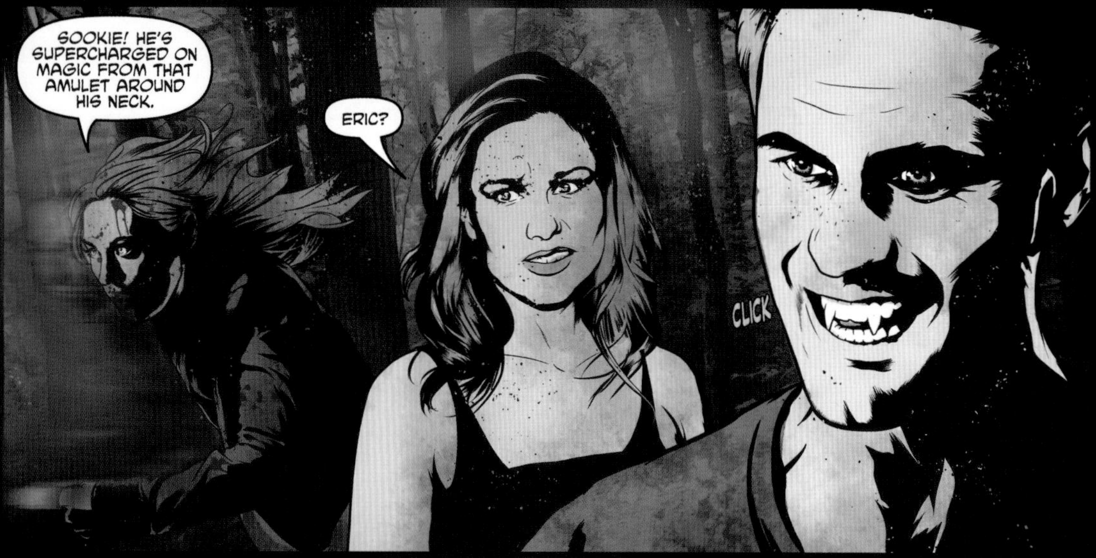
SOOKIE! HE'S SUPERCHARGED ON MAGIC FROM THAT AMULET AROUND HIS NECK.
ERIC?
CLICK

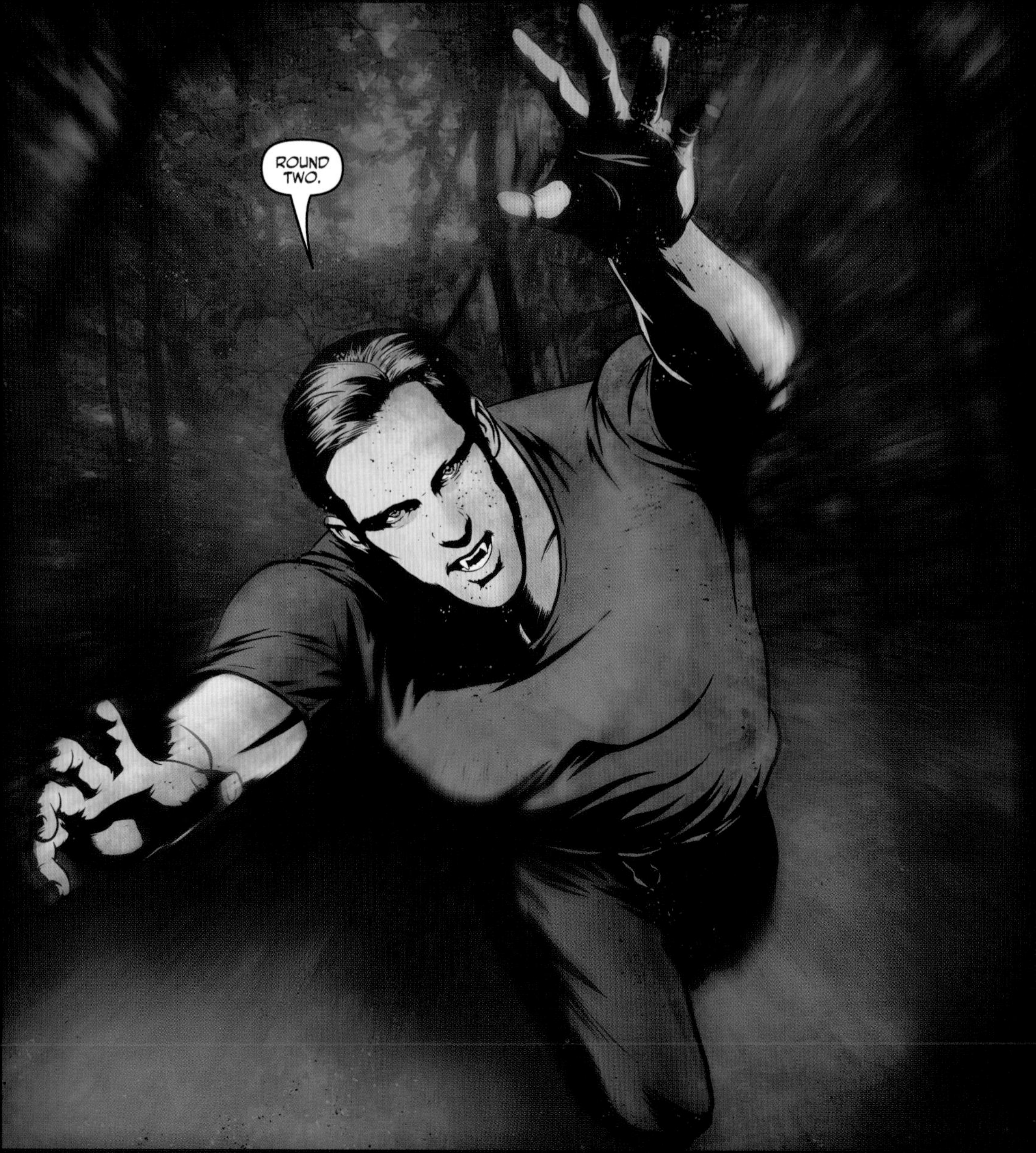
ROUND TWO.

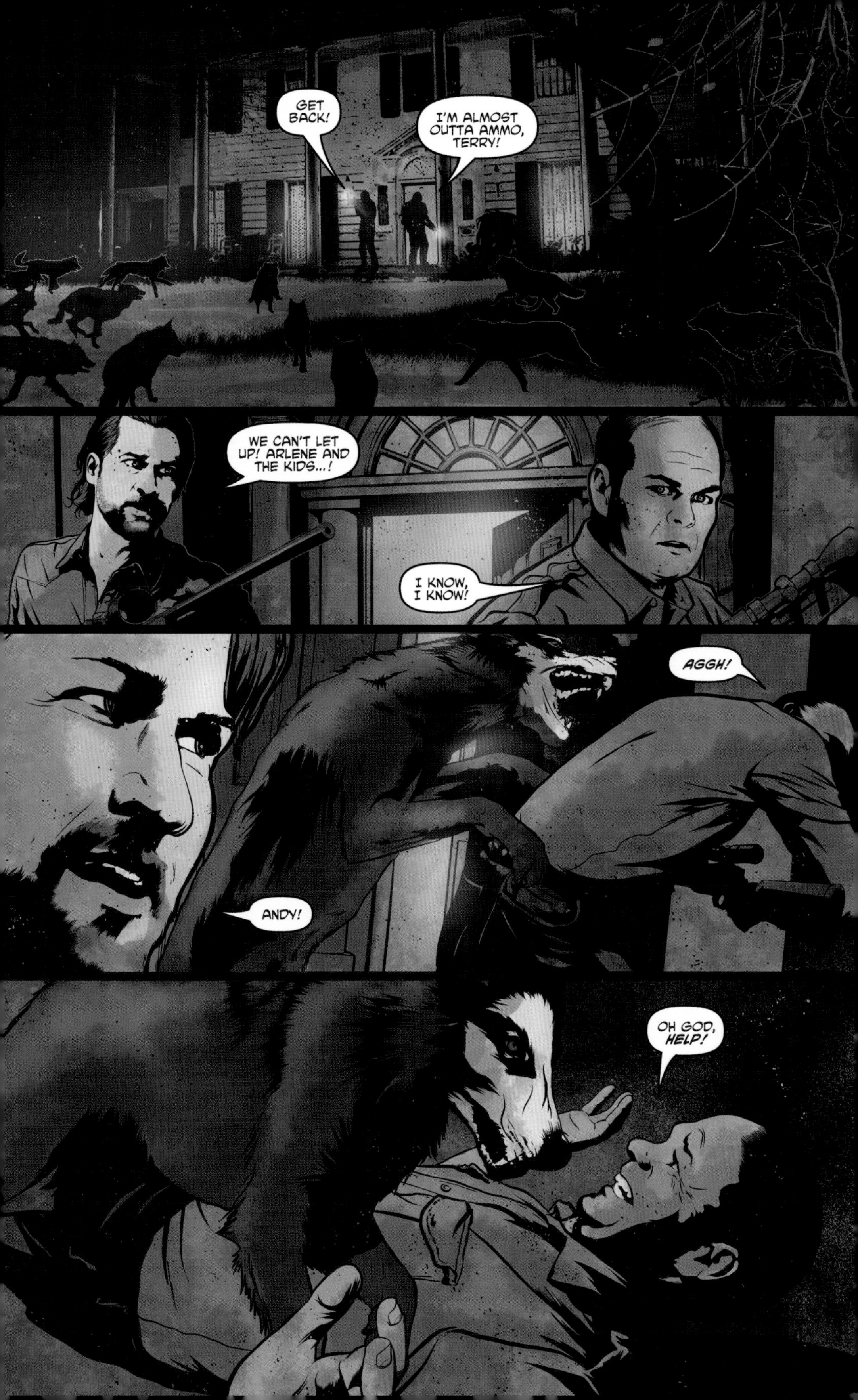
GET BACK!
I'M ALMOST OUTTA AMMO, TERRY!
WE CAN'T LET UP! ARLENE AND THE KIDS...!
I KNOW, I KNOW!
AGGH!
ANDY!
OH GOD, HELP!

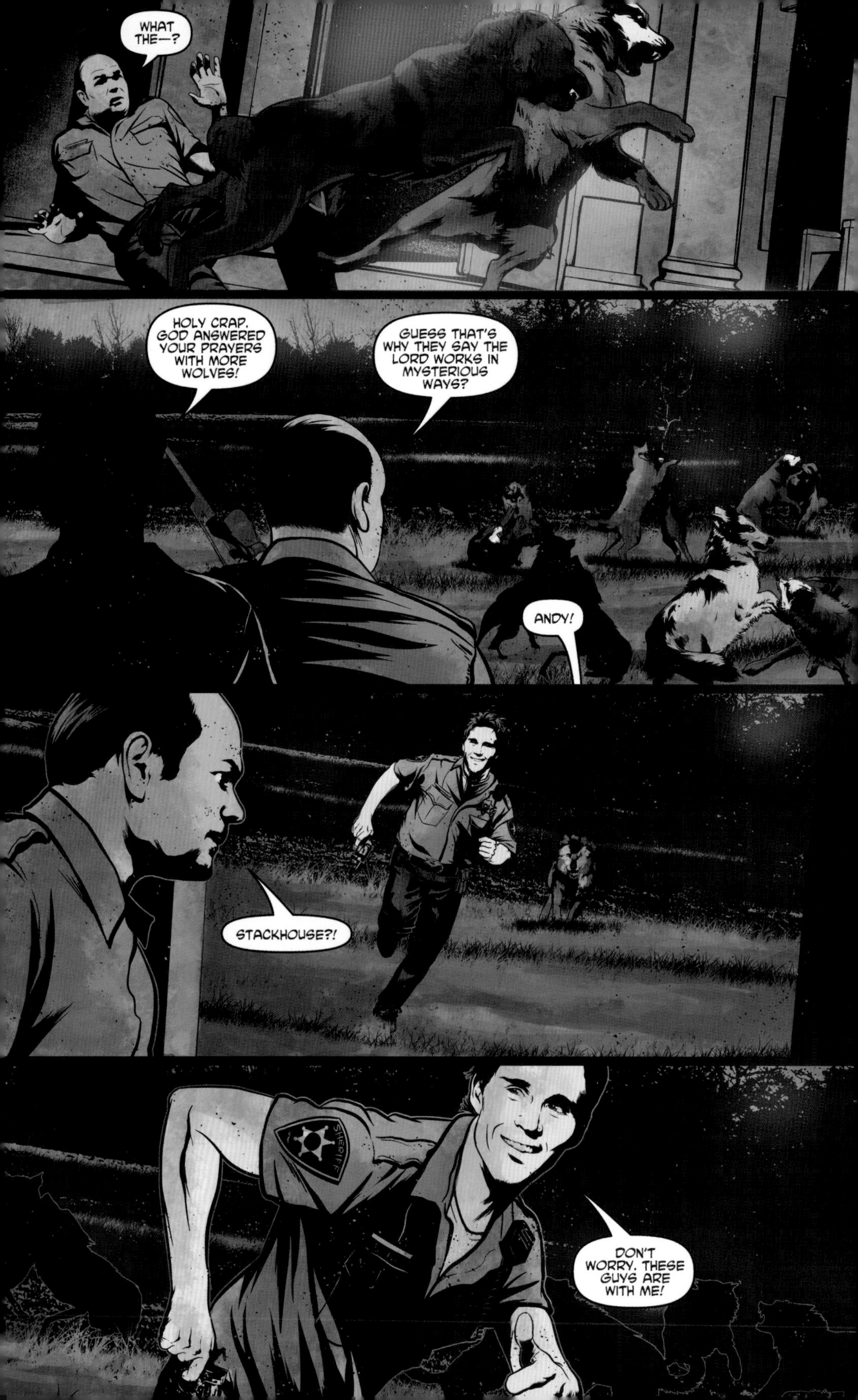
WHAT THE—?
HOLY CRAP. GOD ANSWERED YOUR PRAYERS WITH MORE WOLVES!
GUESS THAT'S WHY THEY SAY THE LORD WORKS IN MYSTERIOUS WAYS?
ANDY!
STACKHOUSE?!
SHERIFF
DON'T WORRY. THESE GUYS ARE WITH ME!

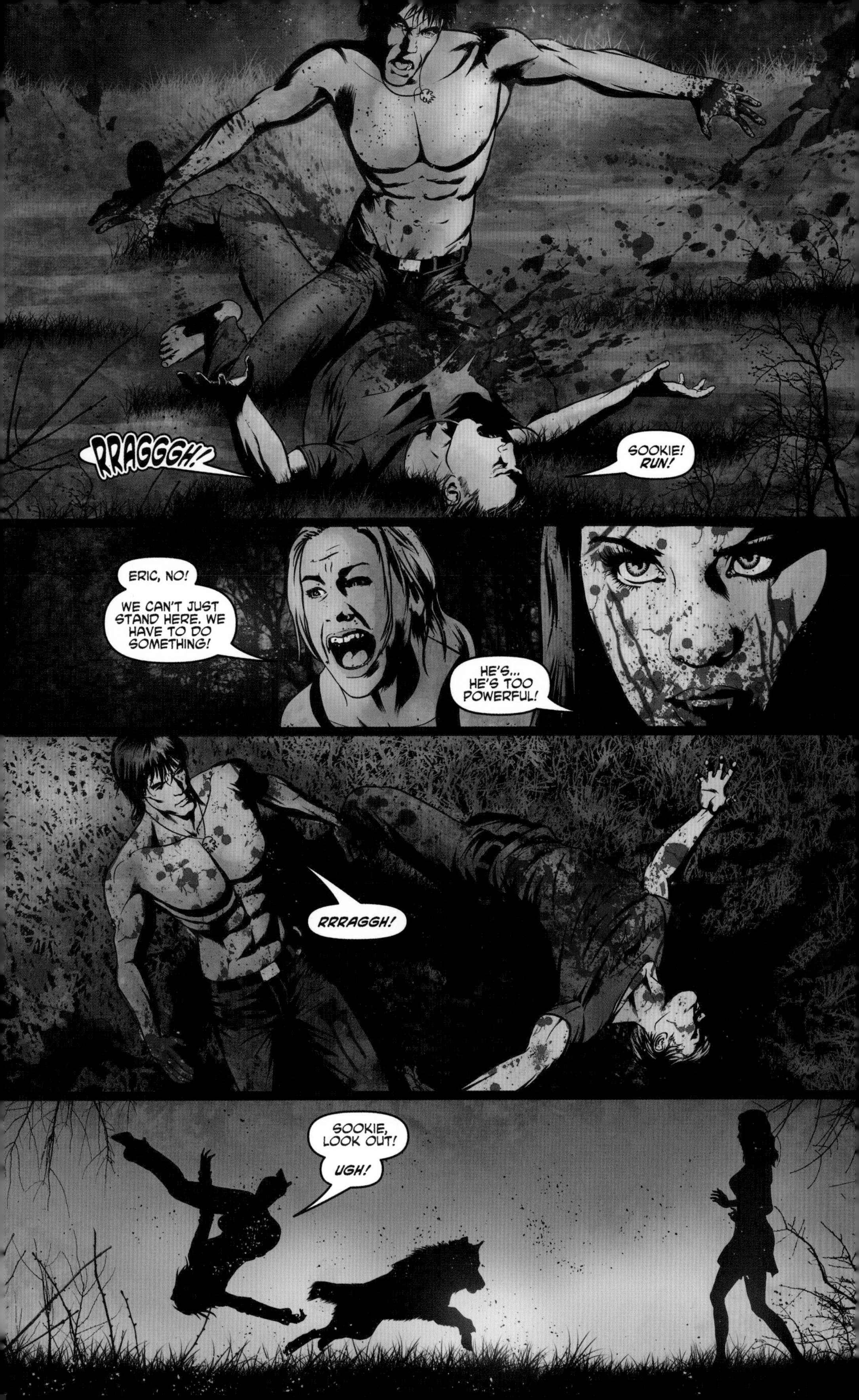
RRAGGGH!
SOOKIE! RUN!
ERIC, NO!
WE CAN'T JUST STAND HERE. WE HAVE TO DO SOMETHING!
HE'S... HE'S TOO POWERFUL!
RRRAGGH!
SOOKIE, LOOK OUT!
UGH!

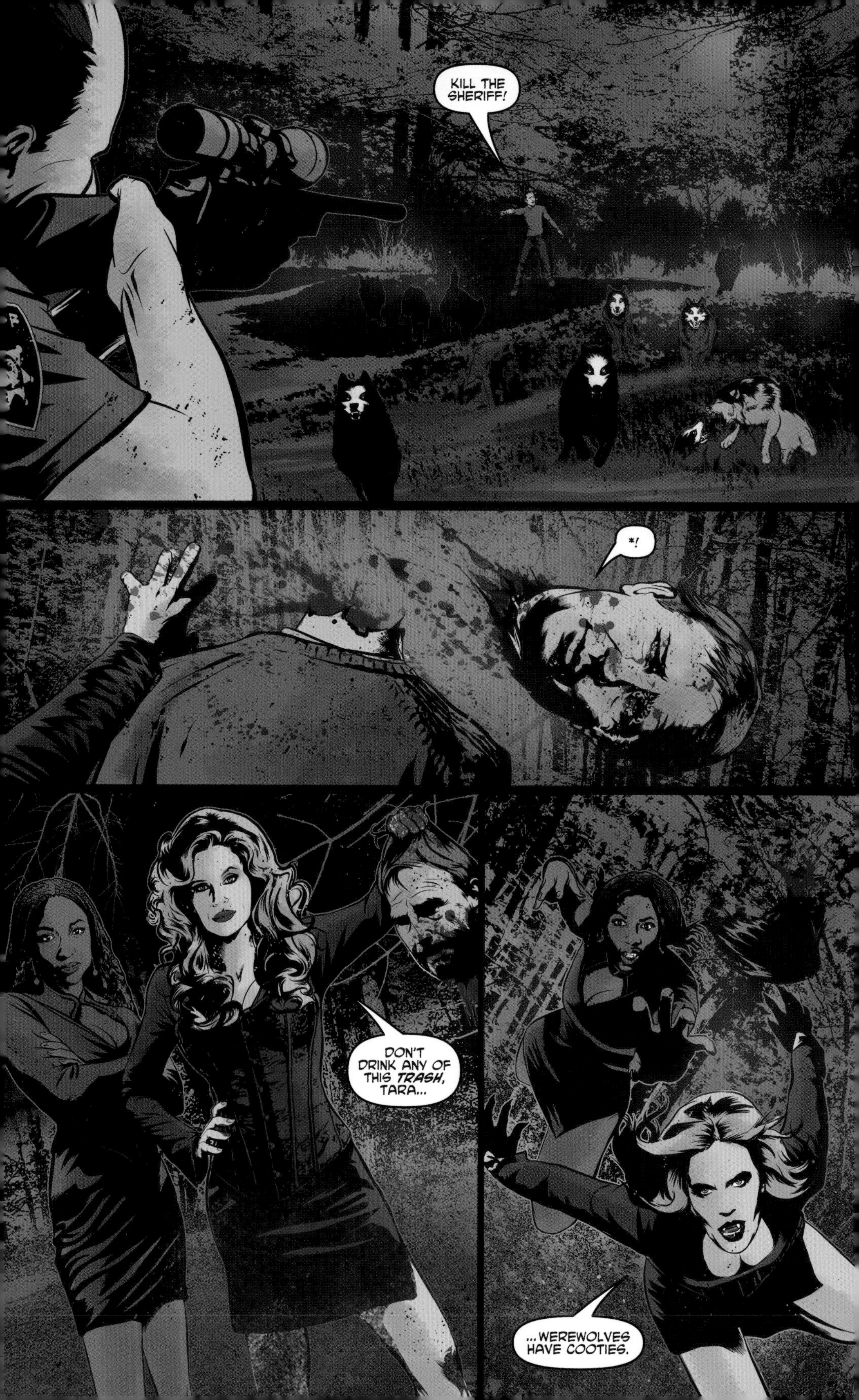
KILL THE SHERIFF!
*!
DON'T DRINK ANY OF THIS *TRASH*, TARA...
...WEREWOLVES HAVE COOTIES.

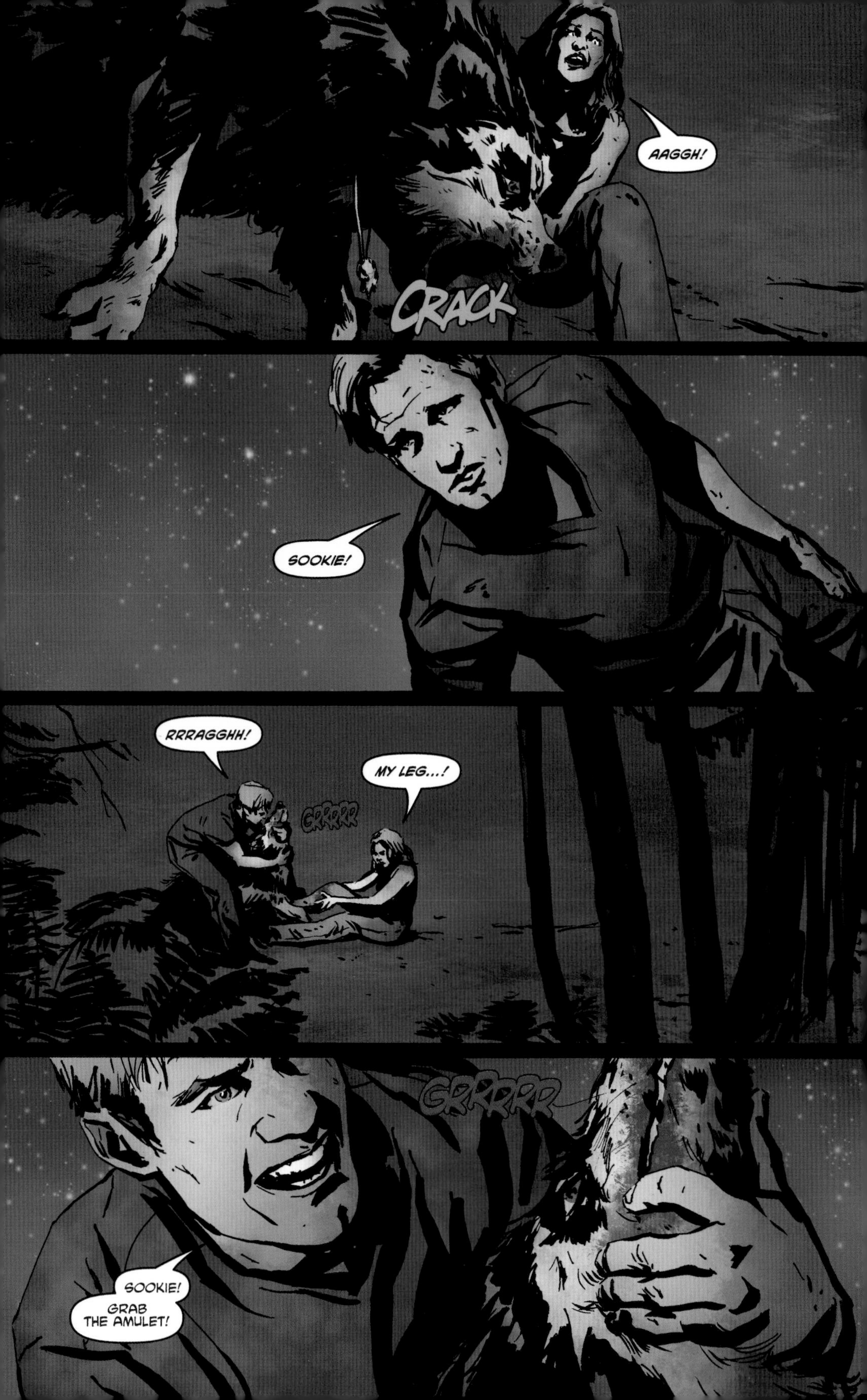
AAGGH!
CRACK
SOOKIE!
RRRAGGHH!
MY LEG...!
GRRRR
GRRRRR
SOOKIE!
GRAB THE AMULET!

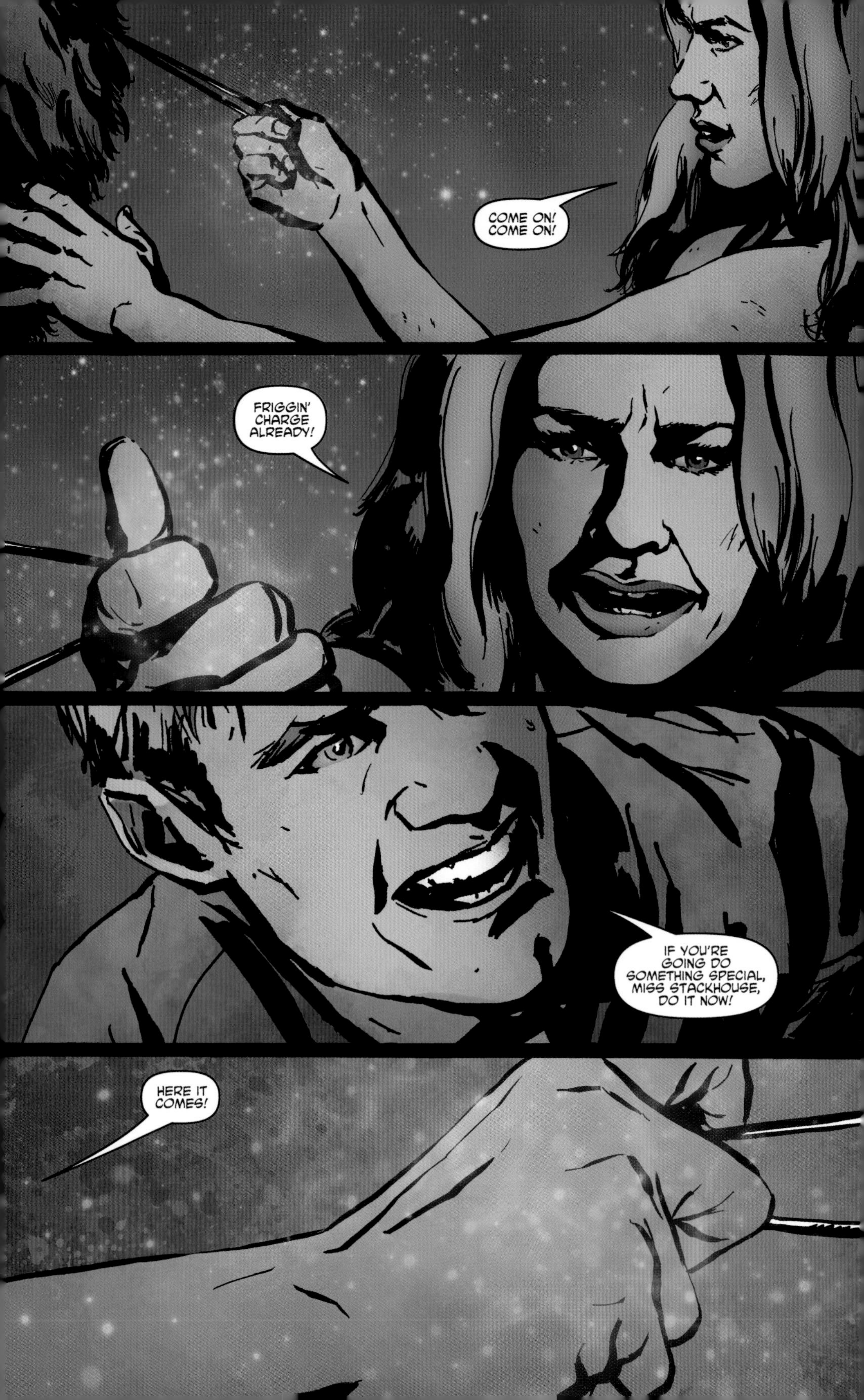
COME ON! COME ON!
FRIGGIN' CHARGE ALREADY!
IF YOU'RE GOING DO SOMETHING SPECIAL, MISS STACKHOUSE, DO IT NOW!
HERE IT COMES!

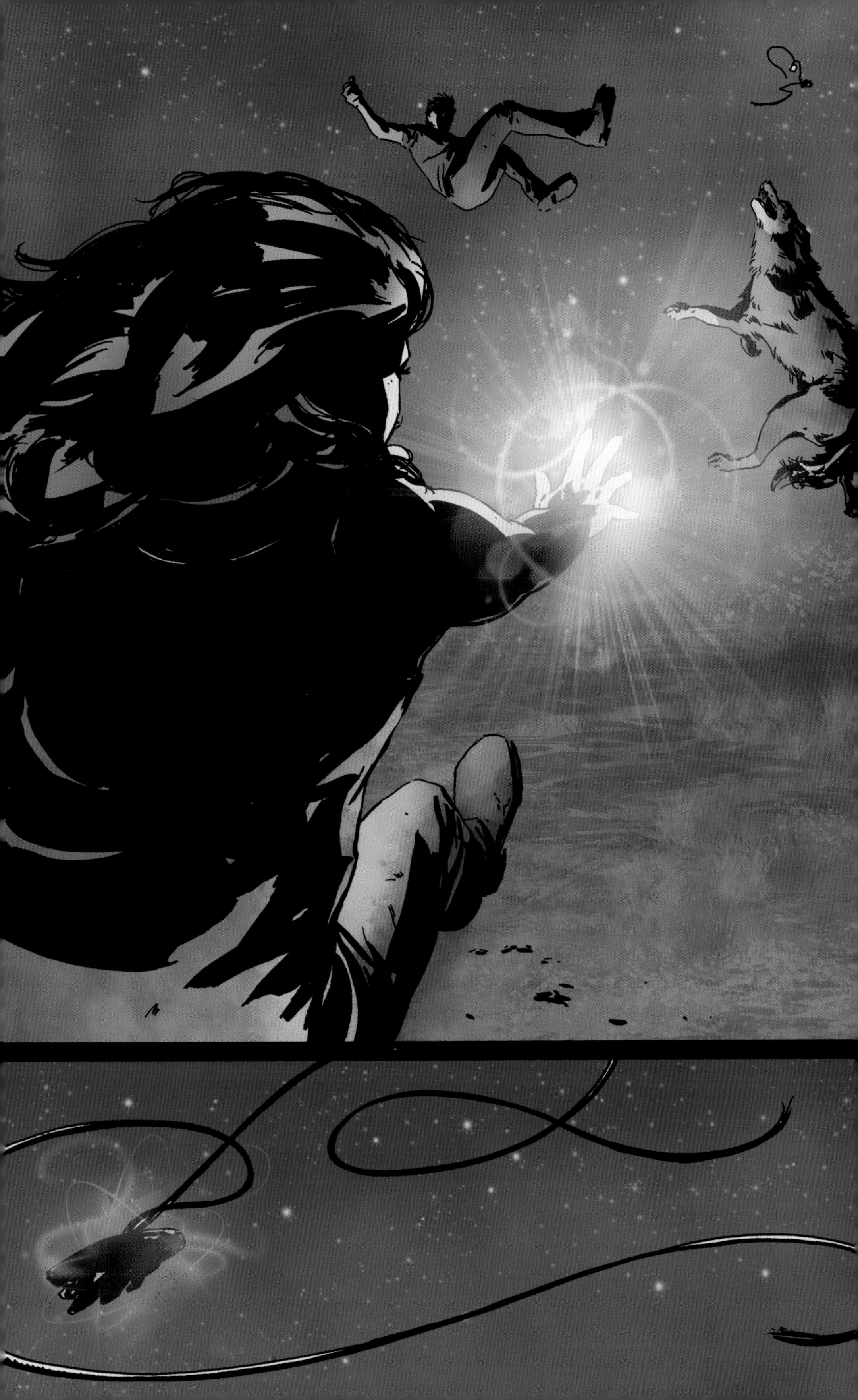

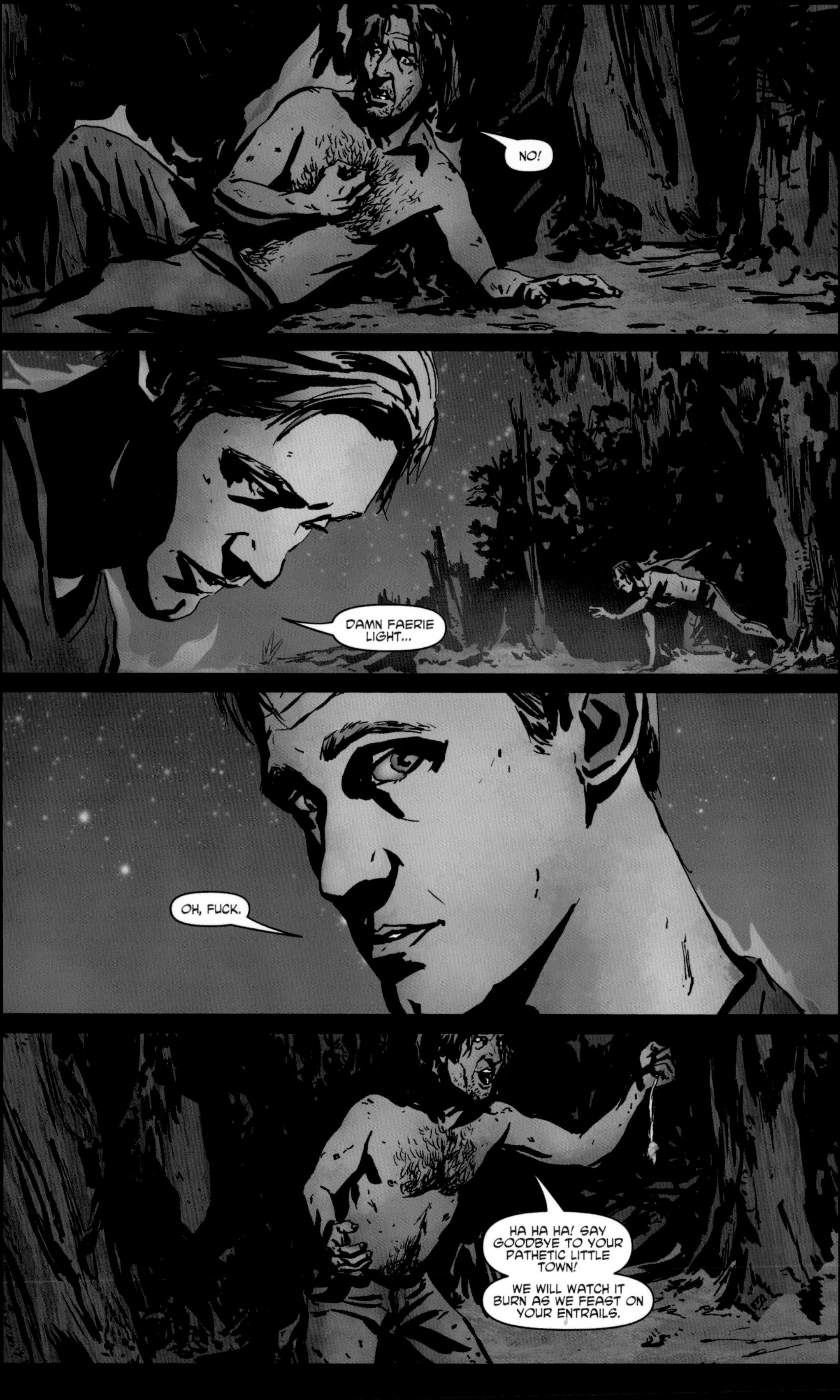
NO!
DAMN FAERIE LIGHT...
OH, FUCK.
HA HA HA! SAY GOODBYE TO YOUR PATHETIC LITTLE TOWN!
WE WILL WATCH IT BURN AS WE FEAST ON YOUR ENTRAILS.

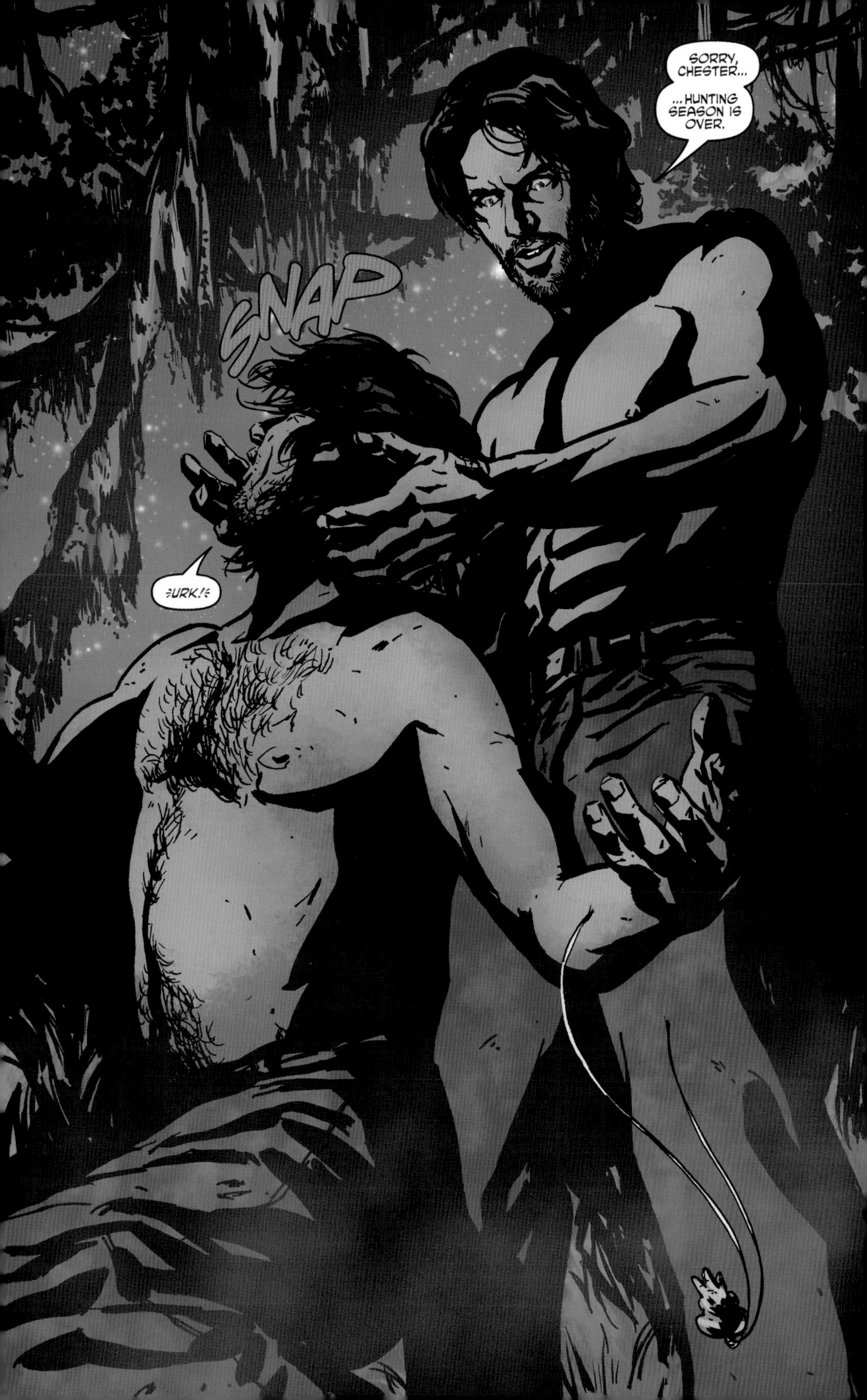
SORRY, CHESTER...
...HUNTING SEASON IS OVER.
SNAP
URK!

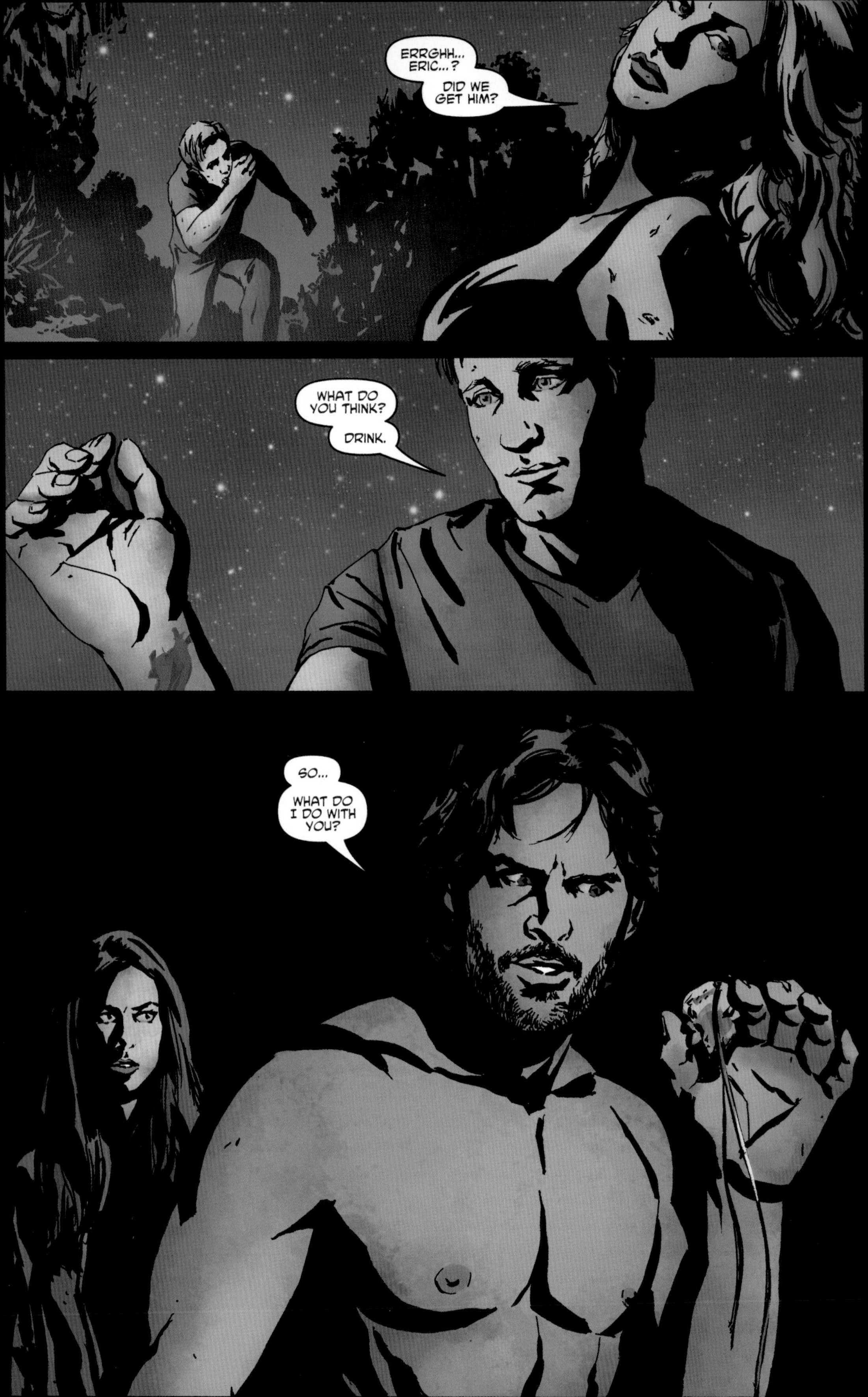
ERRGHH... ERIC...?
DID WE GET HIM?
WHAT DO YOU THINK?
DRINK.
SO...
WHAT DO I DO WITH YOU?

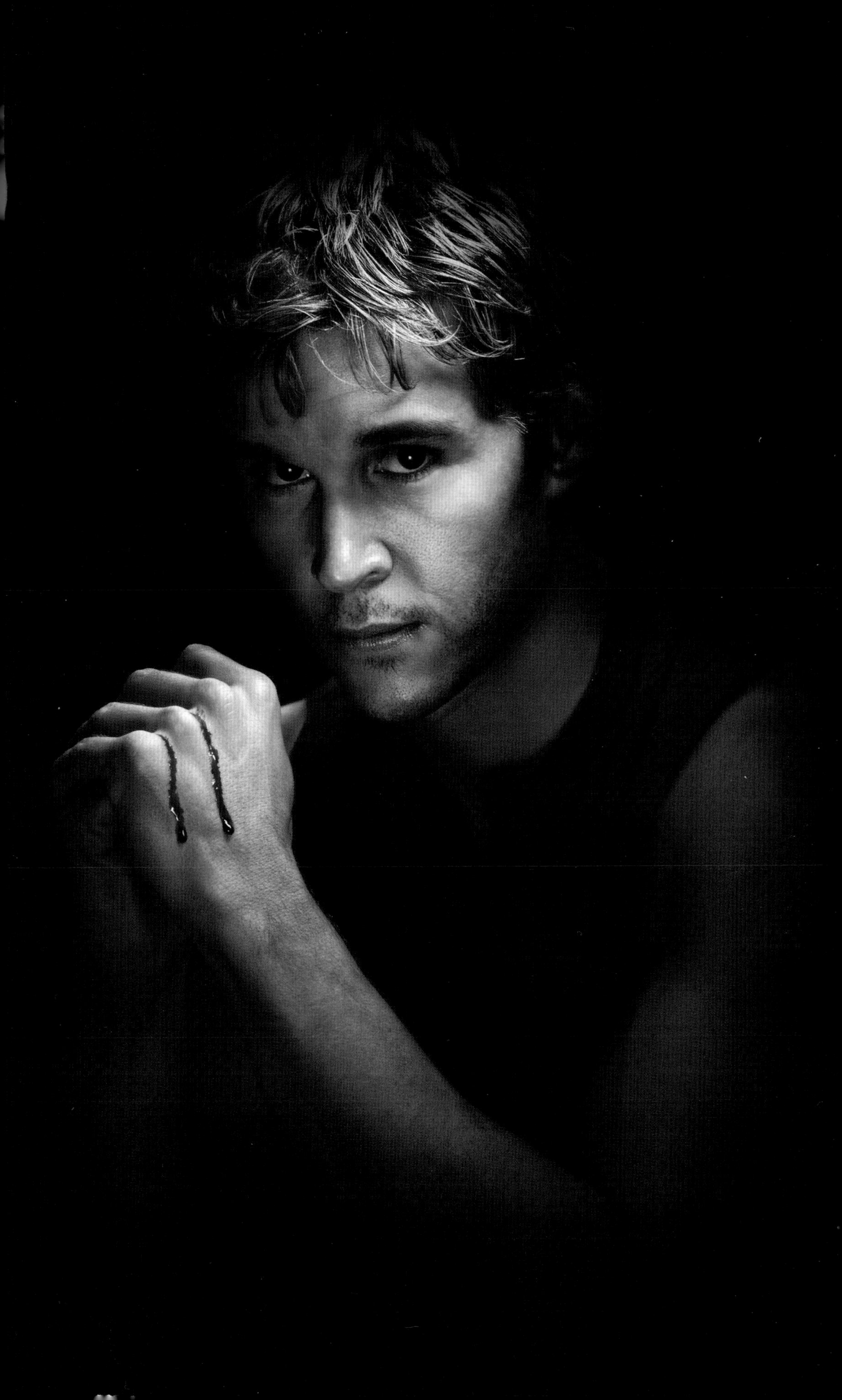

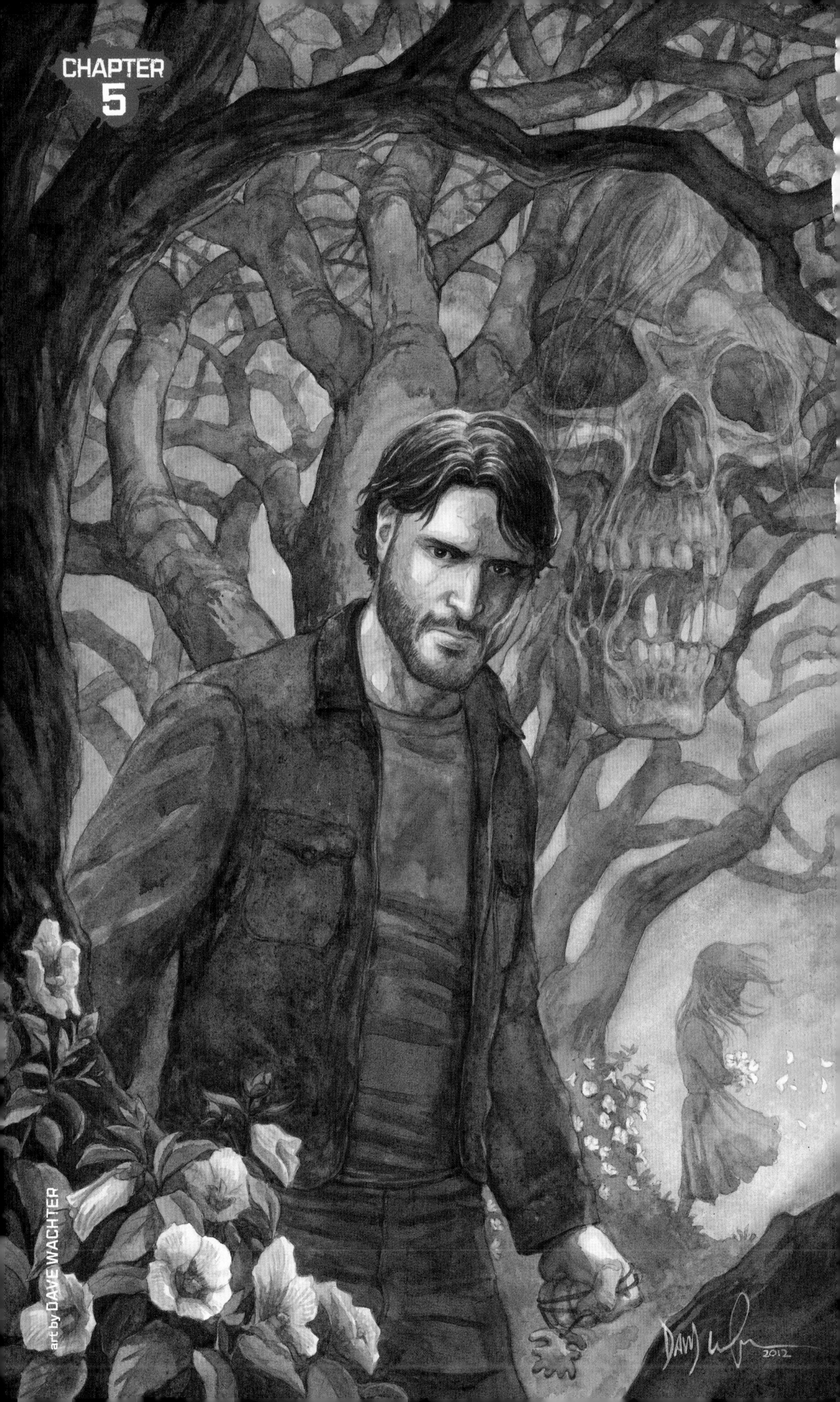

CHAPTER
5
art by DAVE WACHTER
2012

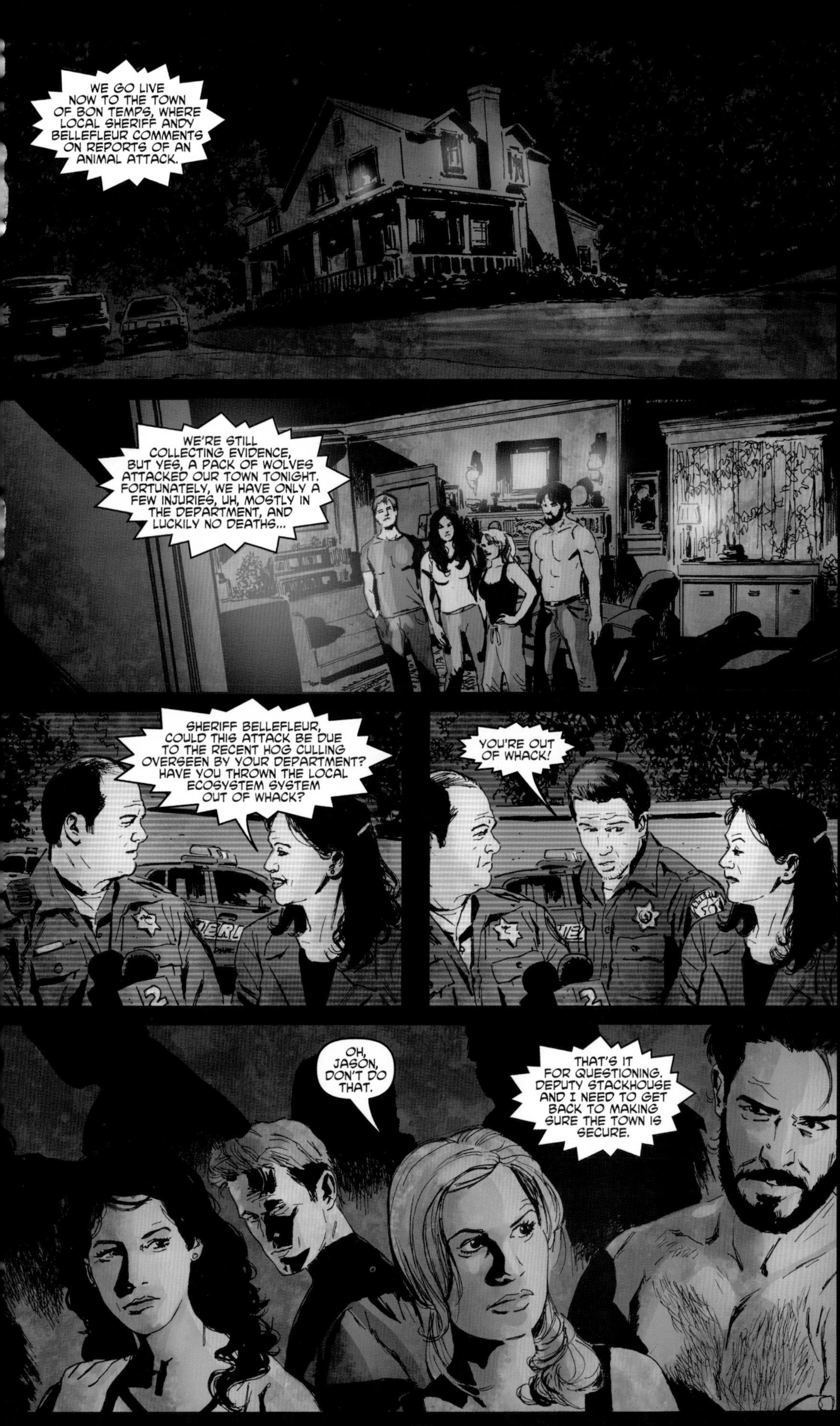
WE GO LIVE NOW TO THE TOWN OF BON TEMPS, WHERE LOCAL SHERIFF ANDY BELLEFLEUR COMMENTS ON REPORTS OF AN ANIMAL ATTACK.
WE'RE STILL COLLECTING EVIDENCE, BUT YES, A PACK OF WOLVES ATTACKED OUR TOWN TONIGHT. FORTUNATELY, WE HAVE ONLY A FEW INJURIES, UH, MOSTLY IN THE DEPARTMENT, AND LUCKILY NO DEATHS...
SHERIFF BELLEFLEUR, COULD THIS ATTACK BE DUE TO THE RECENT HOG CULLING OVERSEEN BY YOUR DEPARTMENT? HAVE YOU THROWN THE LOCAL ECOSYSTEM SYSTEM OUT OF WHACK?
YOU'RE OUT OF WHACK!
OH, JASON, DON'T DO THAT.
THAT'S IT FOR QUESTIONING. DEPUTY STACKHOUSE AND I NEED TO GET BACK TO MAKING SURE THE TOWN IS SECURE.

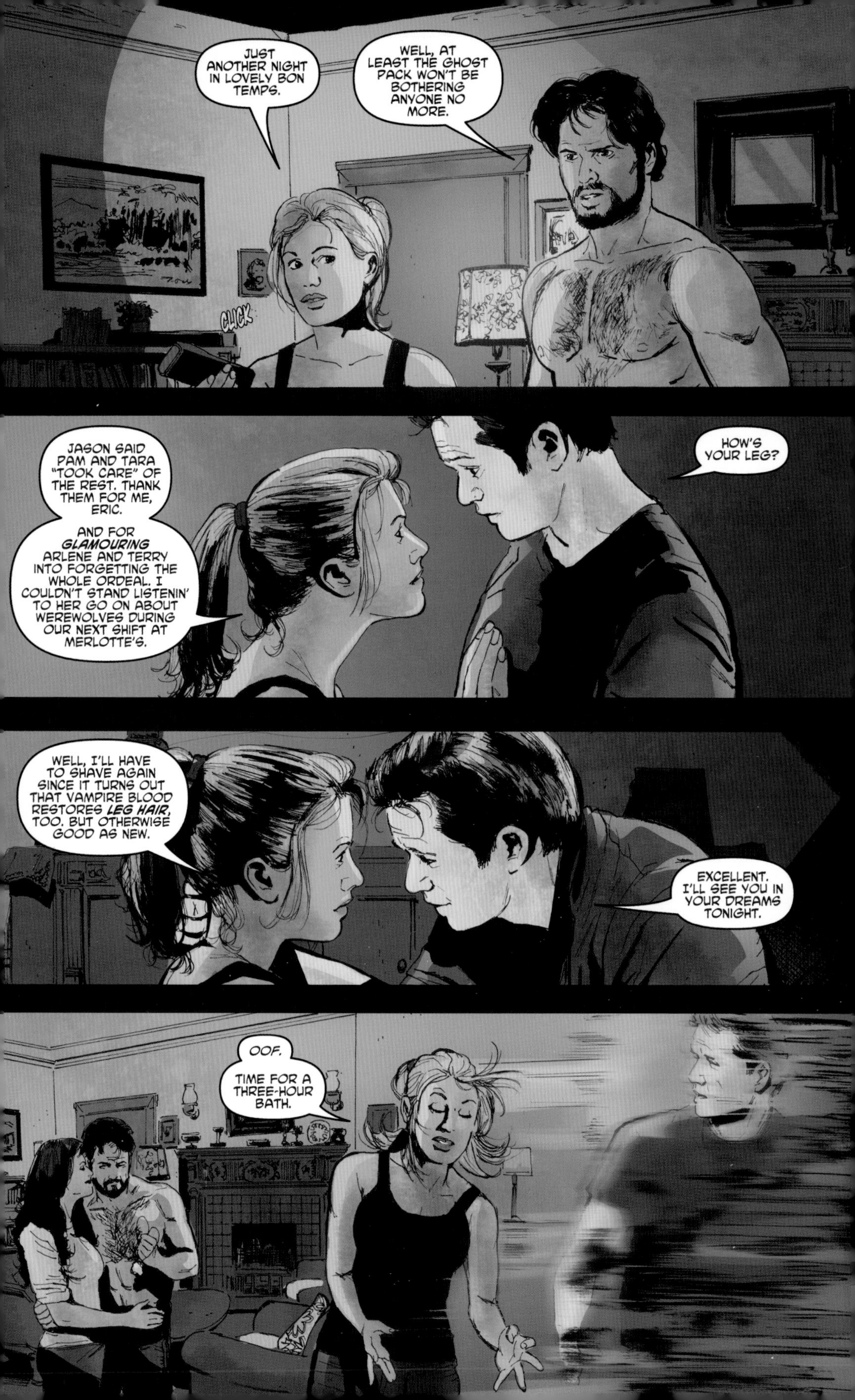
JUST ANOTHER NIGHT IN LOVELY BON TEMPS.
WELL, AT LEAST THE GHOST PACK WON'T BE BOTHERING ANYONE NO MORE.
CLICK
JASON SAID PAM AND TARA "TOOK CARE" OF THE REST. THANK THEM FOR ME, ERIC.
AND FOR GLAMOURING ARLENE AND TERRY INTO FORGETTING THE WHOLE ORDEAL. I COULDN'T STAND LISTENIN' TO HER GO ON ABOUT WEREWOLVES DURING OUR NEXT SHIFT AT MERLOTTE'S.
HOW'S YOUR LEG?
WELL, I'LL HAVE TO SHAVE AGAIN SINCE IT TURNS OUT THAT VAMPIRE BLOOD RESTORES LEG HAIR, TOO. BUT OTHERWISE GOOD AS NEW.
EXCELLENT. I'LL SEE YOU IN YOUR DREAMS TONIGHT.
OOF.
TIME FOR A THREE-HOUR BATH.

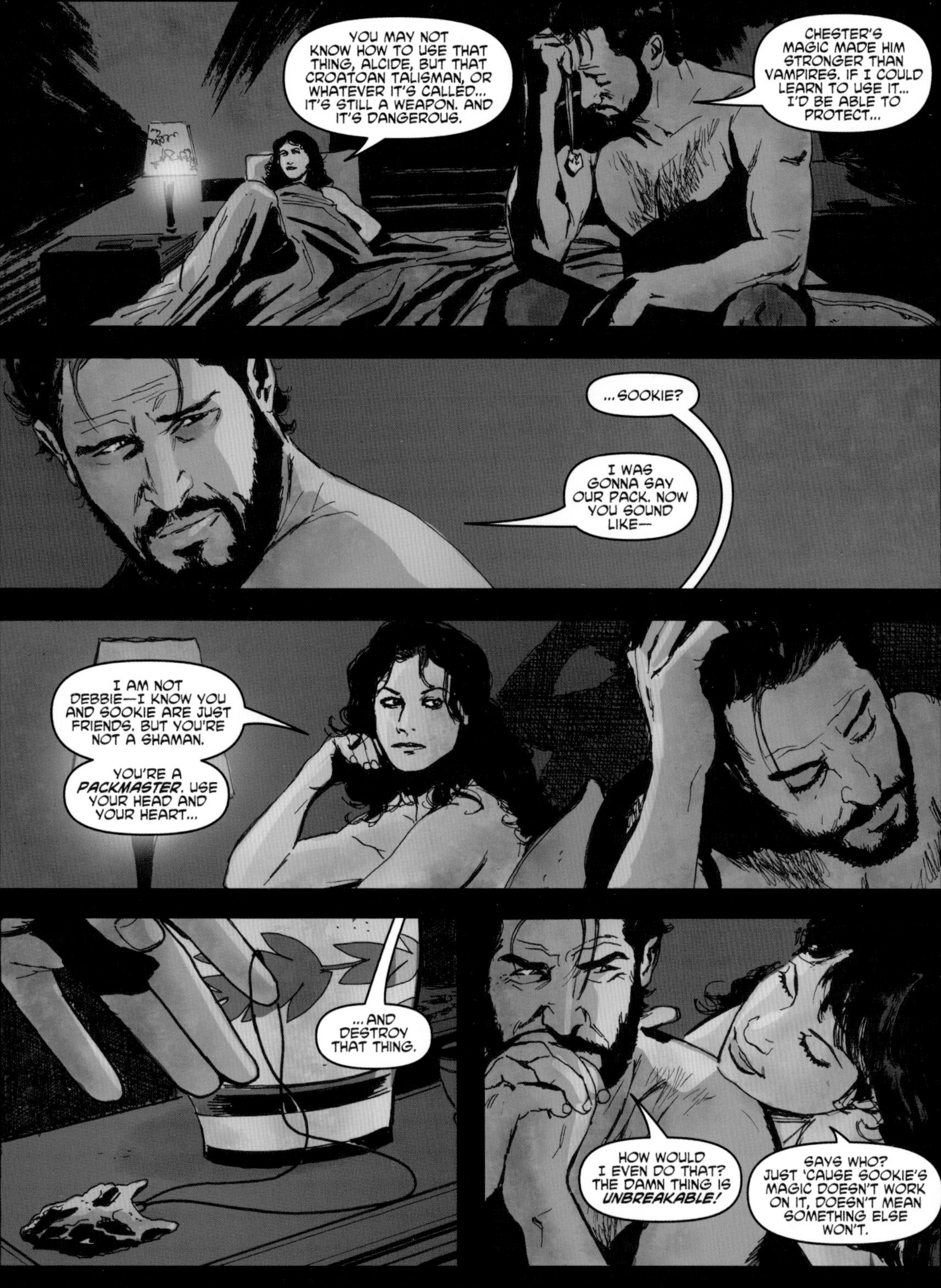
YOU MAY NOT KNOW HOW TO USE THAT THING, ALCIDE, BUT THAT CROATOAN TALISMAN, OR WHATEVER IT'S CALLED... IT'S STILL A WEAPON. AND IT'S DANGEROUS.
CHESTER'S MAGIC MADE HIM STRONGER THAN VAMPIRES. IF I COULD LEARN TO USE IT... I'D BE ABLE TO PROTECT...
...SOOKIE?
I WAS GONNA SAY OUR PACK. NOW YOU SOUND LIKE—
I AM NOT DEBBIE—I KNOW YOU AND SOOKIE ARE JUST FRIENDS. BUT YOU'RE NOT A SHAMAN.
YOU'RE A PACKMASTER. USE YOUR HEAD AND YOUR HEART...
...AND DESTROY THAT THING.
HOW WOULD I EVEN DO THAT? THE DAMN THING IS UNBREAKABLE!
SAYS WHO? JUST 'CAUSE SOOKIE'S MAGIC DOESN'T WORK ON IT, DOESN'T MEAN SOMETHING ELSE WON'T.

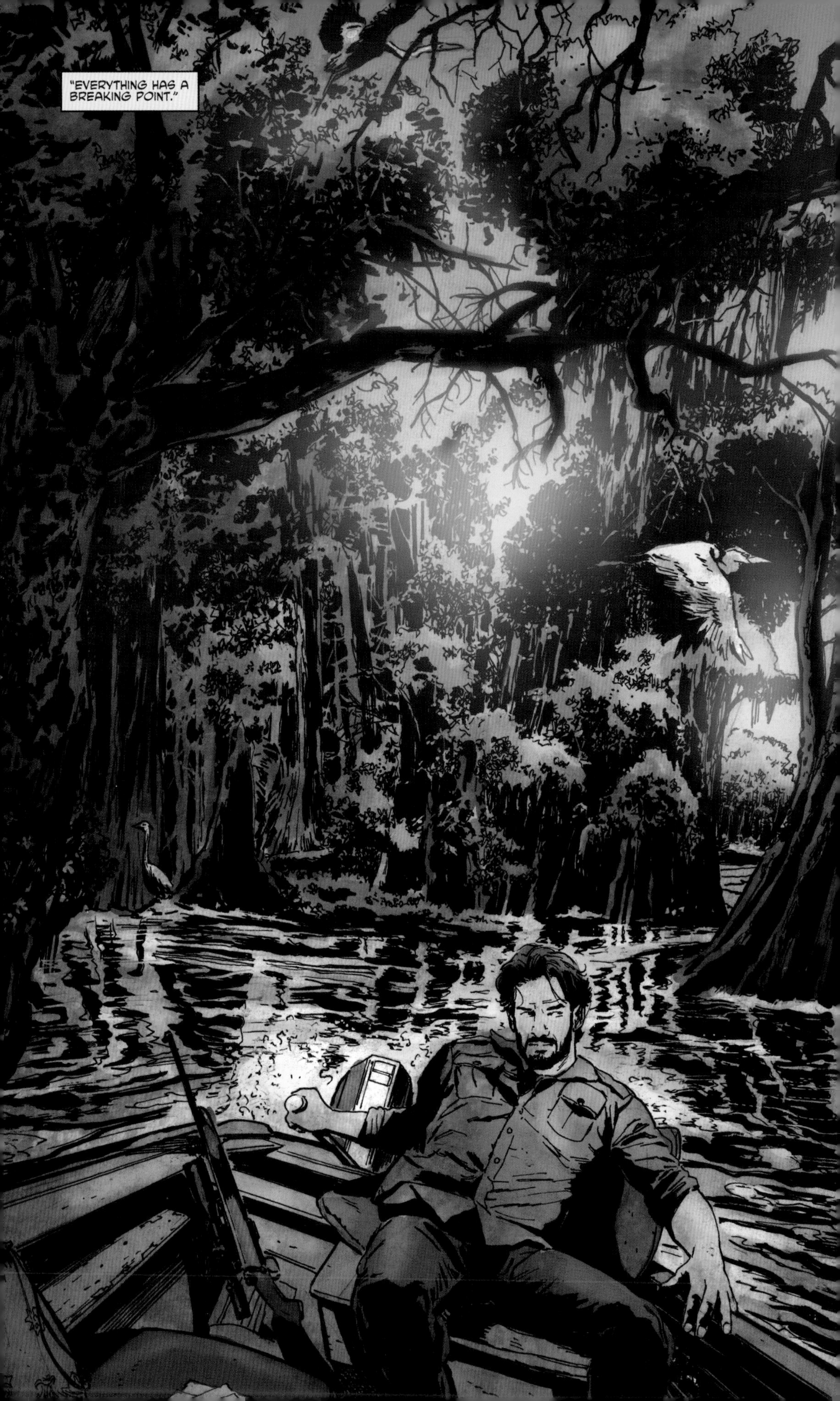
"EVERYTHING HAS A BREAKING POINT."

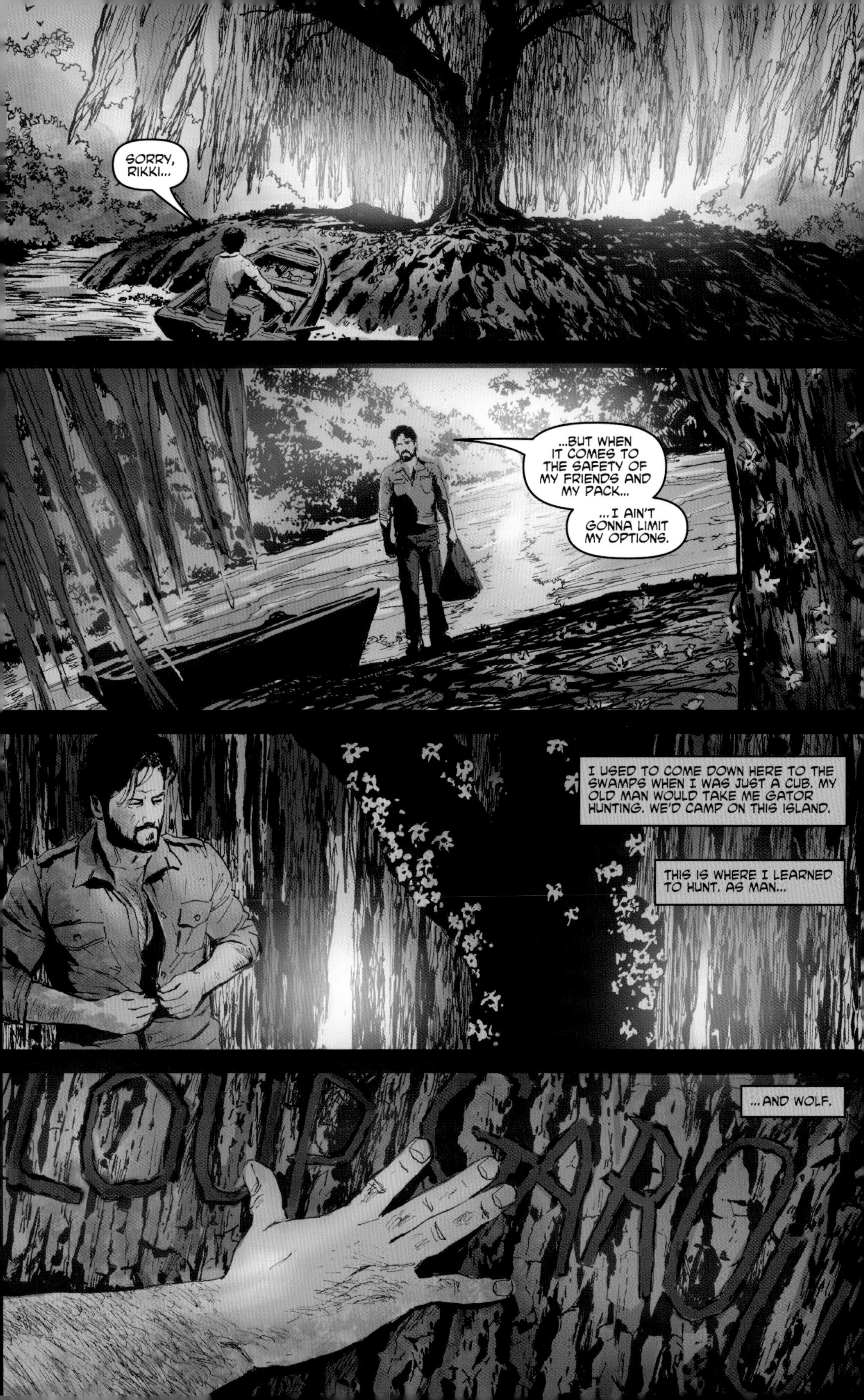
SORRY, RIKKI...
...BUT WHEN IT COMES TO THE SAFETY OF MY FRIENDS AND MY PACK...
...I AIN'T GONNA LIMIT MY OPTIONS.
I USED TO COME DOWN HERE TO THE SWAMPS WHEN I WAS JUST A CUB. MY OLD MAN WOULD TAKE ME GATOR HUNTING. WE'D CAMP ON THIS ISLAND.
THIS IS WHERE I LEARNED TO HUNT. AS MAN...
...AND WOLF.

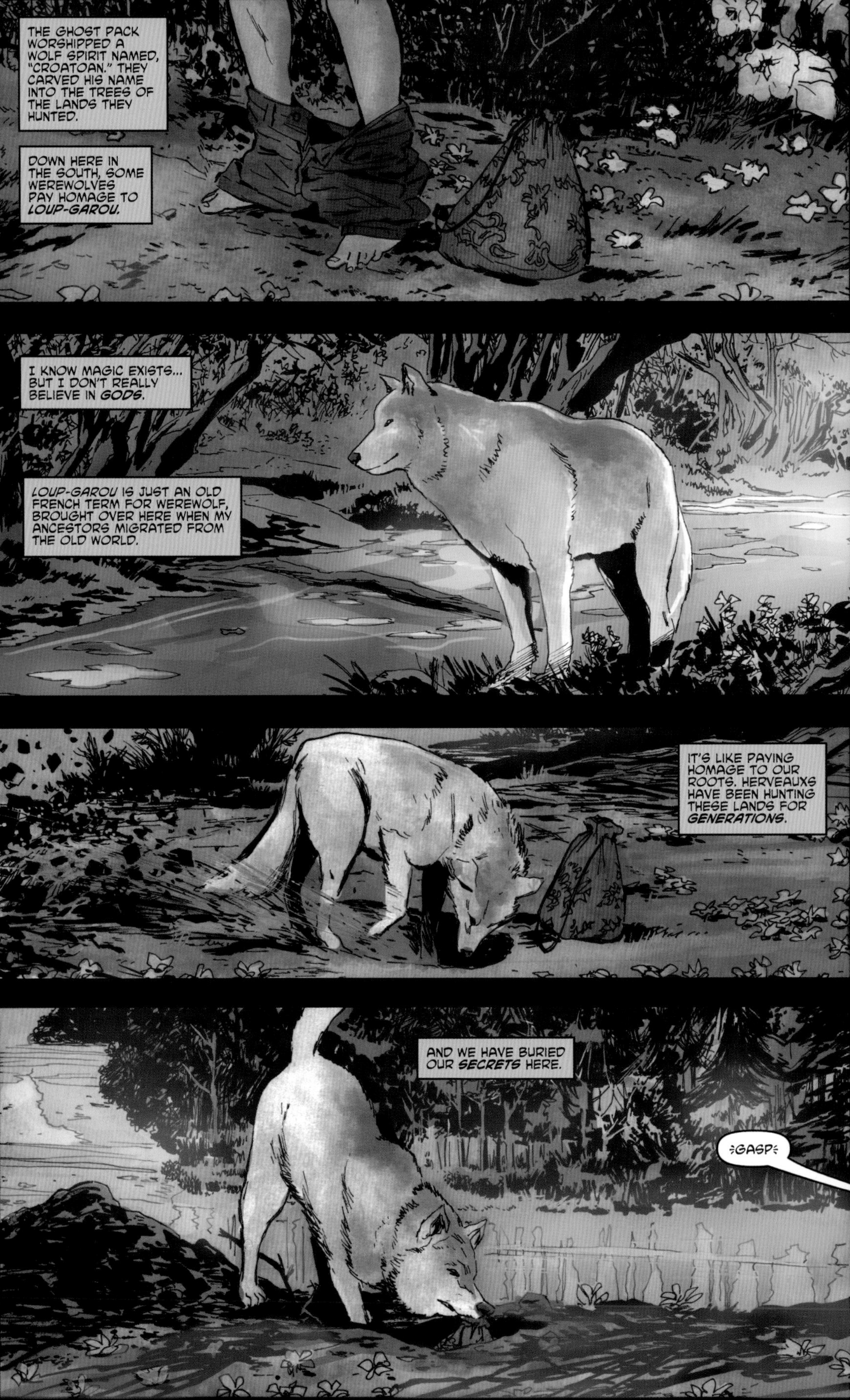

THE GHOST PACK WORSHIPPED A WOLF SPIRIT NAMED, "CROATOAN." THEY CARVED HIS NAME INTO THE TREES OF THE LANDS THEY HUNTED.
DOWN HERE IN THE SOUTH, SOME WEREWOLVES PAY HOMAGE TO *LOUP-GAROU.*
I KNOW MAGIC EXISTS... BUT I DON'T REALLY BELIEVE IN *GODS*.
LOUP-GAROU IS JUST AN OLD FRENCH TERM FOR WEREWOLF, BROUGHT OVER HERE WHEN MY ANCESTORS MIGRATED FROM THE OLD WORLD.
IT'S LIKE PAYING HOMAGE TO OUR ROOTS. HERVEAUXS HAVE BEEN HUNTING THESE LANDS FOR *GENERATIONS*.
AND WE HAVE BURIED OUR *SECRETS* HERE.
GASP

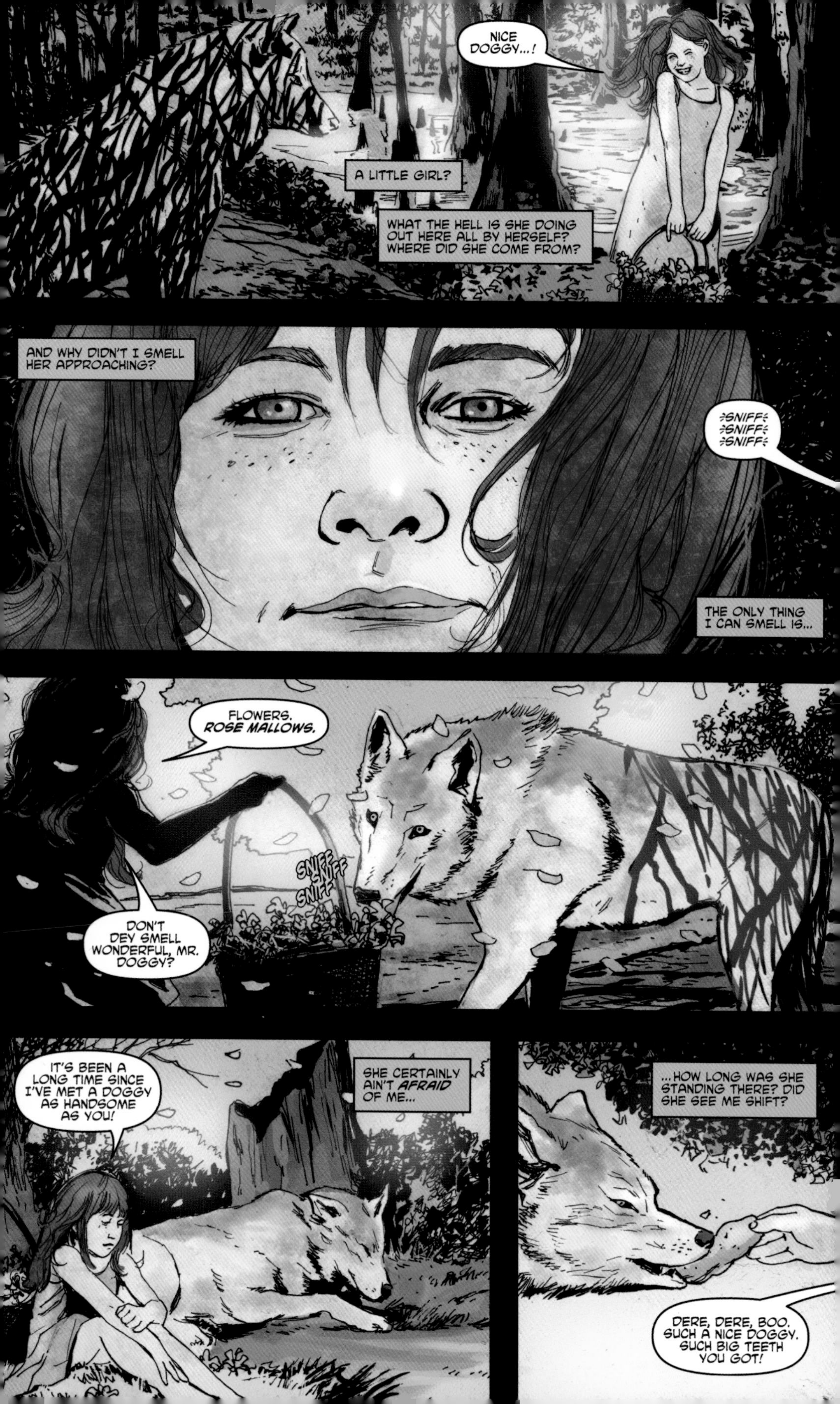
NICE DOGGY...!
A LITTLE GIRL?
WHAT THE HELL IS SHE DOING OUT HERE ALL BY HERSELF? WHERE DID SHE COME FROM?
AND WHY DIDN'T I SMELL HER APPROACHING?
SNIFF SNIFF SNIFF
THE ONLY THING I CAN SMELL IS...
FLOWERS. ROSE MALLOWS.
SNIFF SNIFF SNIFF
DON'T DEY SMELL WONDERFUL, MR. DOGGY?
IT'S BEEN A LONG TIME SINCE I'VE MET A DOGGY AS HANDSOME AS YOU!
SHE CERTAINLY AIN'T AFRAID OF ME...
...HOW LONG WAS SHE STANDING THERE? DID SHE SEE ME SHIFT?
DERE, DERE, BOO. SUCH A NICE DOGGY. SUCH BIG TEETH YOU GOT!

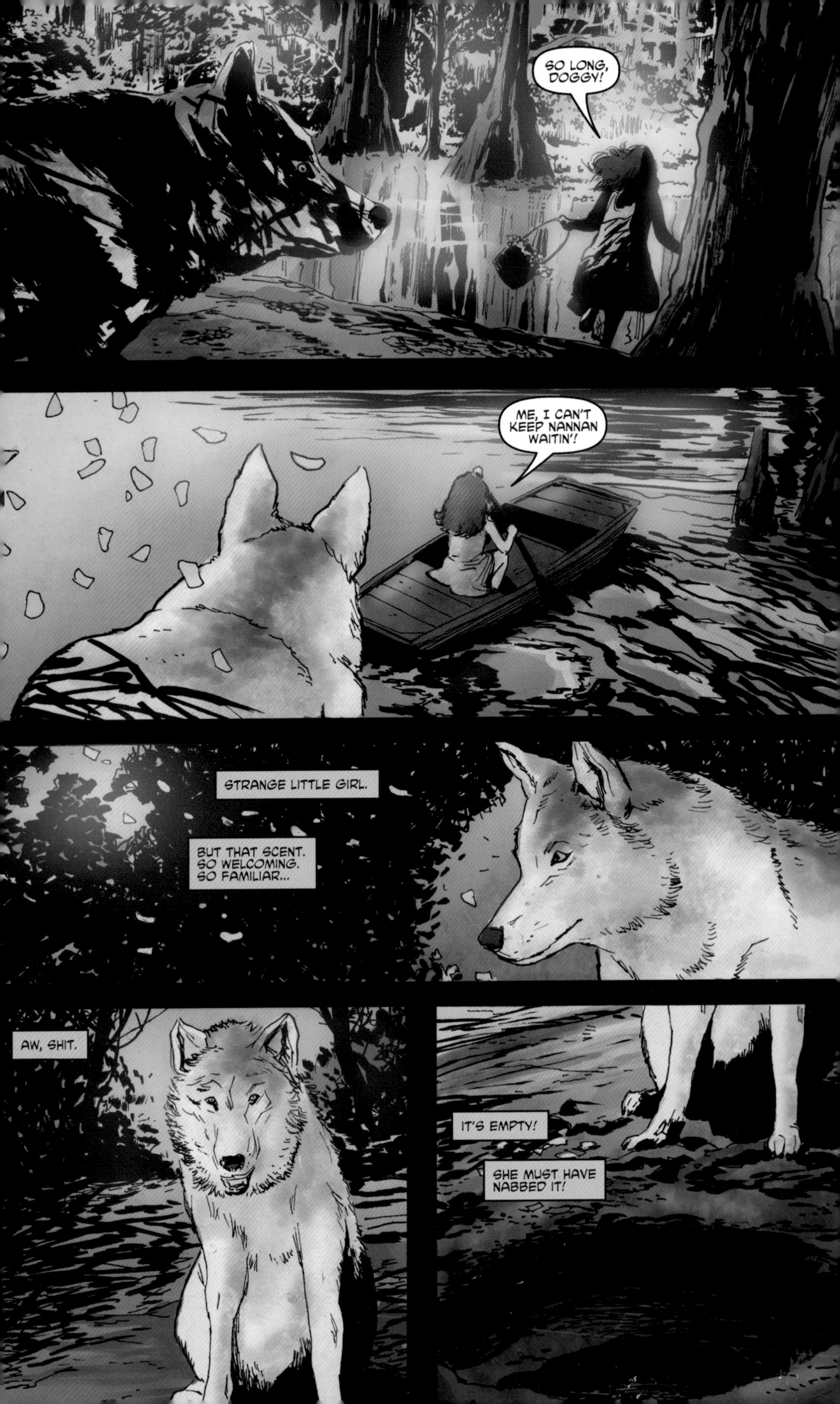
SO LONG, DOGGY!
ME, I CAN'T KEEP NANNAN WAITIN'!
STRANGE LITTLE GIRL.
BUT THAT SCENT. SO WELCOMING. SO FAMILIAR...
AW, SHIT.
IT'S EMPTY!
SHE MUST HAVE NABBED IT!

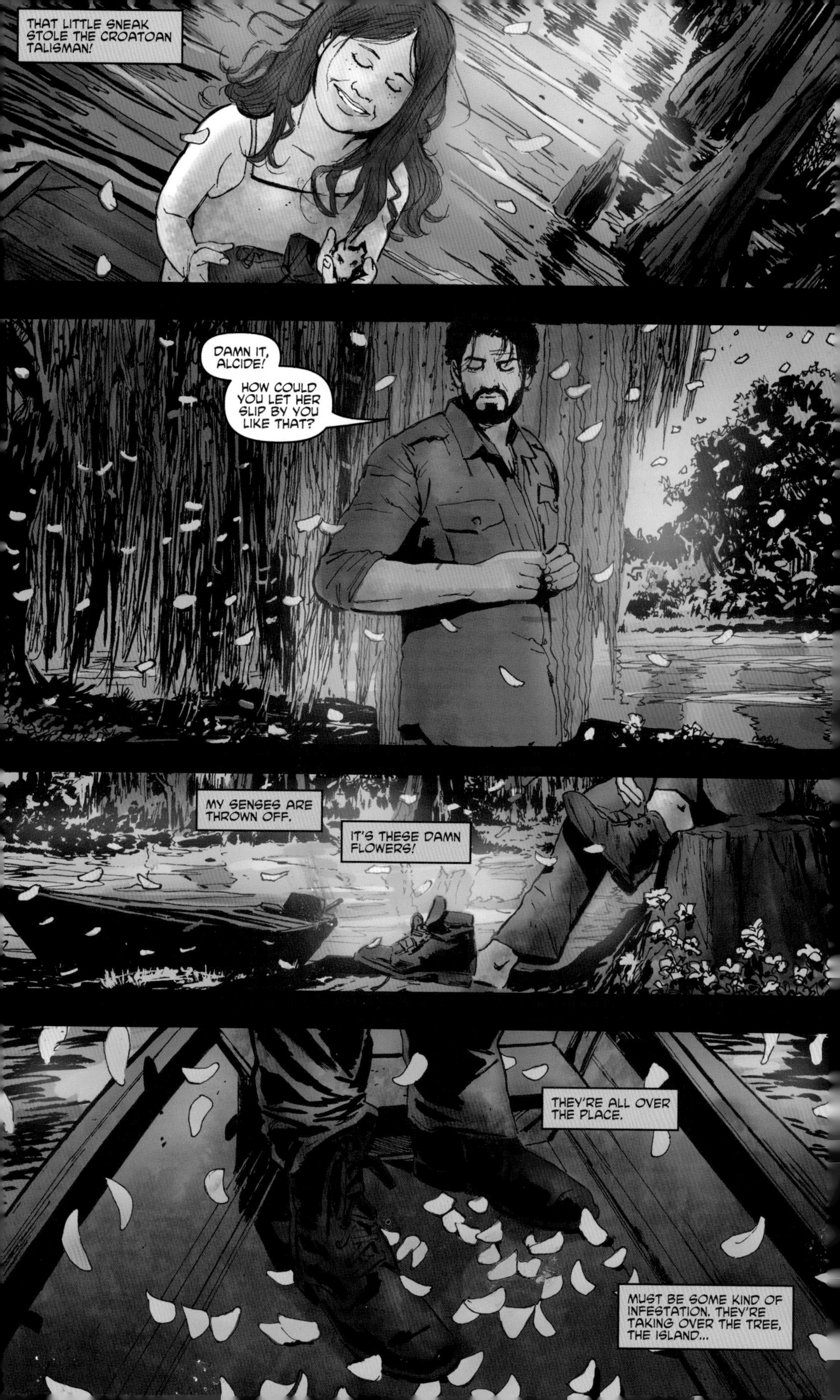
THAT LITTLE SNEAK STOLE THE CROATOAN TALISMAN!
DAMN IT, ALCIDE!
HOW COULD YOU LET HER SLIP BY YOU LIKE THAT?
MY SENSES ARE THROWN OFF.
IT'S THESE DAMN FLOWERS!
THEY'RE ALL OVER THE PLACE.
MUST BE SOME KIND OF INFESTATION. THEY'RE TAKING OVER THE TREE, THE ISLAND...

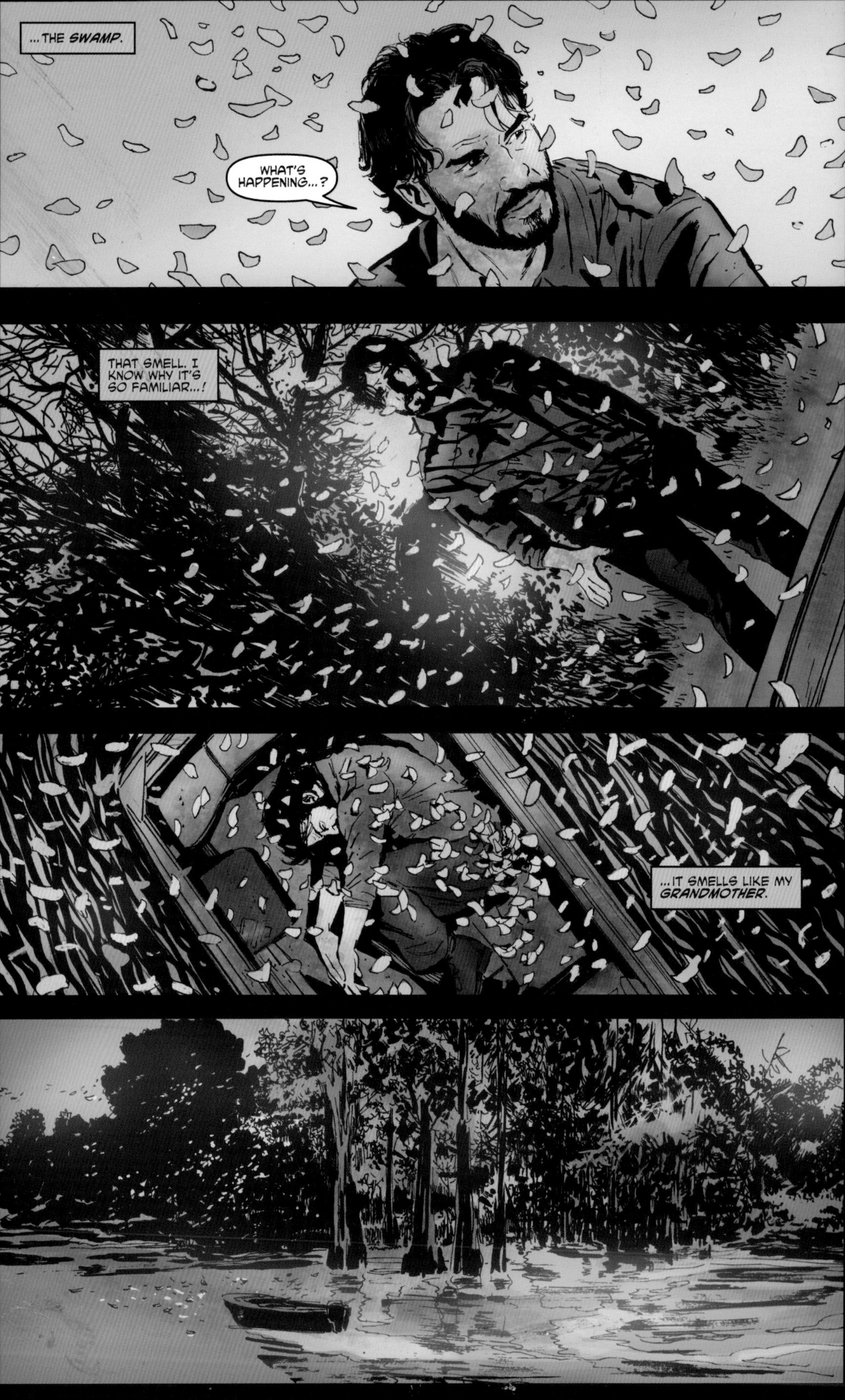
...THE SWAMP.
WHAT'S HAPPENING...?
THAT SMELL. I KNOW WHY IT'S SO FAMILIAR...!
...IT SMELLS LIKE MY GRANDMOTHER.

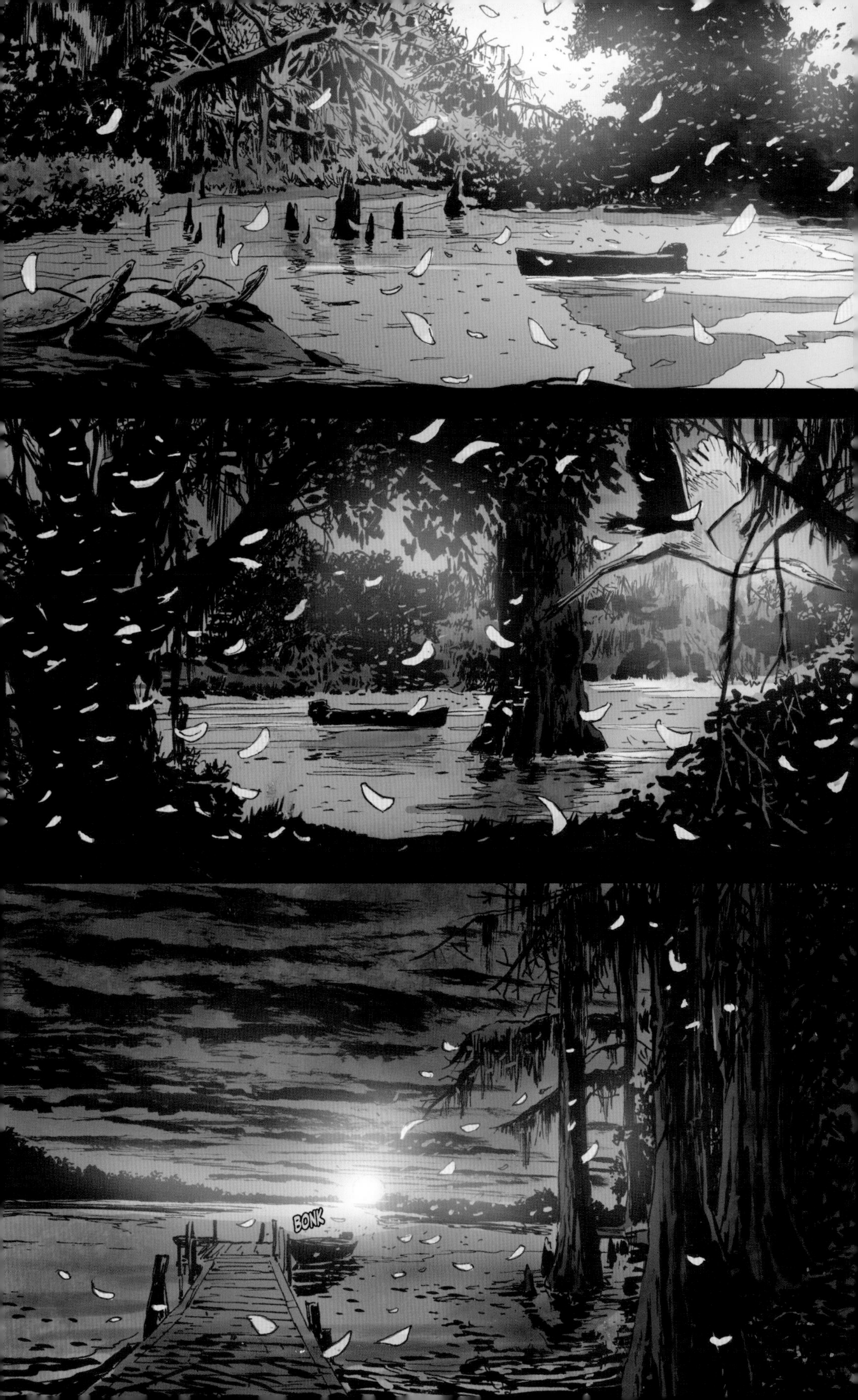
BONK

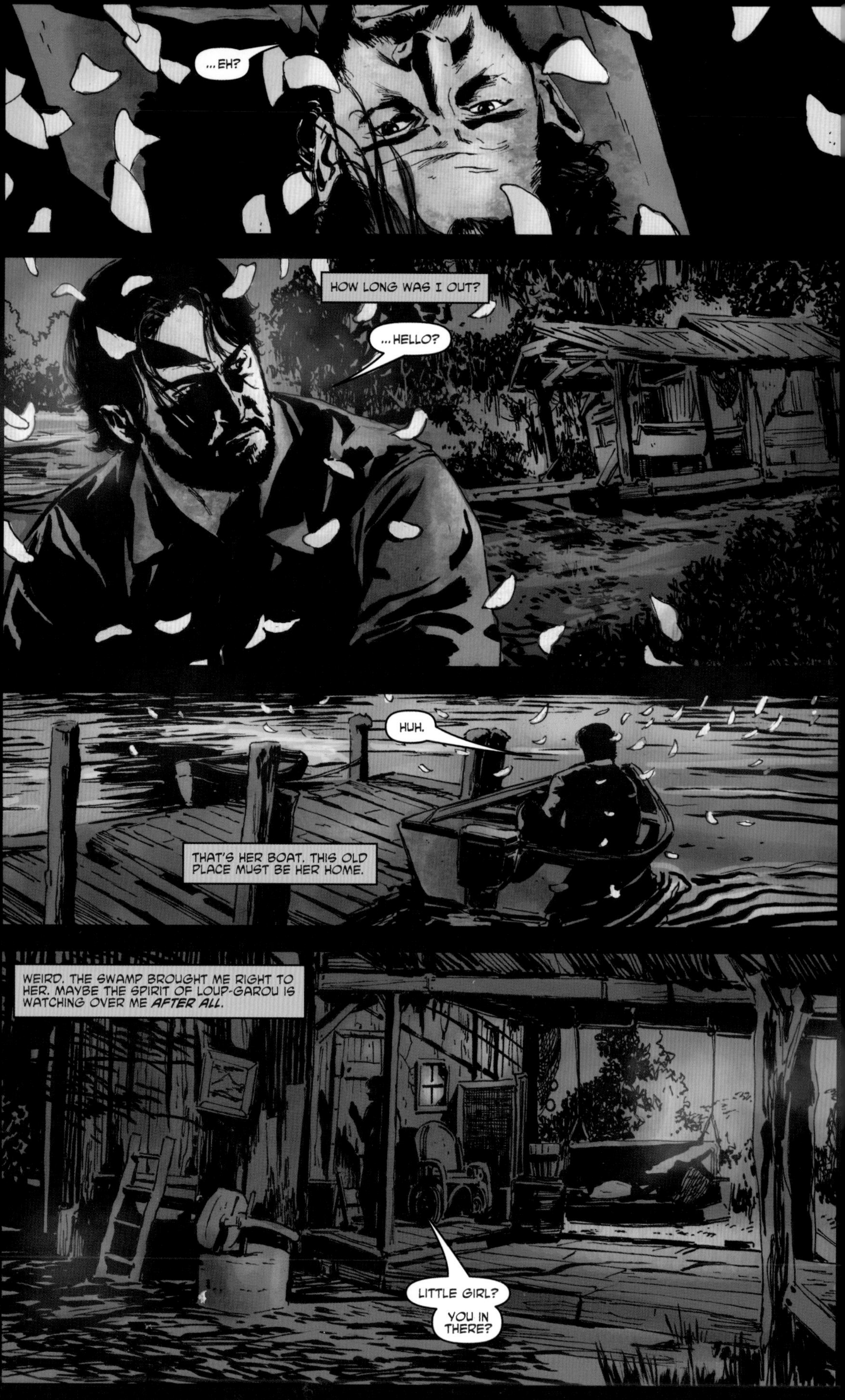
...EH?
HOW LONG WAS I OUT?
...HELLO?
HUH.
THAT'S HER BOAT. THIS OLD PLACE MUST BE HER HOME.
WEIRD. THE SWAMP BROUGHT ME RIGHT TO HER. MAYBE THE SPIRIT OF LOUP-GAROU IS WATCHING OVER ME *AFTER ALL*.
LITTLE GIRL?
YOU IN THERE?

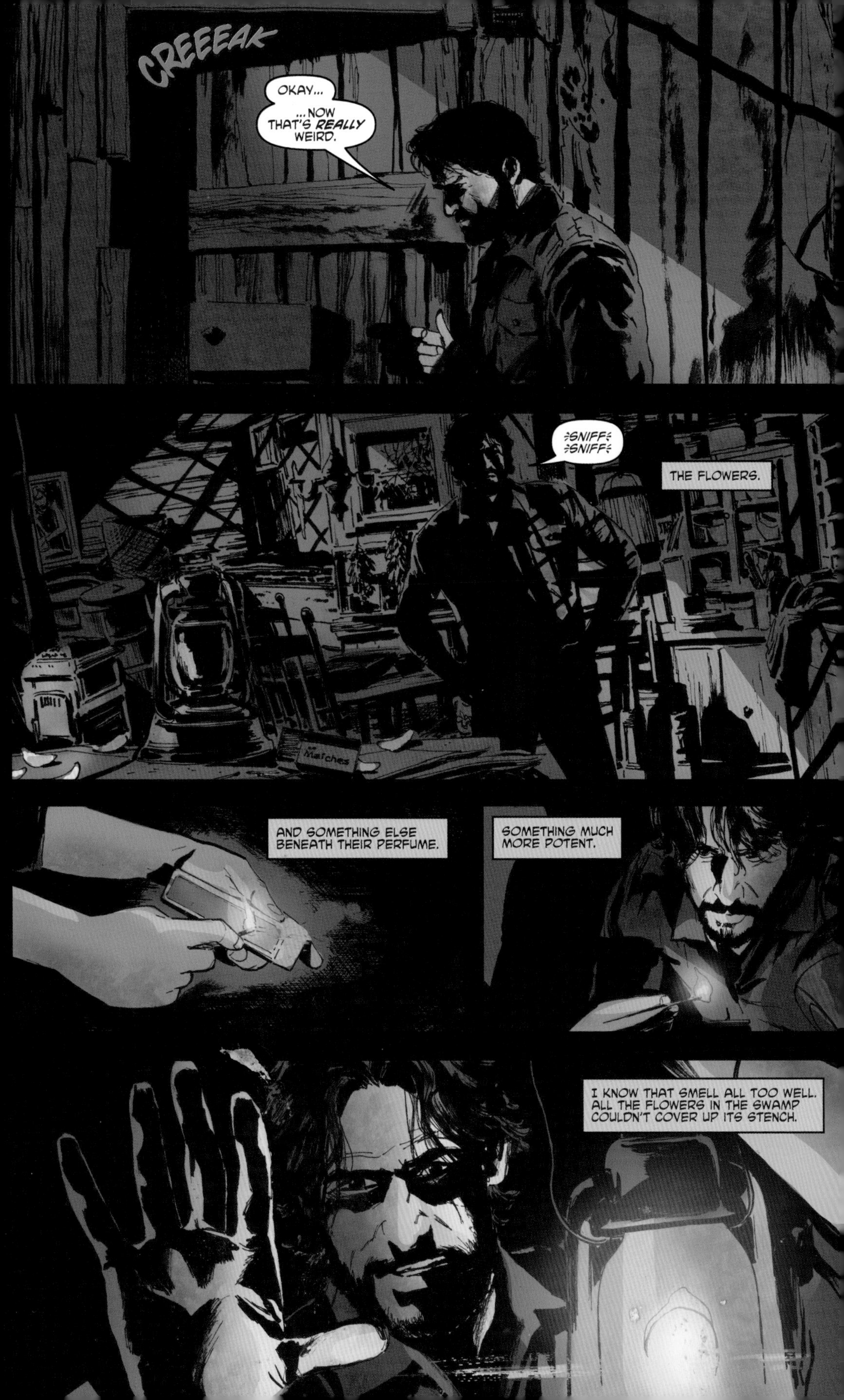
CREEEAK
OKAY...
...NOW THAT'S *REALLY* WEIRD.
SNIFF SNIFF
THE FLOWERS.
Matches
AND SOMETHING ELSE BENEATH THEIR PERFUME.
SOMETHING MUCH MORE POTENT.
I KNOW THAT SMELL ALL TOO WELL. ALL THE FLOWERS IN THE SWAMP COULDN'T COVER UP ITS STENCH.

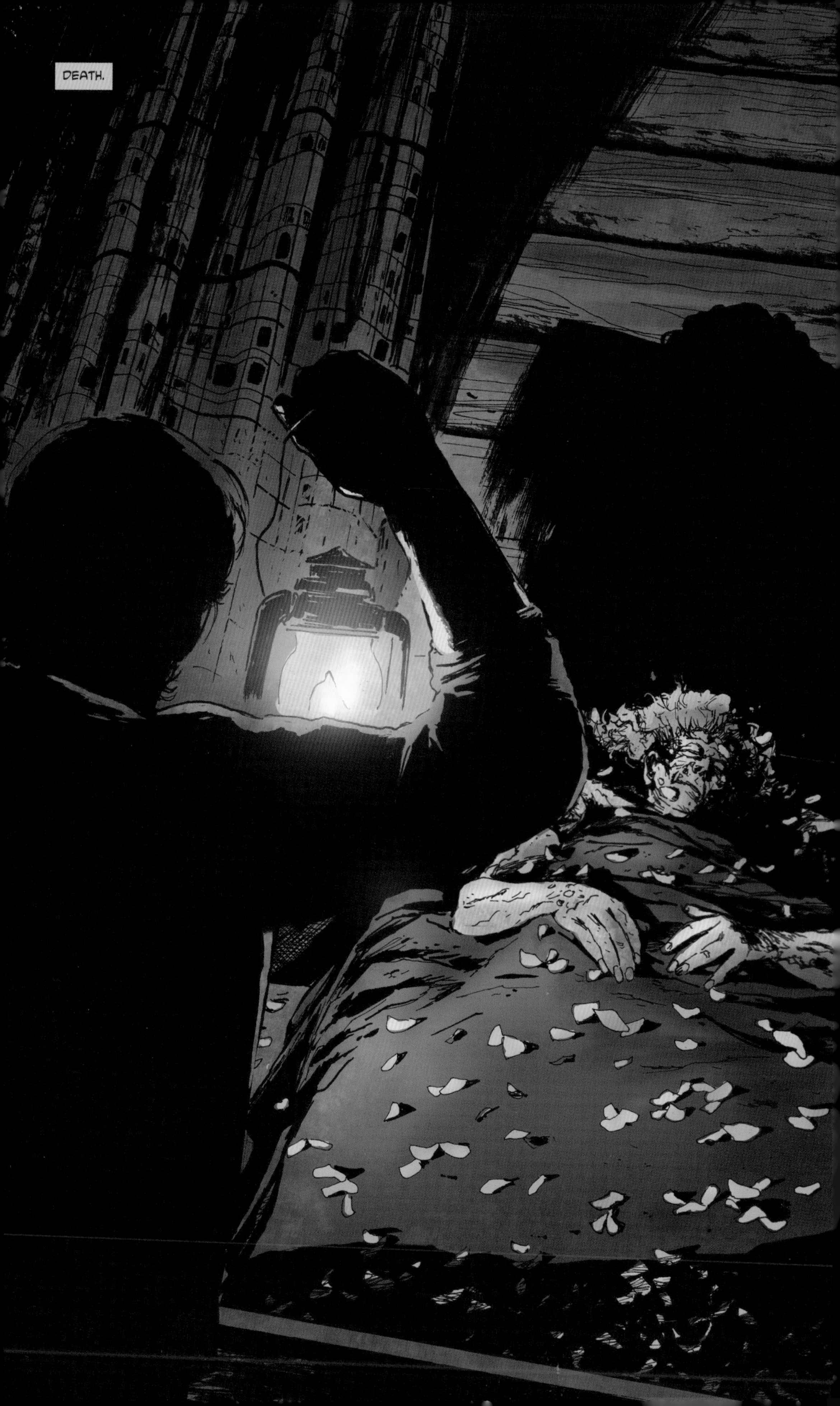
DEATH.

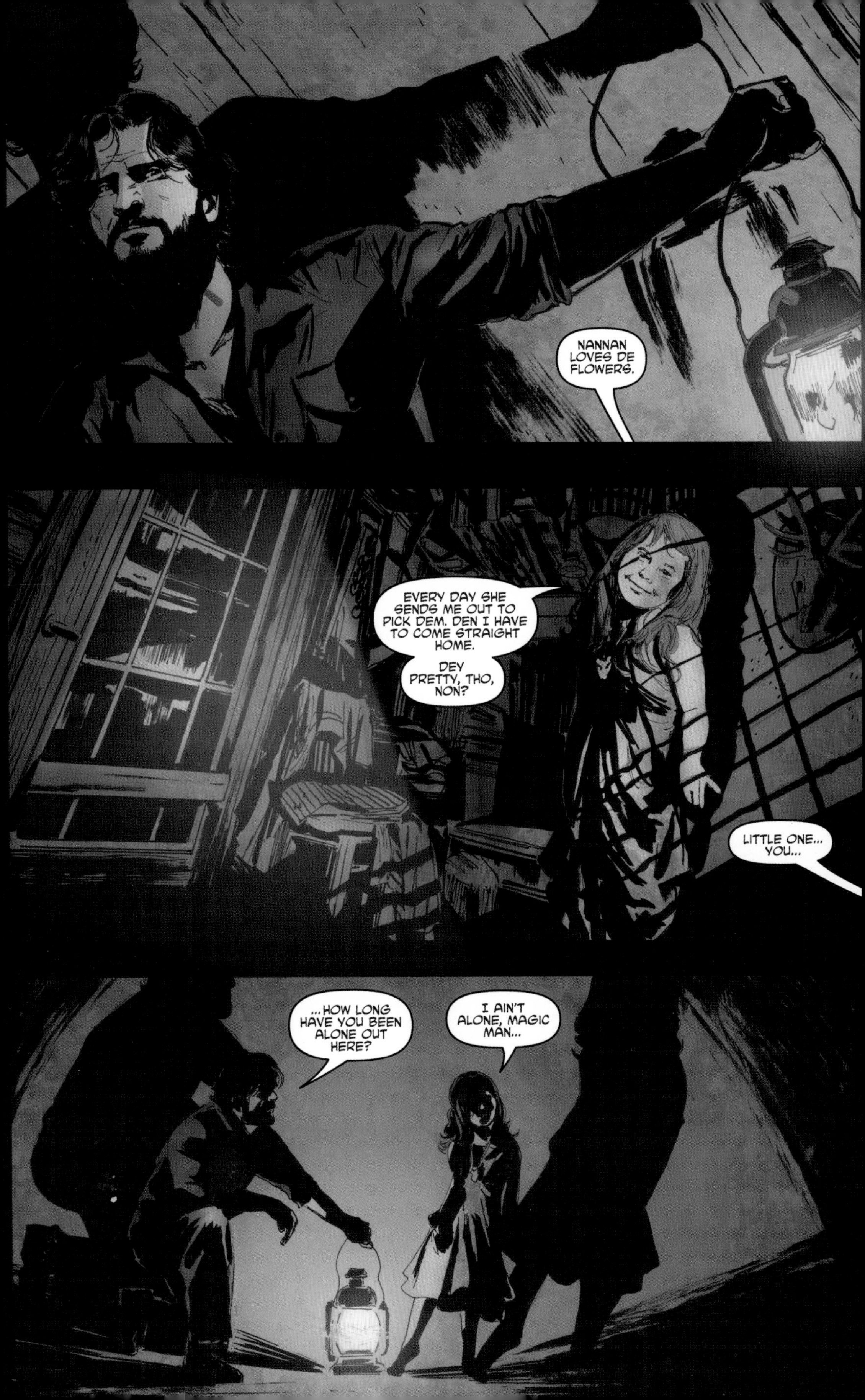
NANNAN LOVES DE FLOWERS.
EVERY DAY SHE SENDS ME OUT TO PICK DEM. DEN I HAVE TO COME STRAIGHT HOME.
DEY PRETTY, THO, NON?
LITTLE ONE... YOU...
...HOW LONG HAVE YOU BEEN ALONE OUT HERE?
I AIN'T ALONE, MAGIC MAN...

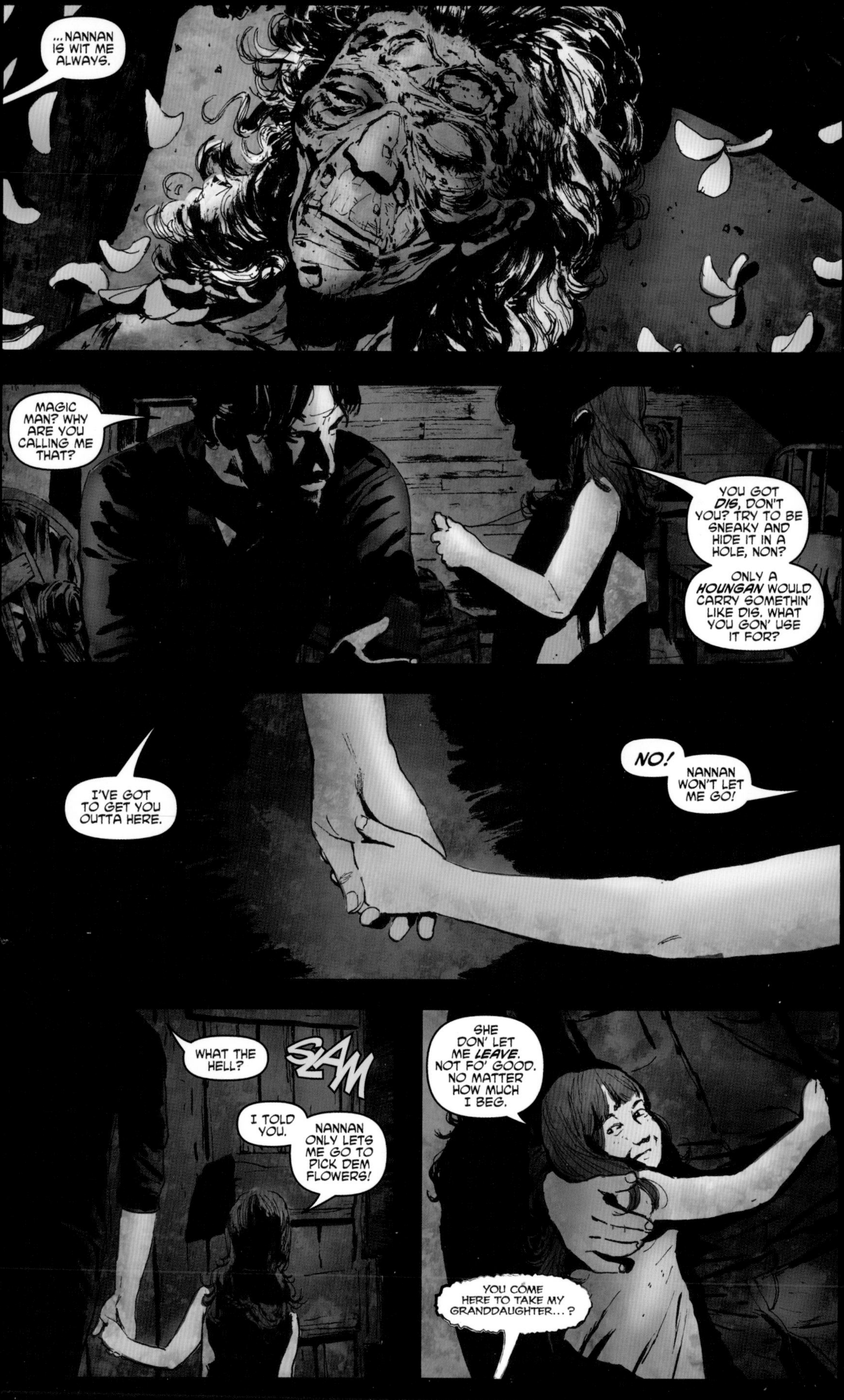
...NANNAN IS WIT ME ALWAYS.
MAGIC MAN? WHY ARE YOU CALLING ME THAT?
YOU GOT DIS, DON'T YOU? TRY TO BE SNEAKY AND HIDE IT IN A HOLE, NON?
ONLY A HOUNGAN WOULD CARRY SOMETHIN' LIKE DIS. WHAT YOU GON' USE IT FOR?
I'VE GOT TO GET YOU OUTTA HERE.
NO! NANNAN WON'T LET ME GO!
WHAT THE HELL?
SLAM
I TOLD YOU.
NANNAN ONLY LETS ME GO TO PICK DEM FLOWERS!
SHE DON' LET ME LEAVE. NOT FO' GOOD. NO MATTER HOW MUCH I BEG.
YOU COME HERE TO TAKE MY GRANDDAUGHTER...?

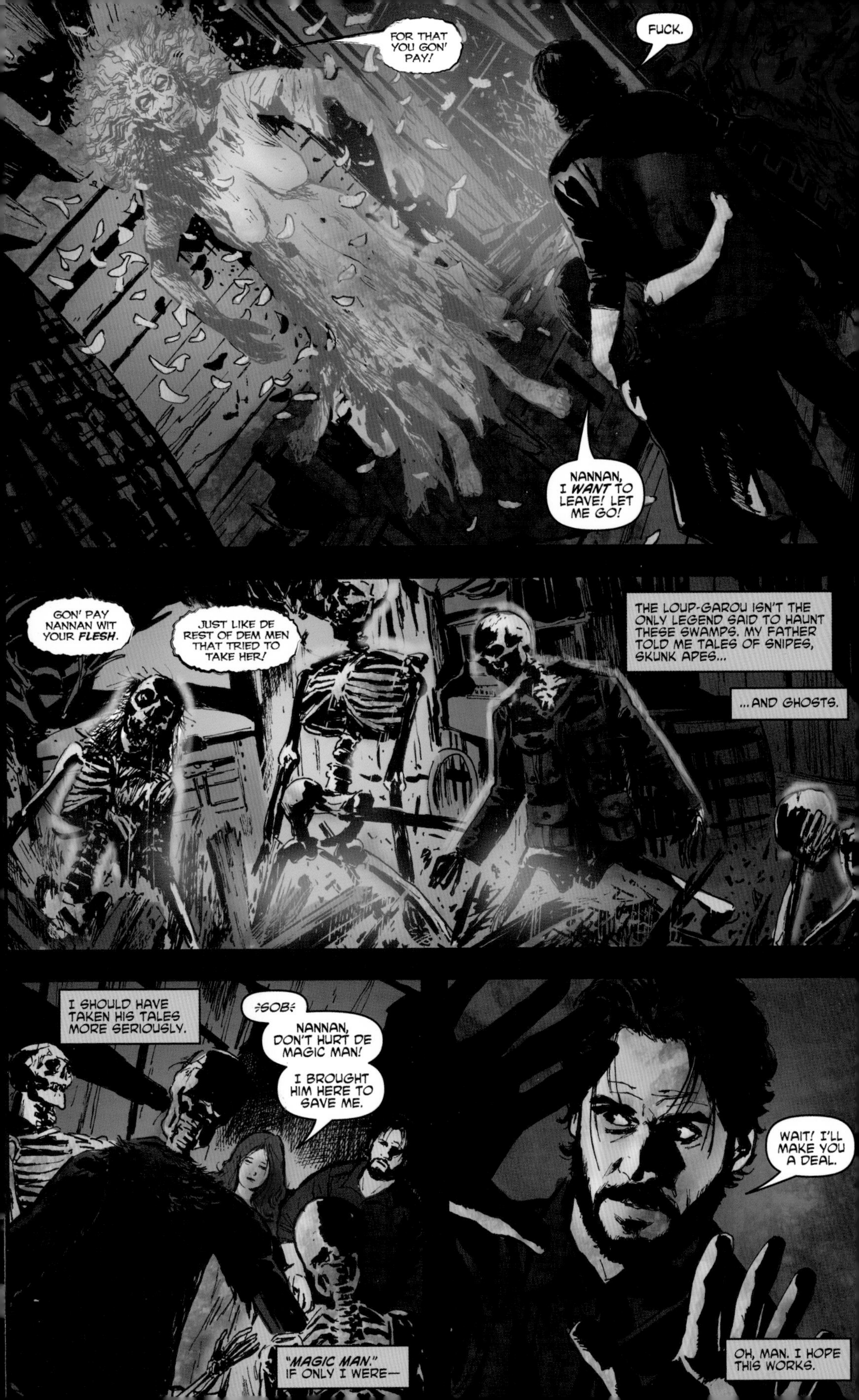
FOR THAT YOU GON' PAY!
FUCK.
NANNAN, I *WANT* TO LEAVE! LET ME GO!
GON' PAY NANNAN WIT YOUR *FLESH*.
JUST LIKE DE REST OF DEM MEN THAT TRIED TO TAKE HER!
THE LOUP-GAROU ISN'T THE ONLY LEGEND SAID TO HAUNT THESE SWAMPS. MY FATHER TOLD ME TALES OF SNIPES, SKUNK APES...
...AND GHOSTS.
I SHOULD HAVE TAKEN HIS TALES MORE SERIOUSLY.
SOB
NANNAN, DON'T HURT DE MAGIC MAN!
I BROUGHT HIM HERE TO SAVE ME.
"*MAGIC MAN*." IF ONLY I WERE—
WAIT! I'LL MAKE YOU A DEAL.
OH, MAN. I HOPE THIS WORKS.

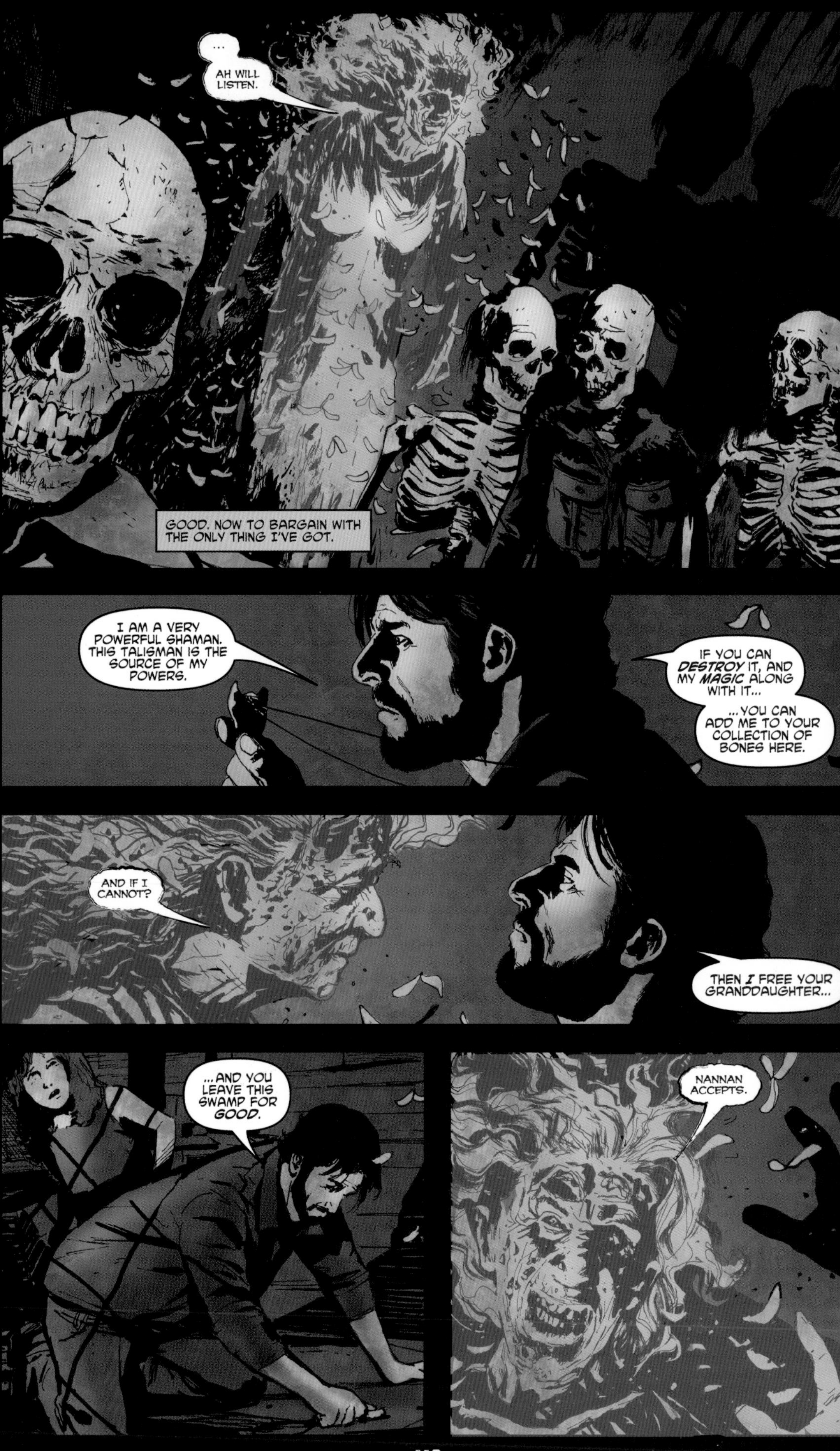
...
AH WILL LISTEN.
GOOD. NOW TO BARGAIN WITH THE ONLY THING I'VE GOT.
I AM A VERY POWERFUL SHAMAN. THIS TALISMAN IS THE SOURCE OF MY POWERS.
IF YOU CAN DESTROY IT, AND MY MAGIC ALONG WITH IT...
...YOU CAN ADD ME TO YOUR COLLECTION OF BONES HERE.
AND IF I CANNOT?
THEN I FREE YOUR GRANDDAUGHTER...
...AND YOU LEAVE THIS SWAMP FOR GOOD.
NANNAN ACCEPTS.

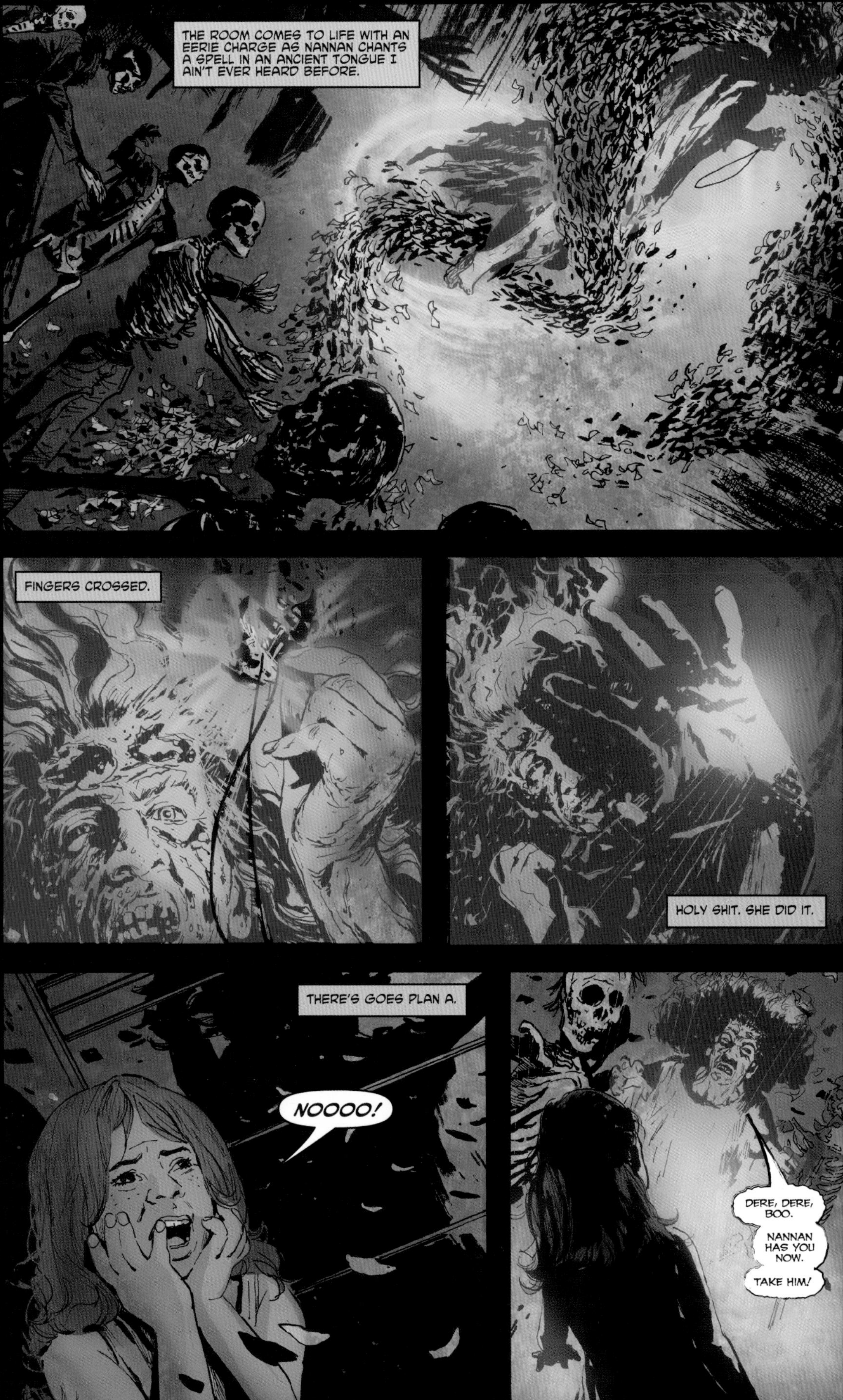
THE ROOM COMES TO LIFE WITH AN EERIE CHARGE AS NANNAN CHANTS A SPELL IN AN ANCIENT TONGUE I AIN'T EVER HEARD BEFORE.
FINGERS CROSSED.
HOLY SHIT. SHE DID IT.
THERE'S GOES PLAN A.
NOOOO!
DERE, DERE, BOO.
NANNAN HAS YOU NOW.
TAKE HIM!

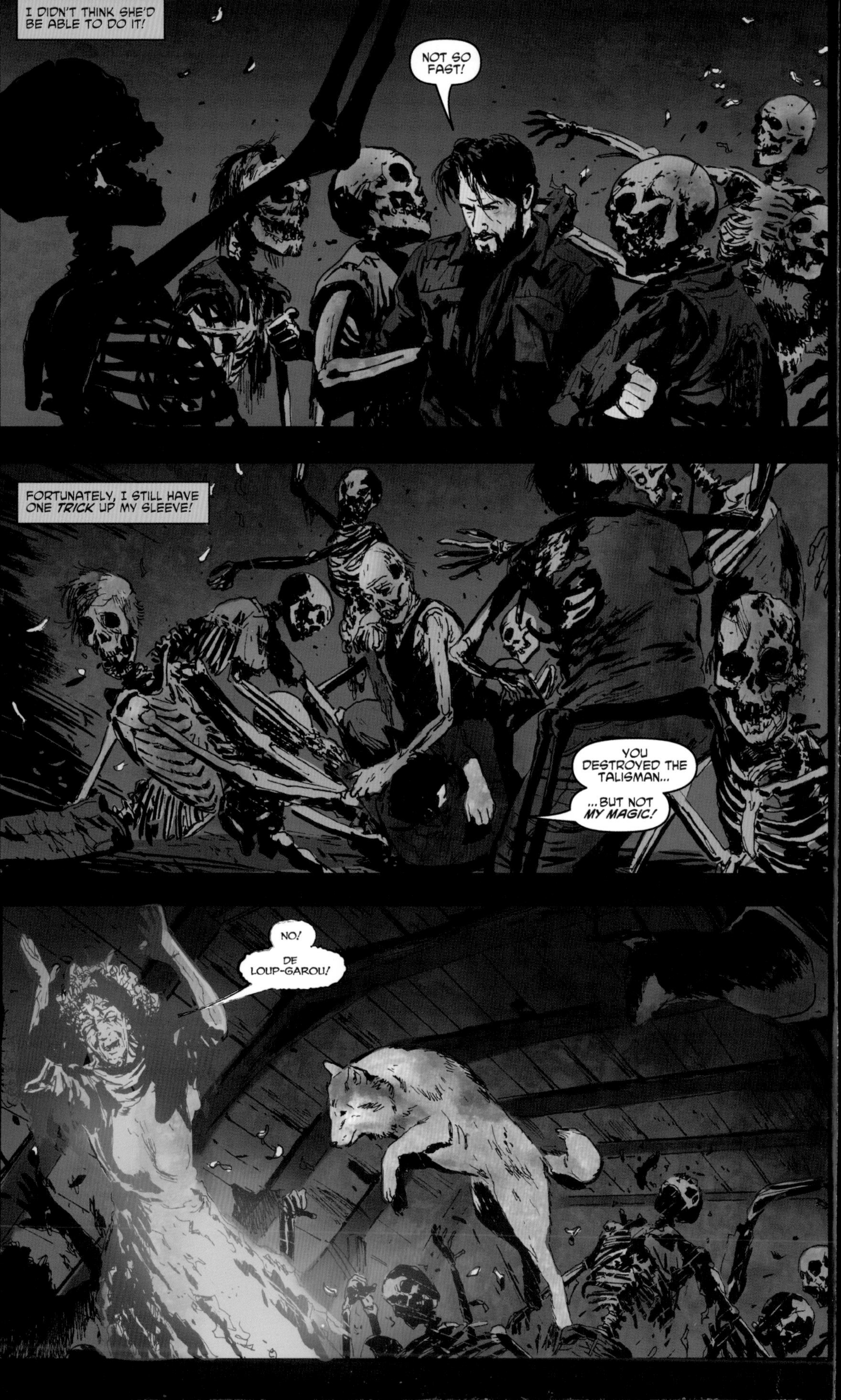
I DIDN'T THINK SHE'D BE ABLE TO DO IT!
NOT SO FAST!
FORTUNATELY, I STILL HAVE ONE *TRICK* UP MY SLEEVE!
YOU DESTROYED THE TALISMAN...
...BUT NOT *MY MAGIC!*
NO!
DE LOUP-GAROU!

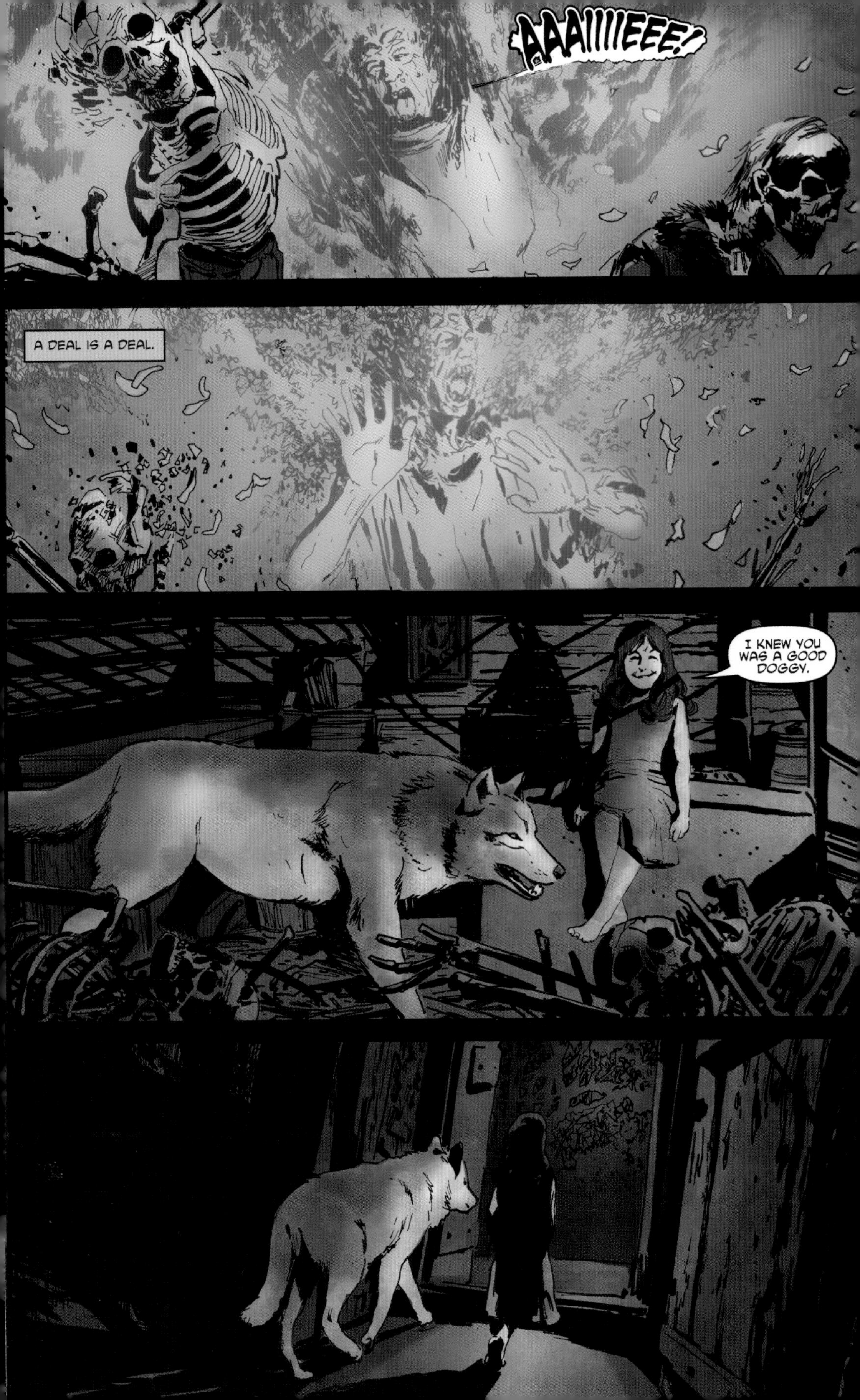
AAAIIIIIEEE!
A DEAL IS A DEAL.
I KNEW YOU WAS A GOOD DOGGY.

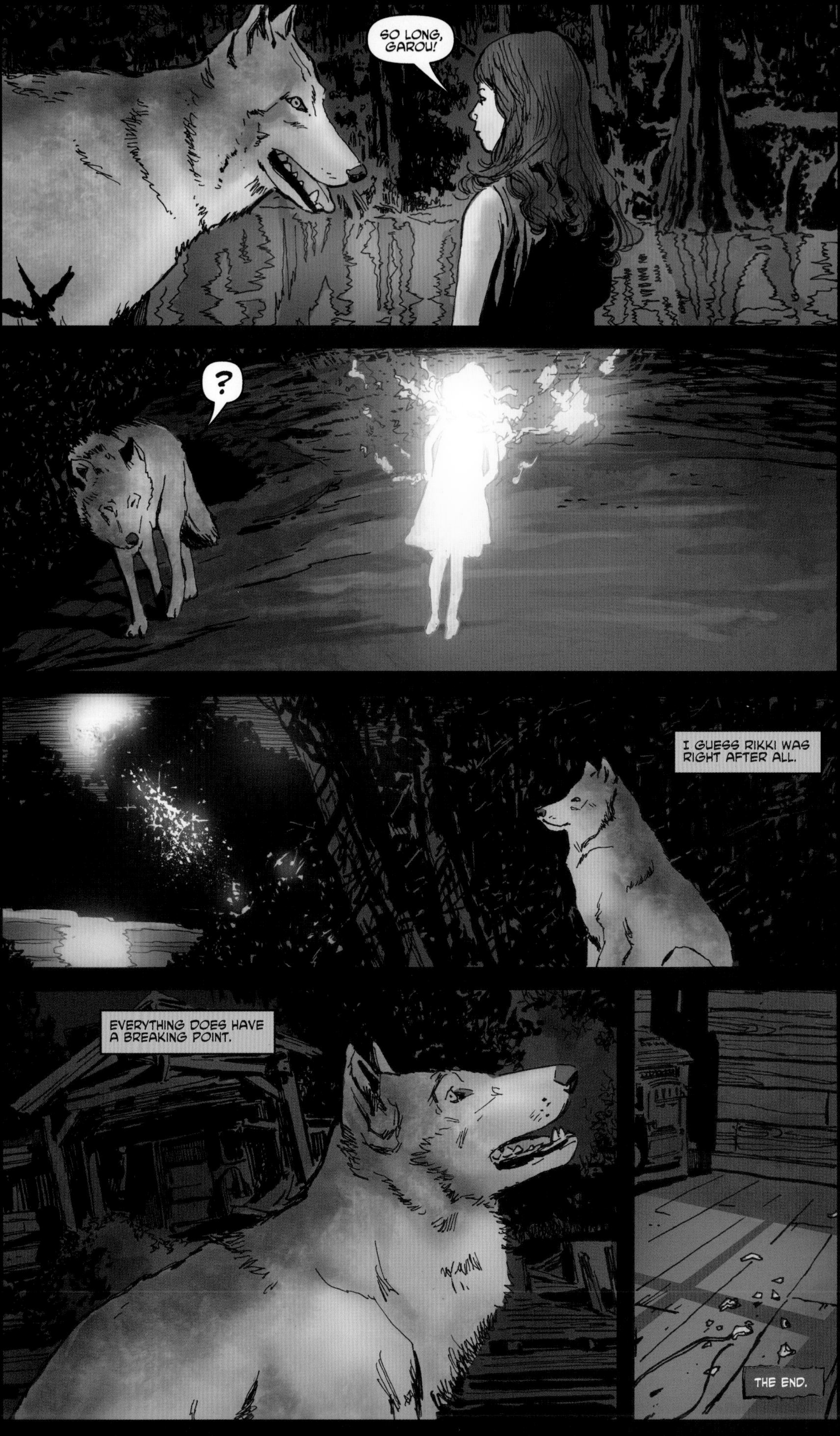
SO LONG, GAROU!
?
I GUESS RIKKI WAS RIGHT AFTER ALL.
EVERYTHING DOES HAVE A BREAKING POINT.
THE END.

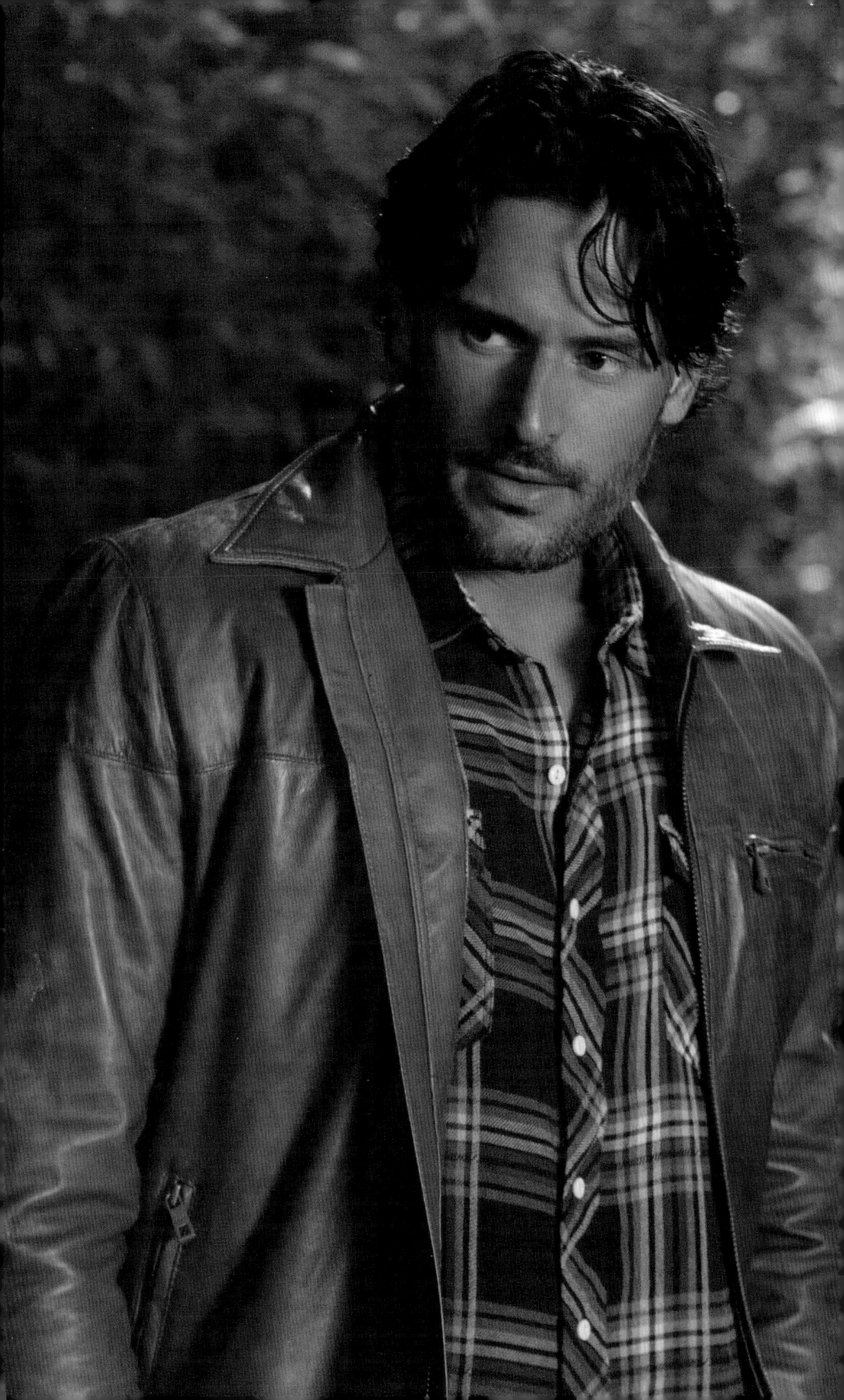

TRUE BLOOD™

SHAKE FOR ME